MAYA REVOLT
AND
REVOLUTION
IN THE
EIGHTEENTH CENTURY

Latin American Realities

Robert M. Levine, Series Editor

AFRO-BRAZILIAN CULTURE AND POLITICS
Bahia, 1790s–1990s
Hendrik Kraay, Editor

BITITA'S DIARY
Childhood Memoirs of Carolina Maria de Jesus
Carolina Maria de Jesus, Author
Robert M. Levine, Editor
Emanuelle Oliveira and Beth Joan Vinkler, Translators

FIGHTING SLAVERY IN THE CARIBBEAN
The Life and Times of a British Family in Nineteenth-Century Havana
Luis Martínez-Fernández

FROM SAVAGES TO SUBJECTS
Missions in the History of the American Southwest
Robert H. Jackson

PILLAGING THE EMPIRE
Piracy in the Americas, 1500–1750
Kris E. Lane

POLITICS AND EDUCATION IN ARGENTINA, 1946–1962
Mónica Esti Rein
Martha Grenzeback, Translator

THE SWEAT OF THEIR BROW
A History of Work in Latin America
David J. McCreery

MAYA REVOLT AND REVOLUTION
IN THE EIGHTEENTH CENTURY
Robert W. Patch

MAYA REVOLT
AND
REVOLUTION
IN THE
EIGHTEENTH CENTURY

ROBERT W. PATCH

M.E. Sharpe
Armonk, New York
London, England

Library of Congress Cataloging-in-Publication Data

Patch, Robert.
   Maya revolt and revolution in the eighteenth century / Robert W. Patch.
      p. cm.—(Latin American realities)
   Includes bibliographical references and index.
   ISBN 0-7656-0411-6 (alk. paper) — ISBN 0-7656-0412-4 (alk. paper)
      1. Mayas—History—18th century. 2. Insurgency—Guatemala—18th century. 3.
   Revolutions—Mexico—Yucatán (State)—18th century. 4. Guatemala—History—18th
   century. 5. Yucatán (Mexico : State)—History—18th century.   I. Title. II. Series.

   F1465 .P37 2002
   972'.6502—dc21
                                                                    2002066518

Printed in the United States of America

The paper used in this publication meets the minimum requirements of
American National Standard for Information Sciences
Permanence of Paper for Printed Library Materials,
ANSI Z 39.48-1984.

∞

BM (c)   10   9   8   7   6   5   4   3   2   1
BM (c)   10   9   8   7   6   5   4   3   2   1

To Beatriz Cáceres Menéndez

There can be no proper relation between one who is armed and one who is not.

—Machiavelli, *The Prince*

Contents

List of Maps

Foreword

The Latin American Realities series presents aspects of life not usually covered in standard histories that tell the stories of governments, economic development, and institutions. Books in this series dwell on different facets of life, equally important as those mentioned, but not often analyzed or described. How have underground economies worked? How have marginalized people coped with hardship and improved their lives? How have government policies affected everyday life? What has been the importance of popular culture? How have social and economic changes shaped the lives of ordinary people?

In *Maya Revolt and Revolution in the Eighteenth Century*, Robert W. Patch positions Mayan culture in the context of Spanish colonialism and examines both this culture and this era from below. Colonialism, he argues, as well as the enslavement of Africans, which went hand in hand with a parallel enslavement in the form of forced labor of indigenous peoples under Spanish rule, was one of the greatest evils in human history. This book asks two key questions: "How did colonialism work?" and "What difference did it make?" His study encompasses four revolts in eighteenth-century Guatemala and one large-scale revolt or revolution in Mexico's Yucatán during the same period. The study explores in depth those who ran the colonial bureaucracy, how those bureaucrats saw the world, how judges dispensed justice, how the Roman Catholic Church functioned, and how the Maya managed to turn the colonial regime against itself. The actions of the Maya, Patch shows us, illuminate history and prompt us to pay attention to them. Although their efforts ultimately failed to drive the Spanish from Maya ancestral land, the Maya negotiated and renegotiated the terms of their domination. The Spaniards stayed throughout the century, and even though their descendants are partly Maya in ancestry, today their culture is more Hispanic than Maya, the price of survival into the twenty-first century.

Robert M. Levine
Series Editor

Acknowledgments

This book was made possible by a Fulbright Foreign Area Fellowship, administered by the U.S.–Spanish Joint Committee for Cultural and Educational Cooperation. I would therefore like to thank the Fulbright Program for its support. I would also like to thank the Academic Senate of the University of California, which provided funds to aid in the transcription of the microfilm of documents from archives in Spain. And I thank those who helped in the transcription, namely, Elizabeth Leonard, Mark Anderson, Eloy Zárate, Lore Kuehnert, and Jason Ward. I hope that the income they earned in return for reading some pretty difficult stuff made their lives as graduate students a bit more pleasant. I am eternally grateful to the staffs of the Archivo General de Indias in Seville and the Archivo Histórico Nacional in Madrid. I would like to thank the many people who read and commented on drafts of chapters, namely, Bruce Castleman, Joseph Green, Keith Cox, Owen Jones, Karen Wilson, Mark Campos, Richard Godbeer, Lucille Chia, Irwin Wall, Michele Salzman, Kenneth Barkin, Piotr Górecki, Alena Simunkova, and Beatriz Cáceres. I would also like to thank the people who have provided me with intellectual advice, inspiration, and comradeship in my professional development, namely, Gilbert Joseph, Sergio Quezada, Pedro Bracamonte y Sosa, Gabriela Solís, Antonio Calabria, Eric Van Young, Eugene Anderson, and especially Stanley and Barbara Stein. None of these people is responsible for the errors that remain.

Introduction

Speak, hands, for me!

—*Casca, in* Julius Caesar, *Act III, Scene i*

Colonialism is one of the most important factors in modern world history. The European people who carried it out justified their actions by claiming that they were spreading Christianity, thereby saving souls from eternal damnation and civilizing backward people contaminated by cannibalism, homosexuality, devil worship, immorality, savagery, and barbarism. Theologians and humanists of the time, while sometimes denouncing the abuses of the European colonists, added moral support to colonialism in their scholarly writings. All of this was consistent with the hubris developing alongside the rise of European civilization as a world force; by 1914 this force had made the world economically and politically Eurocentric.

Then, in the twentieth century, colonialism began to be considered in a new light. Two world wars undermined faith in technology as a measure of civilization and led to the decline of faith in the very Christianity that had always justified colonialism. Paralleling the fall of the religious justification of colonialism was the rise of antiracist ideologies that resulted from the growing acceptance of democratic principles following the defeat of Nazism and fascism. This also undermined support for colonialism and helped convince most European countries still holding colonies to abandon their empires, which in many cases were expensive luxuries anyway. Intense resistance by Africans and Asians settled the issue once and for all.

With the collapse of religious, technological, and racist justifications of colonialism came critical scholarship exposing the exploitation and destruction that were intrinsic parts of, rather than aberrations from, colonial rule. This was paralleled by growing democratization of the academic professions and the decolonization of the social sciences. As a result, colonialism, like the enslavement of Africans, is now considered to have been one of the greatest evils in human history.

Underlying all this was one of the greatest changes in morality in world history. Before the eighteenth century Enlightenment, colonialism and conquest of foreign peoples were defended by Christianity, Islam, and a host of other religions. Now, after the Enlightenment, the situation is reversed. In short, colonialism, like slavery, while once moral no longer is.

Recognizing this change in morality is valuable because it helps move the discussion beyond good and evil and toward important questions like "How did colonialism work?" and "What difference did it make?" Moreover, asking these questions separates the analysis from the approach that vilifies and demonizes not just the colonialists but the entire culture that produced them— a kind of Occidentalism paralleling the Orientalism so often employed by European colonialist thought.[1] The assumptions regarding culture found in this book are that no culture is inferior or superior and that no culture is good or bad, but thinking makes it so.

This book asks the questions "How did colonialism work?" and "What difference did it make?" The latter is probably the more important to answer, but it cannot be addressed without answering the first question. As a result, a good deal of this study will concern how colonialism in fact worked; we can then better approach the more difficult question of its significance and impact.

This book will study colonialism by analyzing it from the bottom up. The subjects of analysis are four revolts that took place in eighteenth-century Guatemala and one revolution that broke out in Yucatán in the same period. A case-study approach has been made possible by the very structure of Spanish colonialism: the Spanish empire was run by a bureaucracy that was dominated for the most part not by humanists (as in China) or soldiers (as in the Ottoman empire) but by lawyers. True, the regional magistrates, governors, presidents, and viceroys were frequently military men, and thus soldiers did play a significant role in the administration of Spanish colonialism. But even regional officeholders of military background were assisted by people known as *letrados*, that is, men of letters with training in the law. The letrados saw to it that the actions of their bosses conformed to the law, even if the latter had to be stretched a good bit. More important, overseeing all colonial administrators were the *oidores*, or judges, of the high courts known as *audiencias*. These men, trained at the most prestigious universities in Spain, were the best representatives of Spanish legalism in America.

The task of the colonial judges was to enforce the rule of law and to dispense justice. Needless to say, they frequently failed. Moreover, the further removed a place was from the center of Spanish legal power the more the local elite or government official was able to rule in an arbitrary, and frequently lawless, way. Nevertheless, the Spanish audiencias made a historical difference. The judges were people with special knowledge who were trained in the same places, often by the same professors, and informed by the same books. They developed a strong esprit de corps and usually retained their commitment to the law despite setbacks to justice. They were a defining element of Spanish colonialism.

The legalism of the colonial regime did not require the Spaniards to get concerned over violations of the law at the local level. A basic principle of Spanish colonialism was the delegation of a great deal of political and judicial autonomy to the Indian villagers who along with city governments formed the basic local units of the Spanish American polity in many areas. But both political necessity and legalism did lead Spaniards to investigate large-scale political disorder in order to prevent the emergence of genuine threats to Spanish authority. Many of the inquests into riots, revolts, and revolutions resulted in documentation that still survives in archives and can be used as a primary source for an investigation at the local level of the functioning of colonialism as both an economic and a political system. Surviving records in indigenous languages, on the other hand, while extremely useful for illustrating key features of Indian culture, society, and government, almost never document the instances when indigenous people challenged Spanish power and authority. Spanish-language sources, therefore, are essential to study the politics of colonialism and Indian resistance.

Approaching the study of colonialism from the bottom up—which in Mexico and Central America means beginning at the village level—has the added advantage of helping us avoid superficiality. Too often scholars have reached conclusions from hasty generalizations based on a large number of cases imperfectly investigated. Many of those generalizations, as we shall see, are valid. But others are misleading or inaccurate and are therefore in need of revision. The approach that begins with a thorough investigation of history at the local level provides a better understanding of the mass of information or data to be used to make historical arguments, generalizations, and conclusions.

Finally, the bottom-up approach allows us to understand history as a process that involved real people rather than statistical data. To be sure, there is a need for statistics in historical research, for they allow for meaningful and accurate generalization. For this reason I have employed statistical data in most of my previous research. I am not arguing here that my earlier scholarship lacks validity; on the contrary, unlike many other historians of my generation, I do not repudiate my youthful work.[2] What I am asserting, rather, is the validity of adding more individuals to my analysis. This will allow the colonized people, who rarely are given a voice in history, to speak up, in a sense. What they have to say, I argue, enriches the endeavor of historical research.

But do "the colonized people" really "speak" in the documents to be examined? Many would argue that they do not. The nature of the documentation was clearly a severe restraint on the free expression of ideas and opinions, and this must be acknowledged from the very beginning of this study. This fact was well understood by those carrying out the inquests, for one of the first official acts of all investigations was the appointment of interpreters. These were necessary because very few Maya spoke Spanish and no Spanish magistrates or investigating judges spoke Maya. The information that we get from the colonized people thus comes to us through one or more interpreters whose accuracy in translation is always suspect. Moreover, as we shall see, the interpreters themselves could be politically motivated and thus they possibly translated only what they wanted and in the way that they wanted.

Added to this problem is that caused by the scribes (*escribanos*) who took down the testimony and drew up the official acts (*autos*) proclaimed in the documents. Rarely were the exact words of a witness written down. Rather, the scribes took down the testimony in the third person ("he said that . . . "; "the said witness answered that . . . ") and often in summary form. The intent was to make a record, not of the exact testimony, but of the gist of the testimony, although exact statements were sometimes written down when thought to be appropriate. As a result, what we are left with is usually a summary of what was said after having been put into Spanish by an interpreter. The opportunities for inaccurate recording, misleading summary, and bad translation add up to documentation that is never very good and possibly very bad.

Next, there is the problem of the objectivity of the investigation itself. Ostensibly witnesses were called to testify, but in reality the process was frequently more of an interrogation of prisoners. Maya women were very rarely questioned at all because females were judged to be unreliable witnesses. The Indians questioned in some cases had already been whipped, and hanging over the heads of all was the threat of judicial punishment, in the form of whipping, exile, confiscation of property, and execution. Under the circumstances it was certainly in the interest of the Maya witnesses to tell the Spaniards—their jailers, judges, and executioners—what they wanted to hear. And had they done so, we could hardly blame them for failing to stand up and give their colonial masters an earful.

For these reasons, the very usefulness of the inquests is to be questioned. Indeed, in certain historical circumstances the documentation from Spanish America is of very limited value. For example, in the highland Andes during and even after the great rebellions of the 1780s it is likely that the inquests had punishment rather than justice as their goal and thus are less useful as sources from other times and places. Similarly, in Mexico during the War for Independence (1810–20) it is once again likely that the judges or military officials who tried insurgent prisoners were more interested in putting down the rebellion through rigorous repression than they were in understanding the motives of the rebels hauled before them. Not all inquests, in short, are as valuable as others.

By the same token, some inquests are more valuable than others. Colonial Yucatán and Guatemala, while having their share of riots, revolts, and rebellions, were never so rebellious or revolutionary as to require long-term and massive repression like that employed in the Andes and Mexico in the late colonial period.[3] True, the large-scale rebellion or revolution in Chiapas in 1712 resulted in large-scale repression that lasted a long time. But this did not spill over into the proceedings regarding revolt and revolution elsewhere in the Maya world and thereby diminish the value of the judicial investigations (although it did have an effect on what happened later in Guatemala, as we shall see). The Maya, in short, were never as rebellious as many modern scholars would want us to believe. Much of what has been written about the Jacinto Canek Revolt in Yucatán in 1761, for example, is either misleading or completely wrong.[4] In any case, the absence of a severely repressive colonial regime resulting from the genuine threat of revolution means that the documentation from most of the Maya world is probably as good as it gets for the purpose of studying the indigenous people resisting colonialism in what were usually nonspectacular ways.

But the proof of the pudding is in the eating, and surely the best way to judge the validity of my use of the documentation is to see the results of my reading of the sources. Once again it must be admitted that the records are problematic and that not all my conclusions will be accepted by all readers. At times I have had to use my imagination and make guesses. Nevertheless, I believe that an imaginative reading of the sources reveals that the Maya found ways to counteract the oppression inherent in the investigations. They sometimes told the Spaniards what they wanted to hear but also told them a great deal that was not solicited or desired. They made their opinions understood even to the most obtuse of Spanish observers. At times they even defied their captors, denied their culpability, accused prosecution witnesses of lying, invented alibis, used their language as a defense of their community, and dared the colonial authorities to punish them.

The Maya also found ways to turn the colonial regime against itself. They made appeals to the high court of Guatemala in order to undermine the authority of a troublesome local colonial official. They hired Spanish lawyers to speak for them and represent them in court. Knowing that the government relied on the taxes they paid, they relied on the government's need to resume payment of taxes; by doing so they contributed to the formation of a colonial state that was so dependent on the Maya for its own income that it was fiscally required to temper justice with mercy. (This was probably less true in colonial Peru, where the state acquired a large part of its income from silver production rather than from tribute.) The actions of indigenous people, of course, did not stop abuse and exploitation, but by forcing negotiation and renegotiation the Maya did succeed in limiting their colonial domination. Their active participation in history, by mitigating the impact of colonialism, made a difference.

Even when the Maya had no real "voice" in what was taking place, their behavior provides good clues as to what was in their minds if not on their lips. Sometimes actions do speak louder than words, and the Maya, like Casca as he stabbed Julius Caesar, let their hands speak for them. We, in turn, must learn to listen.

MAYA REVOLT
AND
REVOLUTION
IN THE
EIGHTEENTH CENTURY

1

The Maya and Their History

The Ancient Maya and the Spanish Conquest

The Maya region is composed of the modern countries of Guatemala and Belize and small parts of Honduras and El Salvador, as well as all or parts of the Mexican states of Yucatán, Campeche, Quintana Roo, Tabasco, and Chiapas. It is located entirely south of the Tropic of Cancer, and thus is in the "tropics." The highland area, however (the mountains of Chiapas and Guatemala), have a temperate climate because of the high altitude, and thus some of the Maya region is decidedly nontropical. Nevertheless, most of the area is in lowlands and therefore is hot and humid virtually all year round. However, since the latitude is considerably north of the equator, there are distinct seasons. The rainy season is from June through October, and the dry season is predominant the rest of the year. All of this means that the Maya lived, and live, in an environment of great diversity ranging from hot tropical rainforests (in the Petén and the Usumacinta River basin) to cold mountains (especially the Cuchumatán Highlands of west-central Guatemala).

The Maya took advantage of their environment to produce a wide range of agricultural and forest products. Agriculture itself began in the region over four thousand years ago, perhaps as long as five or six thousand years ago. Although a variety of food crops eventually were developed, by far the most important was American corn, or maize. This became the staff of life, and was so important to the Maya that their religion taught them that the gods had created human beings out of corn. Maize agriculture was complemented by production of beans, squash, tomatoes, and chili peppers. Animal protein was not always part of the diet, for before the arrival of Europeans the only edible animals were turkey, deer, and iguana. Only the former was domesticated.

To understand the history of the Maya it is vital to take into account the productivity of agriculture. The technology may appear primitive to the mod-

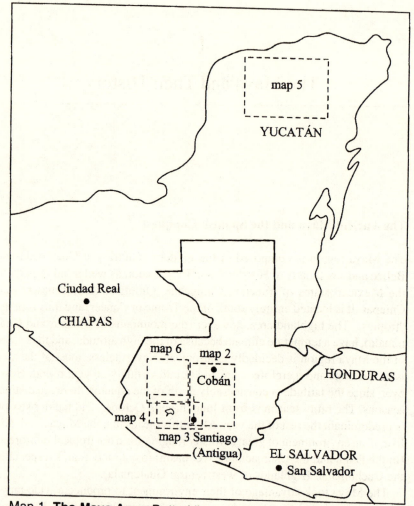

Map 1 **The Maya Area** Dotted lines show location of detailed maps appearing elsewhere in the book.

ern observer, but it was very effective, allowing agriculturalists to produce not only for their own subsistence but also a surplus that was channeled away from the producers through taxation and markets. Agriculturalists got government and cultural activities in return for civil and religious taxes, and goods (salt, flint, tools, etc.) in return for mercantile exchange. The productivity of maize also allowed the Maya the time to produce cotton in addition to food crops. The raw cotton was eventually spun into thread and woven into textiles, which the Maya produced not only for their direct use but also to pay their taxes. Cloth was even used in commercial exchange as a kind of currency. Other Maya forms of money included cacao beans (small change) and jade (for high-value purchases).

As a result of the great productivity of Maya agriculture, a complex society could be supported by the surplus channeled away from the peasants to higher social classes. Maya society eventually became quite stratified, with sharp distinctions made between the farming majority and the ruling elites. Those who ruled developed a strong sense of their special status by emphasizing their lineage and ancestry and by maintaining a monopoly on the skill of reading and writing. They also established a tradition of strong village and regional government and of religious power. The division of society into classes and the institutionalization of political and religious power were characteristics of the Maya that in retrospect helped them survive the extreme dislocation caused by Spanish conquest. At the same time the structure of Maya society and politics provided the Spaniards with the means of controlling the conquered people as well as the mechanisms for extracting wealth from the surplus-producing peasantry.

The ancient Maya were never able to attain political unity. At all times the area was divided into numerous petty states based on capital cities or towns. These engaged in perennial warfare with each other, a practice that served to provide aggressors with captives who could be sold as slaves and exported to other regions, including central Mexico. Some captives, especially high-ranking ones, also became sacrificial victims.

By the early sixteenth century, when the Spaniards arrived on the scene, the Maya area contained a large number of small political states. Yucatán, despite the linguistic unity of the Yucatec Maya, had sixteen or so of these regionally based political units.[1] The highland areas were even more complex, because the people were divided linguistically as well as politically. Some, but not all, of the linguistic groups seem to have formed political units that united all the people of the same language. This was the case among the Cakchiquel and Quiché people of the central highlands of Guatemala, but such political and linguistic unity was not found everywhere.

The results of this political fragmentation were important. On the one hand, it meant that ultimate Spanish victory was virtually certain, for the invaders could pursue a typical policy of "divide and rule": they could make alliances with some people in order to conquer the others and bring all under their control one by one. On the other hand, fragmentation helped delay conquest because for the Spaniards there was no single site to capture or one single government that could be forced to surrender. Conquest took time, which worked to the advantage of the Maya, for over time Spanish enthusiasm for conquest weakened. This was because the area's lack of gold or silver to loot was discouraging, and because the discovery of Peru's resources encouraged many Spaniards to leave the Maya area and seek their fortunes elsewhere. It therefore took over twenty years to bring most of the Maya under Spanish authority, a process that at times—as in the Verapaz region (the northern part of the Guatemalan highlands)—involved a negotiated submission rather than a surrender. In the Petén area of northern Guatemala some Maya remained unconquered and maintained their independence until 1697.[2] Such regional variations, caused in part by preconquest political regionalization, would eventually play an important role in colonial politics.

The Ordering of Colonial Society

The Spanish conquest brought not only violence but also epidemic disease. In fact, the diseases preceded the arrival of the conquistadors and undoubtedly contributed to ultimate Spanish victory. The result of the epidemics of smallpox and other illnesses was a sharp population decline that continued throughout the sixteenth century. The demographic contraction was undoubtedly made worse by the forced resettlement (*reducción* or *congregación*) of the native people into larger, more concentrated settlements, a policy carried out by Spanish priests in order to "civilize" the Maya and make them easier to indoctrinate. Recovery of the population began in most places early in the next century, but then epidemics of yellow fever and other diseases once more caused decline. Only in the eighteenth century would demographic expansion take place in almost all parts of the Maya area.[3]

The institutions of colonialism imposed a structure on Indians all over America, and gave similarity to the history of socially complex, surplus-producing indigenous peoples from Mexico to Peru and even as far away as the Philippines.[4] Nevertheless, local conditions of geography and variations in culture and in social and political structures determined the ways in which native society and colonialism adapted to each other. In the Maya area the absence of gold and silver deposits on a significant scale meant that the Spanish colonists could not enrich themselves as easily as in Mexico and Peru. Spaniards therefore looked for other exportable goods, and at first found one in cacao, much in demand in Mexico and then in Europe. But because cacao could only be produced in the lowlands, which were most exposed to tropical diseases, the indigenous population in the producing areas—Soconusco (the Pacific coast of modern-day Chiapas[5]), the *alcaldía mayor* (high magistracy) of San Antonio Suchitepéquez (the western Pacific coast of Guatemala), and Tabasco (on the southernmost coast of the Gulf of Mexico)—declined more drastically than elsewhere, thus severely limiting the supply of laborers and reducing output and profits.[6] In the absence of an economy based on the export of raw materials, Indian labor was not as valuable as in some other regions of the Spanish empire. The labor draft demanded of the Maya (discussed in Chapter 4) for the most part involved the allocation of workers to local agricultural enterprises rather than to distant mining camps as in Peru and parts of southern Mexico.

Spaniards thus eventually came to realize that the most important source of wealth in the Maya area was the indigenous population and its economy. These the colonists learned to exploit through taxation and commercial exchange. Civil taxes, called tribute, were collected at first in kind (mostly corn, turkeys, cotton textiles, and where possible cacao) and later in silver coin as well as in kind. At first individual Spaniards, as rewards for their participation in the conquest, were given the right to collect tribute from a specific village or villages in return for their services in the conquest. This institution was called the *encomienda*, and the people with the right to collect tribute were called *encomenderos*. As time went on the Spanish crown, which feared that the encomenderos would become too powerful and too independent of Spain, gradually ended the encomienda system and took control of tribute. By the late seventeenth century, most of the Maya of Guatemala and Chiapas paid their tribute to the Spanish government rather than to an encomendero. By the 1720s all encomiendas were abolished in Guatemala and Chiapas; thereafter the Maya paid their tribute to the crown rather than to a private individual. In Yucatán, however, because of the lack of economic resources available to the Spanish colonists, the government allowed the encomienda system to continue to exist until 1785.

The Maya also had to pay religious taxes, which were the ecclesiastical equivalent of tribute. The conquered people paid at first in kind, and later in kind and in money, in the same goods as in the tribute system. The taxes so collected were used to provide for the local church and priest, not for the diocese as a whole. At the same time, Indians were also required to tithe, that is, pay one-tenth of their annual production. Tithes, which Spaniards also had to pay, went directly to the ecclesiastical government of the diocese, and provided an income for the bishop and other priests who administered the church. However, the crown also got a share, usually two-ninths of the total, and thus had a vested interest in seeing that everyone paid what was owed. Nevertheless, the tithe, unlike other religious taxes, had little impact on the Maya. This was because the crown eventually decided that the Indians would pay this tax not on all their production but only on those goods that were not of indigenous origin (in other words, wheat, cattle, sheep, pigs, and chickens). Since the Maya economy was based overwhelmingly on native products, especially corn, the tithe was an insignificant burden on the Indians.

As a result, and because the Spaniards engaged in few productive activities that would produce significant tithe revenues, the Catholic Church in

Guatemala and Yucatán was quite poor. In Guatemala the government paid a subsidy to local priests who otherwise would have found it difficult to make ends meet. Indeed, the clergy was so poor that few people wanted to be priests, and as a result the diocese had to rely on friars who took vows of poverty. As a result, until the middle of the eighteenth century almost all rural parishes in Guatemala and half of those in Yucatán were under the care of Dominicans, Franciscans, or Mercedarians.[7]

Commercial exchange was the other mechanism that the Spaniards used to extract wealth from the Maya. By far the most important practice accomplishing this was the system known as the *repartimiento* (not to be confused with a labor draft also called a *repartimiento*). This came into existence in the late sixteenth century and continually increased in importance until, by the middle of the eighteenth century, it frequently had become the most important mechanism for extracting a surplus from the Maya. The commercial repartimiento was a system of business transactions between Spanish government officials and the Indians under their jurisdiction. The official, usually an *alcalde mayor* (high magistrate), a *corregidor* (magistrate), or a governor, would either sell goods to the Indians at prices favorable to the seller or would buy goods at prices favorable to the buyer. In the first case, the magistrate would usually sell livestock, agricultural tools, or clothing for much more than he paid for the goods and thus make a large profit on the transaction. The second case, the purchase of goods from the Maya, was the most important form of repartimiento. This consisted of the payment in advance, and of course at low prices, for goods that the Indians produced. Most commonly, the alcalde mayor, corregidor, or governor would loan money to the Maya so that they could pay their tribute, and then would collect the debt in cotton or woolen textiles, raw cotton or wool, wheat, cacao, or wax. He would then resell the goods at market prices, which were much higher than the value of the credit given to the Indians. This of course also allowed the magistrate to make a large profit on his dealings with the Maya.

The significance of tribute (whether collected by encomenderos or by the crown), religious taxes, and the commercial repartimiento is that they were mechanisms for the extraction of wealth from the Indians in ways that did not seriously disrupt the Maya economy. The goods in question were almost always those of the native economy; new economic activities that might have been disruptive, such as silver mining, did not have to be introduced. Taxes and the repartimiento, in short, depended not on new structures of production but rather on already existing ones.

Since corn was bulky, expensive to ship, and subject to spoilage, by far the most important native products from the Spanish point of view were cotton textiles, for which the Maya are famous. Cotton was produced throughout the lowlands and then shipped to all Maya communities for spinning and weaving. Spanish encomenderos, officials, and priests demanded partial payment of tribute and religious taxes in cotton textiles.

Eventually the acquisition of cloth manufactured by the Maya became the most important branch of the commercial repartimiento as well as of tribute and religious taxes. Cotton was planted and harvested by men and boys, and spinning and weaving were carried out by women and girls, so tribute, taxes, and the repartimiento ensured that the agents of colonialism tapped the surplus labor of everyone—men, women, and children—in the peasant community.[8]

The royal government prohibited its officials in America from engaging in commercial enterprises within the areas of their jurisdiction. This meant that the repartimiento was illegal. However, the crown did legalize it in Yucatán in 1732, and it remained legal in that province until the 1780s. In Guatemala the repartimiento was legal only for one decade—the 1750s. For most of the colonial period, therefore, this system of economic exchange between the Maya and the Spanish magistrates was illegal. It nevertheless was widely practiced in both Yucatán and Guatemala, legally or otherwise. The repartimiento existed and survived numerous edicts against it because it enabled the poorly paid colonial magistrates to earn extra income and thus was an unofficial encouragement to take up an office with a low salary. The crown in fact tolerated the system, for it permitted the government to pay low salaries and thus keep administrative costs down.

The repartimiento was important because it allowed Spanish corregidores, alcaldes mayores, and governors to acquire valuable goods much below the market price. The cotton textiles acquired through repartimiento, tribute, and religious taxes were of vital importance because, with the exception of wax and a little cacao, they were the only locally produced goods that could be exported to markets near and far within the Spanish American empire. Yucatán's major market was Mexico City and the mining regions of northern Mexico. Chiapas exported some cloth to New Spain, but most of its textiles, as well as those produced in Guatemala, were exported to Santiago de Guatemala (the capital of the Kingdom of Guatemala), to the indigo-producing regions of El Salvador, and to the mining camps of Honduras. In this way the Maya area was incorporated into the major American export economies and hence into the world economy.[9]

Colonialism, therefore, was not a totally destructive process. Indeed, it may even have strengthened certain sectors of the indigenous economy, for it allowed and even encouraged the Maya to continue what they had been doing for millennia. This does not mean, of course, that the indigenous people were not exploited. They were, especially by the repartimiento, which in practice became a coercive kind of putting-out system that forced the Maya to work for the Spaniards at below-market wages, and if they did not deliver the goods they were punished with imprisonment or the whip.[10] Nevertheless, the exploitation involved was well known and understood, and did not entail a change in the organization of life. This, rather than the ostensible absence of exploitation, helps explain the survival of Maya, and indeed Indian, culture after the European invasion. The regions most subject to the coercive repartimiento—highland Guatemala, Chiapas, and Yucatán—are to this day the most "Indian" parts of Latin America.[11]

Colonialism therefore permitted a great deal of continuity between preconquest Maya society and that after the European invasion. It is important to note that although Spanish colonists did set up landed estates (cattle ranches, or *estancias*, and cattle and agricultural properties, called *haciendas*), they did so mostly by occupying land abandoned by the Indians because of population decline. Rarely did the invaders simply throw the native people off the land in order to seize it for their own use. In fact, Spaniards had little use for land because of limited markets in which to sell their products. Moreover, it was in the interest of encomenderos, priests, and the government for the Maya to retain control over land so that they could pay their tribute and other taxes.

For these reasons the colonial regime took steps to protect the Indians as owners of the land. Maya land tenure, which included family as well as village and sometimes lineage property, was therefore officially sanctioned. The Spaniards did not care how Indians owned or used their land, as long as they paid their taxes. Moreover, to prevent individuals from alienating their land and thereby transfer their resources to Spaniards, the crown required that all sales by indigenous people have the approval of both the Spanish and the indigenous village government affected.

The Spanish crown was also aware of the need to protect the indigenous people from theft and other abuses perpetrated by the European colonists. For this reason in many parts of America the government took steps to provide legal aid to the native people. This was usually paid for out of tax revenues collected from the native people, so the legal aid was not exactly free. Rather, the Indians in a sense participated in a kind of legal insurance: they paid, and got service when needed. In Mexico this meant the creation of an institution called the General Indian Court (*Tribunal General de Indios*), staffed by a body of lawyers who devoted all their time to bringing suits in defense of the Indians. A branch of this court was set up in Yucatán, and affected relations between Spaniards and Maya in that province. However, in Guatemala and Chiapas a formal institution was never set up, allegedly because of the poverty of the Indians. However, the crown did eventually appoint a special lawyer called the Advocate of the Poor, who was responsible for defending the Indians (who, it will be noted, were assumed to be poor). Nevertheless, for most of the colonial period only the attorney general was responsible for defending the Indians, and since he had many other pressing duties, the Maya of Guatemala and Chiapas were unquestionably less protected than their Mexican and Andean counterparts from abuse by the colonists and by government officials. And in any case, even where the General Indian Court existed, it served only to limit, rather than prevent, exploitation and abuse by Spaniards.

Still another colonial policy designed to preserve Indian society was the recognition of the indigenous elites as legitimate rulers and nobles. This was done, of course, in return for their cooperation in policing and governing the villages and in collecting tribute and taxes. The Maya elites received tax exemption and a share of tax revenues as their personal income in exchange for carrying out the tasks of government at the local level. The result was that the basic principles of social stratification—the division of society into social classes—survived long after the conquest.

The institutionalization of tribute and the recognition of the legitimacy of the traditional ruling class were fundamental features of Spanish colonialism. In effect, the Spaniards were admitting their own weakness: the crown could not possibly afford to appoint salaried Spanish officials to live in and rule over each of the thousands of Indian villages in America. Tax collection by outsiders, moreover, would have opened up a Pandora's box of abuses. It was much easier and lot more practical to negotiate with the Indians so that essential functions of government were carried out by the people themselves. This was possible, of course, because local governments already existed and had been collecting taxes and enforcing laws for hundreds or thousands of years.

The result was what might be called a colonial pact between the Spanish crown and the Indian societies of America. The indigenous people would pay taxes and provide certain kinds of labor services for Spaniards—in short they would be exploited—but there would be agreed-upon limits on taxes and labor. The Indian governments would collect the taxes and organize the labor drafts, but in return would get a great deal of local autonomy. The villages would continue to rule themselves to a great extent, and even though the colonial regime introduced changes in local government by demanding annual elections of *alcaldes* (Indian magistrates) and *regidores* (councilmen), the indigenous rulers got around this by developing a system of rotation in office—a true circulation of elites—to keep government in their hands. As a result, the normal practice was for the Indians to present the names of the elected alcaldes to the Spanish magistrate or governor for approval. Only rarely, and at great political risk, did the Spanish official veto the election results or interfere with Indian self-government.

This system of allowing considerable political autonomy at the local level meant that only a handful of salaried Spanish officials was needed to rule over a vast empire. In the colonial Kingdom of Guatemala (Central America plus Chiapas), for example, at most twenty-seven Spanish magistrates, high magistrates, and governors ruled over hundreds of thousands of Indians who delivered their taxes to the Spaniards twice a year. This was practical for the colonial regime because it meant that it received revenue at little administrative cost. But it also meant that the Spanish government depended on the indigenous people for an important part of its income. This in turn required the colonial authorities to pay attention to its tax base and hence its taxpayers, who could not be pushed too far or exploited too much without provoking a disruption of tax revenues. The Spanish government thus established its hegemony only by admitting its own weakness as a state.

Despite the important elements of continuity sanctioned and fostered by the colonial regime, colonialism did result in significant change for the Maya. The reducción policy caused considerable dislocation, from which the Maya never made a full recovery. Demographic decline provoked considerable change in the traditional ways of life, leading to the extinction of dynasties and disappearance of whole communities, as well as to the introduction of new patterns of marriage and, presumably, family life. Christianity entailed social and political change, for it deprived the traditional ruling class of full control over religion and religious ritual. Political subordination also eventually undermined the elite by restricting the exercise of power to single communities. Everywhere the old ruling class was subjected to a variety of challenges that caused many members of the elite to lose status and suffer downward social mobility. Nevertheless, the basic principle of social hierarchy and stratification survived quite well, and new people frequently moved up and replaced the old as the latter fell by the wayside. In the eighteenth century a strong, and sometimes wealthy, native elite continued to rule over the commoners, or *macehuales* (from the Nahuatl word *maceualli*) of Maya society.[12] However, as we shall see, that rule was sometimes questioned.

Despite these changes, then, the elements of continuity in Maya society during the colonial period must also be stressed. One of the most important institutions to survive was the social unit comprised of people who believed themselves to be descendants of the same ancestors. This lineage or group of real or fictive kinship that served to define identity, rights, and obligations was called the *molab* among Mam speakers and *chinamit* among the Quiché and Cakchiquel.[13] Eventually the Spaniards used their own term—*parcialidad* (literally a partisan group)—to refer to this unit whenever it was located at a site shared by other such groups. Originally, however, in Guatemala the Spaniards called it a *calpul*, for they had just encountered the Mexican *calpulli* (or perhaps more accurately, the *calpolli*) and believed the Maya institution to be an exact equivalent. The same is possibly the case with the Yucatec Maya lineage group.[14] In colonial documents, both calpul and parcialidad are commonly used. It was also of course a close, if not exact, equivalent of the Andean *ayllu*.

The similarity between the Mexican, Maya, and Andean institutions is striking, and suggests a very ancient origin. Its significance, however, varied from place to place. Several generations of scholars have emphasized the central importance of the calpulli among Mexican Indians because they considered it to be the basic land-owning, suprafamilial institution. Yet, recent research, a large part of which has been about non-Aztec Nahua people, including those outside of the Valley of Mexico, has downgraded its significance. Many calpullis in central Mexico, including those of Nahua peoples, for example, had no lands at all and thus were not the landowning institutions once considered so crucial among indigenous people. The center of scholarly attention is now occupied by the *teccalli* or *tlatocayo* (noble house ruled by a lord called a *tlatoani*) and *altepetl* (city-state) as the basic suprafamilial political, social, and land-owning units.[15] The Andean ayllu, however, continues to hold scholarly attention. Recent research confirms its crucial place in Andean society, for membership in the group defined legal status, and hence tribute obligations, labor services, and rights to the land well into the eighteenth century.[16]

The Maya parcialidad lies somewhere between these extremes. There is no question of its considerable importance as a social, political, and landowning unit in the highlands, where most Maya villages included several, sometimes as many as eight, calpules. This was undoubtedly to a great extent the result of the reducción policy, which gathered people from different parcialidades and required them to live together at a common site. But this did not unify the people in question, and usually each parcialidad tried to maintain itself as a separate entity within its village.[17] As we shall see, this sometimes led to struggles for power and to revolt. In Yucatán, however, fewer villages had parcialidades, and it is likely that many lineage groups lived in several sites at the same time and did not organize themselves into separate parcialidades in each place. In any case, there is little evidence regarding the nature of these lineages, which by itself suggests that they were of lesser importance than the highland calpul and the Andean ayllu. Nevertheless, the Yucatecan parcialidades that did exist were of significance well into the eighteenth century, and one of them was at the heart of the 1761 revolution.

Finally, and perhaps most important, Maya culture survived colonialism and continued to guide thought and action. True, Christianity entailed the imposition of new religious concepts, but to a great extent the native people simply accepted the Christian God and saints as Maya equivalents. Very few of the conquered people ever learned any language other than their own native one, and life in the villages and hamlets, although disrupted by reducción, adhered to traditional patterns. The core of native culture survived the colonial experience. Most importantly for our purposes, the Maya understanding of themselves and the world did not change. They retained their belief that time moved not on a continuum but in cycles, and that their subjection to the Spaniards was only a temporary condition, one that would eventually change.[18]

This deep belief in the past as future was crucial. Not only did it make colonialism psychologically bearable, it also meant that the Maya were ready for their liberation. The survival of religion thus laid the basis for change, for it allowed the Maya to conceive of a world in which they, and not the Spaniards, would be the dominant group. Their belief in the possibility of a "world turned upside down," in which they and their colonial masters would trade places in the social order, constituted a latent although potentially powerful force that could quickly challenge the prevailing colonial order.[19] If they thought that their time of liberation was at hand, as foretold in their religion—a time that they *expected* to come—they could become, almost overnight, revolutionary.

A Revolutionary Prologue[20]

Although the Maya area was not more prone to rebellion than other areas of Spanish America in the colonial period, it was the scene of two unsuccessful revolutions in the eighteenth century, one in Chiapas in 1712 and the other in Yucatán in 1761. I refer to these movements as revolutions because on both occasions the Indians not only revolted against Spanish authority but also challenged the colonial regime's legitimacy by asserting the right to rule themselves. This was a claim to popular sovereignty and thereby qualifies as a revolution in the same way that events in England (in the era 1641–88), the United States (1775–83), and France (1789–99) can be called revolutions.

The events in Chiapas in 1712 serve as a revolutionary prologue to the revolts and the other revolution (that in Yucatán) discussed in this book. Not only did they demonstrate the revolutionary potential of the Maya; they also hung over the Maya area like the sword of Damocles for the rest of the colonial period. In fact, as we shall see, the example of Chiapas influenced events elsewhere, as historical memory affected historical action. For that reason, an understanding of the revolution in Chiapas in 1712 will be useful to put the other Maya revolts and revolution into perspective.

As is to be suspected, Spanish exploitation certainly helped cause events in Chiapas. The revolution broke out almost immediately after the announcement in July 1712 by the bishop, Juan Baptista Álvarez de Toledo, that he would carry out a second episcopal visitation. This caused consternation because his first such visitation, carried out only four years before, had been extortionate in nature: the bishop had forced people to pay hard cash for the sacrament of Confirmation, had jailed those parents who had not wanted to pay, and had charged high fees for giving his approval of the accounts of village *cofradías* (confraternities that owned property and raised money for the religious festivals of their members). The people had not yet recovered from the first episcopal pillaging expedition and feared a second one.

The threat of further exploitation, however, was not the only cause of the uprising. Indeed, as we shall see, the revolutionary organization itself had already been formed even before the announcement of the bishop's second visitation, and only turned to violence when the threat of further impoverishment became real. Moreover, as we shall see in later chapters in this book, revolt against suddenly increased exactions by the colonial regime also took place in Guatemala, yet failed to turn into revolution. Other factors had to exist to transform a revolt against exploitation into a revolution.

In practice Maya revolution was the result of cultural as well as material factors. Scholars usually emphasize the latter, for appropriate material conditions are usually necessary for revolution.[21] Culture, however, frequently gets short shrift in the study of revolution, and in the case of Indians it is usually treated as a given, that is, as background. However, cultural content must be analyzed for the simple reason that it affects history: it shapes a people's understanding of reality and even, at times, determines behavior. Since culture differs greatly from place to place, it plays a major role in determining where revolution breaks out and where it does not. It is herefore imperative to include cultural content as a factor contributing to the outbreak of revolution.

In retrospect, therefore, the observations of a Spanish Dominican who lived through the events of 1712 are of great interest. According to Friar Francisco Ximénez, the highland Maya area in the early eighteenth century, like the Holy Land at the beginning of the Christian era, was a hotbed of spirituality and a breeding ground of heterodox cults. Indeed, Ximénez lamented that although the people of the region were very good, they "suffered from an intolerable illness, namely, that of revelations, for no one, no matter how ordinary, dies without experiencing a revelation . . . and speaking with God."[22] In Chiapas, for example, numerous apparitions were reported, and religious activities were organized around them. At the same time, shamans went about the country and stirred up interest in new forms of spiritual expression. The Church, however, was not blind to what was happening and took vigorous action to suppress all the nonorthodox activity.

Consequently, the report of still another apparition of the Virgin, this time in a Tzeltal Maya village called Cancuc (21 miles [34 kilometers] northeast of the regional capital of Ciudad Real, the modern-day San Cristóbal de las Casas) did not catch the authorities by surprise. The phenomenon started in May 1712 when a thirteen-year-old girl named María López, the daughter of the village sacristan, Agustín López, had a vision of the Virgin, who told María that she wanted to help the Indians and that a shrine dedicated to her should be built at the site of the apparition, just outside the village itself. The girl told her father, and he, with the support of one of Cancuc's Indian alcaldes, recruited a number of the villagers to build the shrine; a cult began growing by leaps and bounds. María López, who started to call herself María de la Candelaria (after the Virgin of the Candelaria), continued to have visions of the Virgin, who talked to her from a vacant room at the shrine. Not all Indians, of course, accepted the veracity of the apparition. But the village officials did, and their support gave some legitimacy to the cult, which continued to grow in strength.[23]

The local priest found out what was going on, declared the apparition to be fraudulent, and had María and Agustín López whipped for their insolence. But this act of repression did not eliminate belief in the apparition, and the townspeople appealed to the bishop and to the royal officials for recognition of the miracle. This, of course, was denied. Instead, Cancuc's Indian alcaldes were arrested and replaced by others who promised to destroy the shrine.

Meanwhile, the cult of the Virgin thrived and attracted pilgrims from surrounding towns. Agustín López contacted Indians who held or had held civil or religious offices in the villages, and these people became the cadres of what would shortly become the revolutionary movement. It is important to note, then, that already existing hierarchies of power and prestige became the mobilizing force of the cult and then of the revolution. In Chiapas, as in Yucatán in 1761, the people followed their leaders.

Among those joining the movement at this time was Sebastián Gómez, who had had his own revelation. He claimed to have ascended into heaven and spoken with St. Peter, who had named him Vicar of Christ and invested him with the power to administer the sacraments, including that of Holy Orders. The participation of Gómez was significant for several reasons. First, he was a Tzotzil Maya (from the village of San Pedro Chenaló), and thus represented the ability of the hitherto Tzeltal-based cult and movement to expand its base of support to include other Maya people. Indeed, eventually five Tzotzil and two Chol Maya villages joined the revolution.

Second, Sebastián Gómez, who now took on the additional name de la Gloria (because he had gone to Glory and returned on a mission from God) added important Christian themes and symbolism to the movement. The powers that he claimed to have were in fact those of the papacy, which also based itself on the Petrine Doctrine ("Thou art Peter and upon this rock I will build My church").[24] The movement therefore would eventually be willing to claim not merely religious autonomy but full-fledged sovereignty. The Maya, far from attempting to purify themselves of all Christian doctrine, in effect believed themselves to be more Catholic than—or just as Catholic as—the Pope. The form, if not the substance, of Christianity had become a necessity.

The transition from revolutionary potential to actuality came about in August as a result of two events. First, the bishop chose this moment to announce his plan for a second episcopal visitation, even though he had been strongly advised to put it off. Second, the original Indian alcaldes of Cancuc escaped from detention, made their way back home, and deposed the village magistrates recently appointed by the Spaniards. They now assumed control in Cancuc, and sent messengers to the surrounding villages to seek their support. In a statement made on August 10, the Indian alcaldes and other leaders of the cult called on the Maya to rise up in support of their religion. In their proclamation they boldly asserted that "there is no king, nor God," referring, of course, to the Spanish king and Spanish God. Sebastián de la Gloria, meanwhile, began the ordination of priests, and became known as the bishop. The revolution had begun.

Realizing the danger that they faced, the movement began to organize an army. The Indian officials of the surrounding villages were called on to mobilize people to serve as soldiers, but when the revolutionary leaders in Cancuc organized the army, they appointed as commanders people who were not members of the political elite. It is possible that this was done so that the people entrusted with military power would be beholden only to the leaders in Cancuc, thereby consolidating that village's status as the head of the insurrection. The actual leadership of the movement, however, was in the hands of the traditional elite of Cancuc.

The mobilization and organization of military forces must have been carried out with extreme rapidity, for within a week the revolutionary army, composed of people who called themselves "Soldiers of the Virgin," was ready to take the offensive. The goal was apparently to bring the highlands of Chiapas under the control of the movement. The army first attacked nearby Chilón, one of several villages that had refused to join the revolution. All the male Spaniards and *ladinos* (non-Indians other than Spaniards, especially mestizos or *mulatoes*) were slaughtered. Then it was the turn of Ocosingo, attacked on August 14. In that village the revolutionaries discovered that all the male ladinos and Spaniards had fled assuming that their families would be safe. Furious over the escape of their primary enemy, the Soldiers of the Virgin massacred all the non-Indian children of the village and took the women back to Cancuc. This was the high-water mark of the revolutionary offensive, for shortly thereafter the Maya had to face a Spanish-led counterattack.

Back in Cancuc, the movement consolidated its power and carried out its revolutionary program. It took control of the money captured in the offensive or donated by the rebel villages and their cofradías. The ladino and Spanish women captured at Ocosingo were forced to marry Maya revolutionaries. This may have been subconsciously a way of taking revenge on the Spaniards. Cancuc was renamed Ciudad Real (Royal City), and the Maya government called itself an audiencia (high court), while the Spanish colonial capital was referred to as Jerusalem—the people of which, it was thought, had killed Christ—and the Spaniards were referred to as Jews, that is, deicides. Even the military took on Spanish nomenclature, for the army commanders were given the rank of captain general. The colonial world was being turned on its head.

Most important, perhaps, the cult of the Virgin of Cancuc became a new form of Christianity. Sebastián de la Gloria called together the Indian religious officials of the rebel villages and ordained them as priests. A new Maya priesthood was thus born, and began to say Mass and administer the sacraments throughout the region. Catholic ritual, including the use of the vestments, was rigidly adhered to. Nevertheless, some people seem to have gone along with this simply to avoid being executed, and most of those ordained by Sebastián de la Gloria were later exculpated by the Spanish authorities. Still, the rebels saw themselves as the true believers of a church founded by Divine intervention in the Christian sense of the term.

The revolutionary leadership in practice found itself challenged from both within and without. Although the movement succeeded in spreading well beyond Cancuc, it had very limited success in appealing to Tzotzil and Chol Maya: only five villages of the former and two of the latter actually joined the revolution, which therefore was for the most part Tzeltal-based. But even among these Maya support was limited to the area just to the north and east of the Spanish capital, in some fourteen Tzeltal villages. The great majority of the Maya of Chiapas, therefore, did not support the revolution. In fact, many joined and fought on the Spanish side, and without such support the Spaniards would have found it extremely difficult, and very expensive, to regain control of the Chiapan highlands.

Moreover, there was a continuous struggle for power within the revolutionary movement. As Friar Ximénez had noted, the people were extremely prone to revelations, and shortly after the founding of the Cancuc cult, sure enough, another Maya woman, Magdalena Díaz, had a vision of the Virgin, this time in Yajalón. This started a new cult dedicated to the so-called true apparition of the Virgin. It inevitably was critical of the one in Cancuc, and began to gain support in some of the villages that had already joined the revolution. This undermined support for the original movement and was a challenge to the revolutionary leaders, who therefore suppressed their rivals and hanged Magdalena Díaz. Then someone else showed up in the highlands claiming to be Jesus Christ; he also was executed. All the time, of course, many Maya refused to abandon their orthodox faith, and some even denounced the cult founded by María López and her father. The leadership had such loyalists killed. Finally, there emerged a full-fledged political opposition, based in surrounding villages and composed of those who disputed Cancuc's right to monopolize leadership and resources. Repression was used against these opponents. All told, the revolutionary leaders in Cancuc executed—sometimes in most gruesome ways—scores or perhaps hundreds of Indians in order to maintain their control of the movement. The enemy within was killed in defense of the revolution.

The greatest danger, of course, was from without. The colonial regime began mobilizing its forces as soon as it had news of the insurrection. Spaniards alone would have been insufficient to put down the revolt, for there were very few real soldiers anywhere in the whole Kingdom of Guatemala. The militia that actually did the fighting was composed mostly of ladinos, mulatoes, and even black slaves, while leadership was in the hands of Spanish officials. Very importantly, large numbers of Maya were recruited, and they had a major part in the military operations. The high magistrate of Chiapas, Pedro Gutiérrez Mier y Terán, was in fact ready to begin a counterattack by the end of August, while the president–captain general of the Kingdom, Toribio de Cosío, raised an army in Guatemala and marched quickly to join forces with those already mobilized in Chiapas.

Although the bishop was so scared that he fled the province, it is obvious from their actions that the alcalde mayor and the captain general had no doubt about their eventual success. The Maya revolutionaries outnumbered the Spanish side, but the latter had the advantages of weaponry—more firearms and swords, while the Maya had mostly machetes, hastily made spears, and clubs—and of leadership experienced in warfare. It is worth noting that neither side, Maya or Spaniard, made any attempt to negotiate with the other. Since both claimed absolute sovereignty, there was nothing to negotiate.

The Soldiers of the Virgin fought a pitched battle against greatly outnumbered loyalist and Spanish forces led by Alcalde Mayor Gutiérrez Mier y Terán on August 25 at Huistán. A Spanish witness later recounted that when fired upon, the Maya revolutionaries "retreated like locusts."[25] The Spanish victory stopped the Maya advance, and Spaniards at the time looked upon the battle as the turning point of the rebellion.[26] Momentum thereafter was against the Maya, and although final Spanish victory was possible only after the arrival of Captain General Cosío's force, the issue was never in doubt. After heavy fighting, Cancuc fell to the Spaniards on November 21. Resistance then shifted to other towns, and the war dragged on into March 1713.

Spanish policy shifted quickly from repression to pacification. During the early months of the war, few prisoners were taken, and on the day that Cancuc fell all the rebel captains who were captured were hanged without benefit of trial. The next day, however, Cosío offered to pardon all who would surrender immediately. Many did so, but others, including practically all the revolutionary leadership and those who had severely compromised themselves, continued the struggle in the countryside. The colonial forces eventually captured many people and then held trials to determine degree of guilt. All captains, revolutionary leaders, and individuals known to have participated in killing Spaniards, ladinos, or Indians, were hanged, drawn, and quartered. Those who had joined the movement but had done nothing else specific were usually given floggings and sometimes exile as well. Still others were found not guilty and freed. María López, whose vision had given cultural meaning to the revolution, died in childbirth before she could be captured. Sebastián Gómez de la Gloria, the leader of the revolutionary church, escaped and was never found.

The events in Chiapas demonstrate the great importance that culture played in revolution in the Maya area. True, the economic motive—the threat of further exploitation by the bishop—was significant, but to emphasize the economic alone is to ignore the existence of a revolutionary organization prior to the announcement of the bishop's episcopal visitation. Moreover, the purely economic interpretation does not take the Maya's own actions seriously. Indeed, the Maya may have resented the attempt to extort more money from them, but their attempt to take over both church and state and to achieve recognition of a local apparition of the Virgin demonstrate that more was involved than resistance to economic exploitation.

Revolts and revolutions, of course, can have numerous causes. The events in Chiapas reveal the Maya at their most revolutionary. Most acts of resistance to colonialism, however, were not revolutionary. The rest of this book seeks to find out why revolt and revolution took place elsewhere in the Maya area and what those events can tell us about the Maya experience with colonialism.

2

Reputation, Respect, and Role Reversal: Verapaz, 1735

The God who created you also created them.

—Martín May, Indian of the village of San Juan Chamelco, speaking to
Spanish High Magistrate Manuel Barrueta, 1735[1]

PARTICIPANTS

* = key figure
+ = died in uprising

Mayas

Martín May, former alcalde (village magistrate) of San Juan Chamelco
Juan Toc, alcalde mayor's translator
Gaspar Butz, senior alcalde of San Juan Chamelco
Juan de la Cruz Chuc, former alcalde of San Juan Chamelco
Marcos Cuq, former alcalde of San Juan Chamelco
*Esteban Siquiq, person alleged to have pushed the alcalde mayor
*Sebastián Bol, former alcalde of Cobán
*Domingo Putul, alcalde of Cobán
Tomás Contreras, indio ladino, informer
*Pedro Salá, principal of Cobán
*The people of San Juan Chamelco
*The people of San Pedro Carchá
*The people of Cobán

Nahuas

The militiamen (archers) of Salamá

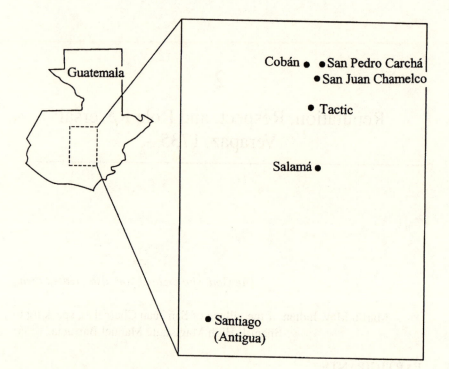

Map 2 **Cobán and Vicinity**

Spaniards

Pedro de Rivera, captain general and president of the audiencia
*Manuel Barrueta, alcalde mayor (high magistrate) of the province of Verapaz
Manuel Ordóñez, lieutenant of the alcalde mayor
"Manuelito" Ordóñez, son of Manuel Ordóñez
Juan Ramón Texedor, relative of the alcalde mayor
Fray Diego Pacheco, curate of San Juan Chamelco and San Pedro Carchá
Fray Bernardino Ceballos, priest in Cobán
Fray Gregorio Suárez, friar who calmed down the people from San Juan Chamelco
Fray Juan Asañón, friar who calmed down the people from San Pedro Carchá
Antonio López Morato, Peruvian Spaniard, resident of Cobán
Juan de Coto Mézquita, resident of Cobán
Nicolás de Santa Cruz, carpenter, resident of Cobán

Lic. Isidro López de Ereiza, fiscal (attorney general) of the audiencia
Joseph González de Rivera y Rancaño, corregidor of Chiquimula de la Sierra
*Lic. Antonio de Paz y Salgado, special investigating judge
Juan Antonio de Pedrosa, legal defender of Sebastián Bol and Pedro Salá
Luis de los Reyes, legal defender of Domingo Putul

Ladinos

+ Juan Augustín de Sauza, mulato who worked for the alcalde mayor and
who detained the people trying to get to Santiago
Augustín Salvador de Guzmán, mulato, important witness to events
Miguel Larios, mestizo
Luis de Paz, mulato barber who disguised himself as a Maya woman
+ Nicolás de Paz, resident of Cobán
+ Jacinto Zapatero, resident of Cobán
Petrona Matamoros, mulata, resident of Cobán, sister of Miguel Matamoros
+ Miguel Matamoros, mulato, resident of Cobán
Juan de Moto Torres, brother-in-law of Miguel Matamoros
Tomás Eusebio Esquivel, mulato weaver of Cobán

A colonial society is like all others in one fundamental way: it is based on
institutions and mechanisms that channel to elites the wealth produced by
the working population. This basic reality is usually justified in one way or
another, however, so that brute force is only rarely required to keep a working class or peasantry in its place. Normally there is some degree of acceptance, however reluctant, of class rule and the channeling of wealth to the
higher social strata. Brute force is usually unnecessary. Most systems of social stratification thus rely on a sometimes unsteady balance of consensus
and coercion, the latter backing up the former.

Spain's rule over millions of Indians in America lasted so long—three
centuries in the case of Mexico and only slightly less in Central and South
America—because the Spanish American elite succeeded in establishing that
balance of consensus and coercion. The indigenous population in most (but
not all) of Spanish America resigned itself to colonialism. To be sure, the
European conquerors almost always used brute force at first to conquer the
Indians and set up the colonial system, and thereafter they relied on coercion
to maintain their control over the conquered people. But eventually violent
resistance was worn down or overwhelmed, and the Indians agreed to the
peace settlement offered by the Spaniards. In return for tribute, labor, and
submission to Spanish authority, the native people received Christianity (from
the Spanish point of view, that was a big deal), peace (in the sense of the
absence of war), considerable political autonomy at the local level, and perhaps

most important, their survival not merely as individuals but as unique societies complete with their own social classes, political ideologies, land tenure, and culture—all of which the Spanish state tried to protect and perpetuate.

To be sure, this colonial bargain in the long run worked very much to the advantage of the Spaniards. Indian societies became progressively poorer, and changed in ways detrimental to their members. Eventually even the Spanish state did less and less to protect indigenous society and more and more to exploit it. But all that was unpredictable at the time the colonial system was set up. Spaniards could no more foretell the impoverishment of the Indians than they could their own imperial decline from the seventeenth century onward.

Moreover, not all of the colonial bargain was negative for the Indians. Peace—a *Pax Hispanica*—meant the end of the interminable bloody warfare that had characterized much of America, especially Mexico and Central America, in the millennium before the arrival of European invaders. Furthermore, the colonial bargain required the Spaniards to establish limits on exploitation. Indians, in turn, saw the establishment and maintenance of such limits as their right. Consequently, attempts by Spaniards to go beyond the boundaries and limits of exploitation meant, from the Indians' point of view, the violation of their rights.

The colonial bargain—Indian acceptance of colonialism in return for special rights—thus led to the establishment of what might be called the moral economy.[2] As long as Spanish exploitation stayed within certain limits, the indigenous people would resign themselves to the inevitable; they would pay their taxes and perform certain labor services (although they would also find ways of getting around the latter). But when Spaniards made demands that transgressed those limits, they violated the moral economy. Indians saw such demands as immoral and hence unacceptable. The result was resistance. Sometimes this was violent. Most of the time, however, the native people realized the danger of violent rebellion and chose more subtle forms of resistance. They resorted to what James Scott has called the weapons of the weak: "foot dragging, dissimulation, false compliance, pilfering, feigned ignorance, slander, arson, sabotage, and so forth."[3]

This chapter concerns the Spanish violation of the moral economy in Guatemala's Verapaz region (the northern part of the central highlands). The ensuing revolt caused the death of four people, and likely would have resulted in the demise of the Spanish provincial high magistrate (*alcalde mayor*) and of several others had they not fled to the church for safety and had the Indians not respected the sanctuary of the holy ground. Two entire villages— men and women, old and young, *principales* (elites) and *macehuales* (commoners)—and a large part of a third participated and caused some material damage. But most damaged of all was what the Spaniards called their "reputation": their position of authority. By saying and doing things that placed them on an equal footing with the Spaniards, the Indians challenged the Spaniards' position and subjected the Spanish magistrate to treatment hitherto reserved strictly for the indigenous people. The mere restoration of order would not suffice to restore the Spaniards' position. They also had to reestablish their reputation, without which their authority was in question and their right to rule in dispute.

However, reestablishing authority also meant reestablishing consensus, and it was not easy to accomplish both at the same time. Brute force would not have worked as well as subtlety, for the Spaniards faced a serious constraint: the most important source of governmental revenues was tribute, that is, the taxes paid by the indigenous people. Everything had to be done to get the Indians to resume paying their taxes as soon as possible. The exercise of Spanish power therefore was always tempered by this fiscal reality. Paradoxically, the colonial pact that allowed the colonists and the government to live like parasites at the expense of the Indians also limited Spanish power. The activities of the indigenous people—paying their taxes or not paying their taxes—helped determine the nature of politics in colonial America. State formation, in short, was the result not simply of imposition from above as the result of conquest, but also of negotiation, renegotiation, and resistance from below. The Indians, in other words, were active participants in political struggle and helped determine the nature of colonial politics because Spanish power depended on them.

Colonialism Without Conquest

Verapaz is one of the most fertile regions of Guatemala. Although the province is mountainous, its altitude is not as high as that of the Huehuetenango just to the west (the site of a revolt discussed in a later chapter). The climate, therefore, while chilly is moderate, neither cold nor tropical. The terrain is hilly and lacks the precipitous mountains that to the west make agriculture difficult. The plentiful rainfall enabled Verapaz to produce a wide variety of crops, including not only the typical Mesoamerican foods (maize, beans, squash, etc.) but also cotton. Indeed, in the preconquest and colonial eras this was one of the main cotton-growing regions of Latin America. Much of the crop was exported to other provinces of Guatemala. A large part, however, remained in Verapaz and was woven by local Maya women into cotton textiles, the province's principal export. It was largely through cotton that the region was incorporated into the Guatemalan and world economies.

The people of the northernmost part of Verapaz were Maya Indians who spoke the Kekchi language. We shall therefore call them Kekchi Maya, although technically Kekchi is simply a linguistic term. Nevertheless, it makes sense to use a word to distinguish these people from others, for as we shall see with other indigenous groups, Maya who spoke the same language frequently manifested solidarity with each other. That solidarity between different villages within the same language group was one of the distinctive characteristics of the Maya, a factor that distinguishes them from many other indigenous people of America.

Thirty-four years after the revolt discussed in this chapter, the archbishop of Guatemala, Pedro Cortés y Larraz, visited Verapaz and commented on its land and people. He noted the fertility of the soil and praised the people for their industriousness. He also reported that the Kekchi Maya were exceptionally devout Christians, although he complained that they demanded the last rites of the Church at the slightest incidence of illness.[4] (Perhaps they viewed the rites as having medicinal as well as spiritual value.) At the time of the archbishop's visit there was no apparent evidence of the revolt that had taken place three decades earlier, but, as we shall see, Christian devotion did play a role in the thinking and acting of the rebellious Kekchi Maya in 1735.

Verapaz is a region with a somewhat unusual history. It is one of the few places with a large indigenous population that was never conquered by the Spaniards in a military campaign. The great and famous missionary, historian, and political advisor, Bartolomé de las Casas, after being appointed bishop of the region in the early sixteenth century, convinced the Kekchi Maya to submit peacefully to Spanish rule. To be sure, Spaniards did have to use force to maintain their control over the region in the centuries after las Casas.[5] Nevertheless, the lack of violent conquest unquestionably contributed to the growth of Indian belief in their own rights as part of the colonial bargain, and thus played a role in the outbreak of the revolt of 1735.

The capital of the province was Cobán. In Spanish documents it is referred to—somewhat grandiosely—as "the Imperial City." Its title of city dated from the sixteenth century when Cobán was made the see of a diocese. That status was taken away in 1608, for it was found to be more convenient to the Church to have the region under the ecclesiastical control of the diocese of Guatemala. Cobán was left with its fancy title and with a large convent of Dominicans, successors to the great missionary efforts of las Casas.

There is no information available regarding the population in 1735, but thirty years later, when Archbishop Cortés y Larraz made his episcopal inspection, that prelate estimated Cobán's Indian population at between ten and eleven thousand. In the 1730s the provincial capital would have been somewhat smaller, but would still have been a very large town. The surrounding villages of San Juan Chamelco and San Pedro Carchá (located just a few miles to the southeast and east respectively of Cobán) were considerably smaller. In the 1760s each had an Indian population of about two thousand.[6]

Verapaz was one of the most Indian provinces in all of Spanish America. Archbishop Cortés y Larraz reported that very few non-Indians lived in the region. In 1735, however, it would seem that *ladinos* (people who were neither Indian nor Spanish) were somewhat more numerous, especially in the provincial capital. When the Spanish high magistrate got into trouble in that year, he succeeded in mobilizing a squad of two dozen able-bodied men from among the non-Indian people of Cobán. A few were officially referred to as "Spaniards," although that term meant people of Spanish ancestry born in America as well as those born in Spain itself. Indeed, one of these men was a native of Piura, Peru. On the other hand, as we shall see in later chapters, it was not uncommon for people from other Spanish colonies to be found in Guatemala.

Practically all the non-Indians in Verapaz therefore were called ladinos. This term is now used in Guatemala to refer to all non-Indians, but in the colonial period the word had a narrower definition. It did not include Spaniards. Rather, ladinos were almost entirely mixed-race people, that is, mestizos and mulatoes. Most of those in Cobán seem to have been the latter. At the same time, a few Indians were called *indios ladinos*, by which was meant Indians who were bilingual in an indigenous language and in Spanish. They were always distinguished from the mestizos and mulatoes.

The non-Indians of Cobán were unlike the Indians in important ways. They were mostly artisans by profession and probably did not engage in agriculture like the Maya. Many of them were bilingual in Spanish and Kekchi, while all but a handful of Indians were monolingual. Finally, the ladinos considered themselves to be members of a different group. They certainly dressed differently, and because of their partly African origin they undoubtedly looked different too. Indeed, the Indians frequently did not know the mulatoes' surnames but knew some of them well enough to call them mulatoes. Finally, they were not subject to tribute and most importantly behaved like members of a different group. For the Kekchi Maya, the ladinos and Spaniards were "other" people and were identifiable as such.

At the same time, the Maya villagers were easily identifiable as Indians. Ladinos somehow knew that particular people were from specific places. Perhaps the Maya had already begun to dress as they do in modern times, each village having its own distinct and recognizable clothing. In any case, when people from the surrounding villages of San Juan Chamelco and San Pedro Carchá came to Cobán one Sunday in January 1735, the non-Indians of the provincial capital recognized their origin.

Village of origin was not the only way that the Indians identified themselves. Each settlement was composed of several social subunits, each of which was called a *calpul*. What members of calpules believed they had in common was descent from a common ancestor. Many villages in the Maya area were originally composed almost exclusively of people from the same calpul. The Spaniards, however, found the numerous scattered Maya settlements to be inconvenient and conducive to both barbarism and heresy and thus carried out a policy called *congregación* or *reducción*. They forced the resettlement of small villages into larger ones. The Maya, however, usually refused to give up their loyalty to their clans. Therefore, even in the new larger settlements the people maintained their clan structure. Calpules, in short, survived colonialism.

Maya social institutions clearly become evident in the documentation of the revolt of 1735 in Verapaz (and in the uprising in Tecpán in 1759 discussed in the next chapter). San Juan Chamelco was composed of three calpules, named Santo Domingo, Santa Catarina, and San Luis, which were in addition to the principal calpul of San Juan. The names were derived from the patron saints of the churches in the neighborhoods where the clan members lived. Clans, in other words, tended to occupy specific spaces within the village. San Pedro Carchá was composed of the principal calpul as well as those of San Pablo, Santiago, and San Sebastian. Cobán had at least six calpules, but only four of these were mentioned in the records: Magdalena, San Marcos, San Bartolomé, and the principal one of Santo Domingo.

In some cases a clan would have self-government within the village. This helps explain why some villages would have not two Indian magistrates (*alcaldes*), as Spanish law specified, but three or more such officials. Indeed, during the revolt one of the Indian magistrates of Cobán suggested that he go to Santiago (modern-day Antigua), the capital of the Kingdom of Guatemala, accompanied by the six other calpul leaders of the village.[7] Spanish colonialism, in short, could affect settlement patterns but could not always eliminate Maya social organization. The survival of clans, as we shall also see in later chapters, proves that.

At the time of the revolt in 1735, Verapaz was governed by High Magistrate Manuel Barrueta. Provincial magistracies, or *alcaldías mayores,* were usually purchased by Spaniards, both from Spain and from Spanish America, and Verapaz was one of the most expensive posts in the Kingdom of Guatemala. In 1728 Barrueta paid 4,500 pesos to be high magistrate of the province, and occupied the post from 1732 through 1736. During that time his annual salary was 770 pesos, which means that his cumulative income in five years, after taxes, was 2,951 pesos.[8]

Barrueta, like all purchasers of provincial magistracies, bought the post in order to be able to carry out business activities that he backed up with the power of his office. In Verapaz this meant participation in the production of cotton and cotton textiles. The normal practice was for the high magistrates to advance money or credit to the Indians to that they could pay their tribute. In return, the Spanish officials were paid in raw cotton and in cotton textiles, products that were sold outside of Verapaz. Since the goods that the Indians delivered in payment of debt were evaluated well below market prices, the Spanish officials made a profit by selling the cotton and textiles at prices well above what he had paid for them. In 1738 the president of the Kingdom of Guatemala submitted a secret report in which he estimated that the high magistrate of Verapaz could earn some 8,000 pesos per year through these *repartimientos*.[9] That, of course, explains why Barrueta was willing to buy a post that yielded a cumulative salary less than what he had paid for it.

It should be noted that the political power exercised by the Spanish officials was essential for the business. In theory, of course, any businessman could lend money to the Indians in return for repayment in kind. But private merchants rarely entered into such deals because they found it hard to make the indigenous people pay their debts. Indeed, they found it hard to make anyone pay up, and thus high magistrates in Mexico who loaned money to Spanish or other non-Indian prospectors in silver-producing regions frequently had to write off as losses many of the loans that could not be collected.[10] Government officials, however, had means that private merchants lacked: the power of the state. High magistrates therefore could and did threaten, arrest, and flog the Indians in order to make them pay their debts. This gave Spanish officials an advantage over private merchants, and explains why so much business with the Indians was conducted by high magistrates.

Manuel Barrueta was probably a Spanish-born Basque. He must have been a man of prospects. When he purchased his post in 1728, he was an official resident of the colonial capital of Santiago, and by the year of the revolt he had married the daughter of Don Tomás Arana, the *oidor decano* (senior judge) on the *audiencia* (high court) that ruled over the kingdom. This of course resulted in a conflict of interest when the audiencia had to investigate Barrueta. We shall later see how this was resolved.

Barrueta was the only salaried royal official in Verapaz. However, the job required helpers and therefore the high magistrate hired an assistant, called a *teniente* (lieutenant). Barrueta's assistant was Don Manuel Ordóñez, who had already acquired experience in the business of the magistrates of Verapaz. In the 1720s he had served as the legal representative of a previous high magistrate, who had granted Ordóñez his power of attorney to act for him in Santiago.[11] Barrueta's lieutenant in turn was aided by his son Manuel (called Manuelito by those who knew him), who worked as a scrivener (*escribiente*). The high magistrate was also helped by a relative of his named Juan Ramón

Texedor; and because he could not speak Kekchi, Barrueta also employed a translator named Juan Toc. All these people had to be paid out of Barrueta's own pocket. The expenses were considered to be the costs of doing business.

Tax Relief, Rumor, and "Revolution"

The revolt in Verapaz was caused, paradoxically, by a measure that the Spanish government introduced to help the Indians of the kingdom by eliminating an abuse. One of the ways (in addition to the repartimientos) that provincial magistrates made money was to collect taxes in kind and then resell the goods; this yielded a profit because the goods were officially evaluated well below the market price. In the few cases in which commutation (payment in money) was permitted, Indians were forced to pay at rates that were above the market price and hence exploitative.

In 1734 the audiencia decided to reform the tributary system in two important ways. First, it allowed the Indians the option of paying in money or in kind. Second, the evaluation of goods was changed to reflect real prices. In Verapaz the new evaluations were important. In the past Indians were allowed to commute some taxes in maize to money, but to do so thay had to pay three reales per fanega. The reform lowered that payment to two reales, a tax reduction of one-third. However, the change in question affected only what was defined as tribute in a narrow sense; another tax, called *recudimiento*, may or may not have been affected. The high magistrate insisted that the new evaluations did not affect the recudimiento tax, and eventually the audiencia supported his reading of the law.

However, the priests of Verapaz read the law in a way that was favorable to their parishioners. The Dominican Friar Diego Pacheco, the curate of San Juan Chamelco and San Pedro Carchá (the villages just a few miles from Cobán) informed the people of the change and of how it affected them. Since the priest was never called as a witness, we have only the Kekchi Maya version of what was said.[12] What is clear is that the parishioners of San Juan Chamelco concluded that their taxes had been lowered.

Sometime later High Magistrate Barrueta got into what was called an "altercation" with Gaspar Butz, the Indian senior magistrate of San Juan Chamelco. Butz, who like almost all Indians did not know his age (although the Spaniards estimated him to be seventy years old), refused to acknowledge that his village owed anything beyond what it had already paid in taxes. Barrueta insisted on his interpretation of the audiencia's reforms, and when Butz remained adamant, the high magistrate ordered the three Indian magistrates to be flogged for their insolence. Butz was given 100 lashes (for as we shall see many times in this study, age did not exclude an Indian from corporal punishment), and the others got sixty. The Maya leaders were then jailed in Cobán.[13] This probably happened on Friday, January 28, 1735. By Sunday morning the officials of San Juan Chamelco were still in jail, where the Spanish magistrate was holding them until they agreed to pay their village's debts.

Meanwhile, back in San Juan Chamelco news of the flogging and jailing of their magistrates became known to the villagers. They were not leaderless, for although their elected officials were in jail in Cobán, there still existed a body of people known as "*principales* and *chinames.*" The former were quite simply the principal people of the village, an all-male group that included several former Indian magistrates. *Chinam*, a word common in many Mayan languages, means lord, and in the records it was always used in conjunction with *principal*. In short, the "principales and chinames" were the lords and masters of the village. All the others, except for elite women and children, were called *macehuales*. Because of this social and political structure, the villagers did not need their current Indian magistrates to act; instead, they themselves acted. The "principales and chinames" decided to go as a group to Santiago.[14] Only those too feeble to travel, such as eighty-seven-year-old former Indian magistrate Martín May (the only Indian who knew his exact age), stayed behind.

The "lords and masters" later claimed that they were going to the colonial capital to thank the president for having introduced the tribute reform. This was not entirely credible. But they were undoubtedly telling the truth when they said that they would also ask the president for clarification of the reform and for a copy of the tribute schedule (the *tasazión*). That way, they claimed, they would be able to find out "many truths" about their taxes. The schedule would help them, for as former Indian magistrate Juan de la Cruz Chuc explained, "without the tribute schedule, we were blind."[15] Moreover, unless they had it in writing their high magistrate would not believe them, for, as former Indian magistrate Marcos Cuq put it, "he always has a hard head."[16]

It is important to note, then, that the events culminating in revolt did not begin simply as resistance to taxation. The people had paid taxes before, and fully expected to pay them in the future. Action was taken in fact in defense of rights: the belief that Spaniards should not exploit them arbitrarily. Barrueta's actions were understood to be arbitrary and illegal, and hence were a violation of the moral economy and of the colonial bargain. The Indians' first response, in fact, was to seek the intervention of higher Spanish authority. It was thus in defense of their rights that the Maya took action.

At the very time that the "lords and masters" of San Juan Chamelco were making their decision, the same class of people in nearby San Pedro Carchá was doing the same thing. The village Indian magistrates had also at first refused to pay what Barrueta had demanded, but they eventually gave in and paid up. The village leaders therefore were not arrested and flogged. Nevertheless they were interested in the tribute reform and therefore the Indian magistrates and principales met in the village hall to discuss what to do. They decided to send a delegation to the colonial capital in the company of that from San Juan Chamelco.[17] This joint action could hardly have been a coincidence. Some communication between the two villages—that is, collusion or "conspiracy"—must have occurred.

There were therefore two village delegations of principales and chinames that set off together—probably on Friday, January 28—for the colonial capital. They got about halfway there when they were stopped. Somehow High Magistrate Barrueta had found out what was up and had quickly dispatched a ladino named Juan Augustín de Sauza to apprehend them. Sauza carried with him a written order to the Indian magistrates of all the villages along the way to arrest the people from San Juan Chamelco and San Pedro Carchá. The ladino overtook them at the Sierra de Chuacús (which divides Verapaz from central Guatemala). Some of the Indians managed to flee and avoid capture, and this group eventually made it to the capital. There they met with the provincial (elected leader) of the Dominicans and even succeeded in getting an audience with the president, Captain General Pedro de Rivera, although nothing is known about what was said at the meeting.[18]

Most of the delegates, however, were stopped by Sauza, who demanded that they turn over the petition they were carrying to the president. The Indians denied they were carrying any such petition, so Sauza conducted a thorough search of their backpacks. He found nothing.[19] It is possible that the petition was in hands of those who escaped capture and made it to Santiago. It is also possible that there was no written petition. What this incident clearly demonstrates, however, is the high magistrate's fear that the Indians would lodge a formal complaint against him with the president. No official, of course, likes people under his jurisdiction appealing to higher authority or bringing outsiders into local conflicts. Barrueta's reaction was typical of a provincial magistrate.

The ladino, whom the Indians referred to simply as Juan Augustín Mulato—for that is how they saw him—then brought his prisoners back to Cobán. He also took advantage of them. He forced them to carry sacks of flour and sugar and pots of honey to the provincial capital.[20] It is likely that someone paid him, but not them, for the labor. But Sauza would soon pay with his life for what he did and for what he was thought to have done.

After having spent the night in jail in the village of Tactic, the prisoners arrived in Cobán on Saturday, January 29. There Barrueta informed them that because they had left their village with evil intentions he would have them whipped. The high magistrate did not carry out his threat immediately, and the prisoners were put in jail along with the Indian magistrates, who were still there refusing to agree to Barrueta's tribute demands. But none of them would remain in jail much longer.

News of these developments reached San Juan Chamelco and caused great consternation. Now not only the village magistrates but practically all the "principales and chinames" were being held in jail in Cobán. But once again captured leaders were replaced by new ones. The wives of the prisoners demanded action, and were joined by the children and everyone else, including the macehuales, of the village. Even eighty-seven-year-old former village magistrate Martín May joined in, and the people en masse left San Juan Chamelco for Cobán.[21] They arrived in the provincial capital on Sunday morning at nine o'clock on January 30.

The appearance of practically everyone from San Juan Chamelco caught nearly everyone in Cobán by surprise. Manuel Barrueta immediately made one of his two intelligent decisions of what would be for him a bad day: he sent his relative Juan Ramón Texedor to the houses of all the Spaniards and ladinos of the village with orders for every able-bodied man to come to the Casas Reales (the government buildings in the town square where the jail was located). The non-Indians were to come armed.

Since it was Sunday, many people were easy to find. Augustín Salvador de Guzmán, a mulato, remembered that he was "at home drinking chocolate" with several other people (his friends?) when Barrueta's relative showed up asking for his help. With him was the Peruvian Spaniard Antonio López Morato. Juan de Coto Mézquita, also a Spaniard, was at church, as was the mulato barber Luis de Paz, who was in company with Juan Augustín de Sauza, who the day before had delivered his prisoners to the high magistrate. The latter two men had gone to visit the Dominican Friar Bernardino Ceballos. Also at church were the mestizo Miguel Larios and the Spanish carpenter Nicolás de Santa Cruz, a resident of Santiago, who was there to attend Mass.[22]

Within a short time after being summoned, about two dozen non-Indians were in the main plaza in front of the Casas Reales. They came armed with machetes, long knives, and shotguns. Nicolás de Paz probably had his *trabuco*, or blunderbuss, which would be fired later in the day with fatal consequences. The ladinos and Spaniards were positioned to defend the government buildings, while in the meantime the villagers of San Juan Chamelco, armed with lances, clubs, and rocks, built a barricade in front of the Casas Reales. It is unclear whether the Indians did this to protect themselves from a ladino attack or to prevent anyone from getting out of the government buildings.

By the time the ladinos had assembled, Barrueta had already sent his translator, Juan Toc, out to try to pacify the Indians. But he had no success. Then the high magistrate himself had a discussion with some individuals who appeared to be leaders of the people from San Juan Chamelco. Martín May, the elderly former Indian magistrate, spoke for these people. The conversation, he later remembered, took place in the corridor in front of the Casas Reales. At the inquest May did not report what Barrueta said, but he did put into the record what he told the high magistrate. He said that all the people of his village had come to plead for the release of their principales and village magistrates, who had done nothing to warrant flogging. Then, in what must have been one of the most dramatic moments of the inquest, May reported that he told Barrueta that the whipping of the village magistrates was an action "never seen nor heard of in all my years, and the God who created you also created them."[23]

We cannot be certain that May actually said that to Barrueta. But he clearly made that statement at the inquest. Here, then, is an opportunity to hear the authentic voice of the Kekchi Maya under colonialism. May was pointing out the fundamental equality of human beings, and by doing so he was questioning one of the fundamental principles of colonialism: the inequality between Spaniards and Indians.

To do this, the elderly former village magistrate of San Juan Chamelco appealed to the highest authority: God. Paradoxically, the Divinity in question was that introduced by the Spaniards. Moreover, the Christianity of Martín May was nothing less than the ultimate justification of Spanish colonialism. The Spaniards, after all, were the only Europeans who asked themselves whether it was just to conquer and rule over the indigenous people of America. They answered, of course, in the affirmative, but with a vital sine qua non: Christianity for the Indians.[24] Yet in Verapaz in 1735 we see that Christianity could be turned against the colonial masters. May did this by claiming equality before the Christian God. Christianity, in short, proved to be a double-edged sword: on the one hand it justified colonialism, but on the other it included principles and concepts that in certain conditions—as we shall also see in a later chapter—were subversive of the social order and even revolutionary in nature.

After May's confrontation with Barrueta, nothing happened for a while. Several Spaniards and ladinos asked what was going on, and the high magistrate said that he did not know. Spaniard Juan de Coto and ladino Augustín Salvador de Guzmán then asked the Indians the same question, and were told that the people of San Juan Chamelco had come to free their village magistrates and principales, whom the high magistrate had arrested because he mistakenly thought that they had gone to the colonial capital to cause him trouble.[25] Meanwhile Barrueta, inside the Casas Reales, was heard to mutter that "those Indians . . . have shamed me and lost respect for me."[26] Respect, we shall see, was important for colonialism.

Eventually Augustín Salvador de Guzmán offered to try to calm down the people in the plaza. Barrueta's lieutenant, Manuel Ordóñez, discouraged him, however, saying "you don't know the way these Indians are and the shameful things they have called us."[27] The high magistrate later complained that the people had called him a crook (*ladrón*), and he told Guzmán that the Indians "have become demons." The ladino eventually asked three times for permission to deal with the Indians before Barrueta finally agreed, saying "well, if you dare to try, go ahead."[28]

Augustín Salvador de Guzmán then convinced the Spaniard Juan de Coto and the ladinos Juan Augustín de Sauza, Miguel Larios, and Luis de Paz, all of whom spoke Kekchi, to accompany him. They asked someone who appeared to be a leader what the problem was, and that person replied that the people had not come to cause trouble but only to get their village magistrates and principales released from jail. The ladinos then convinced the Indians to lay down their clubs and rocks while they went back to convince the high magistrate to free the prisoners.[29]

Barrueta now made his worst decision of the day. He got angry, and after refusing to release the prisoners in return for an end to the standoff, he decided to stand by the door and taunt the Indians, holding a dagger in one hand and yelling "come and get them, Indian dogs!"[30] When, days later, the high magistrate finally got a chance to report events in Cobán, he must have realized his bad judgment, for he told the audiencia that he had called on the Indians "with total calmness and affection" ("con todo sosiego y cariño").[31] But at the time of his report he was in the village of Salamá (about 25 miles south of Cobán), and was then ordered to go to Santiago; as result he could not return to Verapaz to influence or "orchestrate" the testimony of the Spaniards and ladinos during the inquest.

The non-Indians therefore told a different story when they had their chance. Augustín Salvador de Guzmán said that he had warned the high magistrate three times not to go out in front of the Indians to taunt them, "because once they lose respect for you, all will be lost." The Peruvian Spaniard Antonio López Morato also said that Guzmán had warned Barrueta "many times" not to do it, because if he did, the Indians would lose respect for him.[32] No one supported the high magistrate's version of events.

What happened next is confusing (as events frequently are during civil disorder), but what is clear is that the taunting by the high magistrate had an effect. Several Indians approached Barrueta and a youth named Esteban Siquiq was either pushed into or tried to push the high magistrate. Barrueta used his dagger to slash Siquiq on the wrist. The youth began to bleed and screamed that he had been wounded. There was an uproar, and a scuffle between the Indians and the ladinos broke out. Several ladinos and twenty-two Indians were wounded, although none seriously. Augustín Salvador de Guzmán later said that some Indians from Cobán joined in with those of San Juan Chamelco. Between twenty and thirty succeeded in entering the Casas Reales. Then out of nowhere appeared the Dominican Friar Gregorio Suárez, who first calmed the Indians down and then convinced Barrueta to release the prisoners. The Indian magistrates and principales of San Juan Chamelco, reunited with their people, went home.[33] The uproar ceased, and Cobán suddenly became quiet.

At this point it should be noted that the people of the provincial capital had thus far done little. True, some may have joined the people of San Juan Chamelco, but for the most part the absence of Cobán people is striking. It turned out that the Indian magistrates of the provincial capital were holding their people back. Barrueta thought that they would come to his aid, but they did not. When asked at the inquest why not, the village magistrates responded that Barrueta had given them no orders to do anything, and that in any case Friar Suárez succeeded in calming everyone down with no one getting killed. But the high magistrate had learned an important lesson: he could not count on the people of Cobán or their leaders to rescue him. He would eventually take them to task for that.

It was probably at this time that the high magistrate sent a message to the village of Salamá asking for aid. That village, the people of which were not Maya but rather spoke the Nahua language, was the home of a militia unit of archers (*flecheros*, i.e., people who shoot arrows). These "indios flecheros" were reliable allies of the Spaniards, and shortly after receiving the message the militia unit was mobilized and began to move.

All might then have returned to normal in Verapaz had not a rumor arrived in the village of San Pedro Carchá. No one knew who reported events to the other village, but afterward the Spanish government tried hard to find out. It was unsuccessful in doing so. In any case, according to the rumor Barrueta and his ladino allies had killed several people from San Juan Chamelco during the battle in Cobán. It was also reported that the non-Indians had beaten up or killed Friar Suárez. This was, of course, untrue. The people of San Pedro Carchá, however, believed the rumors and decided to take action.[34]

But what did these villagers have to do with what had happened in Cobán to the people of San Juan Chamelco? Juan de Coto Mézquita, a Spanish resident of Cobán, certainly thought that it was strange. He later said that the actions of the people of San Pedro Carchá in support of their fellow Kekchi Maya were "notable."[35] The Spanish government tried to investigate this at the inquest, for it was disturbing to find out that Indians might manifest solidarity with each other. And solidarity is exactly what was being manifested. The only explanation that any of the participants, whether from San Pedro

Carchá or elsewhere, had was that these people thought of themselves as "friends" and "neighbors" of those of San Juan Chamelco.[36] They were interested in the same issue, that of taxation believed to be illegal, and they were in effect the same people because they spoke the same language. They would probably not have done the same for any other Indian group, and indeed Spanish rule in Verapaz was eventually restored by the Nahua-speaking people of Salamá.

Supposedly, during acts of resistance to Spanish colonialism, Indians showed little or no solidarity with people outside their own narrow village.[37] This may have been true in central Mexico and central Peru, but it was not true in the Maya area. In fact, as we shall see in later chapters, Maya people of the same linguistic group frequently showed solidarity with each other and participated in joint activities. Indeed, we have already seen that San Pedro Carchá people had joined with those of San Juan Chamelco in sending a delegation to Santiago to find out "truths" about tribute. Now they were showing solidarity again with their "friends" and "neighbors" of the other village.

It was around 3:00 P.M. on that same Sunday that the people of San Pedro Carchá arrived in Cobán. They came armed with clubs, machetes, lances, and bows and arrows. Their arrival was a noisy one, and caused Tomás Contreras, an Indian of Cobán and former secretary of the village government, who happened to be at the Dominican church-convent at the time, to think that something must have been going on among the unmarried adult men who were carrying out their Sunday duty of cleaning the orchard of the convent.[38]

The people of San Pedro Carchá must have had a menacing aspect about them, for Barrueta took one look at them and made his second, and last, intelligent decision of that day: he fled to the Dominican church-convent. Accompanying him were his lieutenant Ordóñez, several Spaniards, and ladinos who had been alerted in time. The high magistrate and the others had to run for their lives, for the people of San Pedro Carchá were shooting arrows at them. Several ladinos were wounded because the main door of the church was closed and they had to run to the side door, thus exposing themselves to even more arrows. Nevertheless, no one was hurt badly, and the Indians were left outside, continuing to shoot arrows and throw stones at anyone who showed his face. But they did not break in. It would have been difficult but by no means impossible to do so, for the doors could have been battered down. The Indians, in short, chose to respect the right of sanctuary.

Meanwhile, not all ladinos at the Casas Reales succeeded in fleeing, for a group of about fifteen was trapped inside. When the people from San Pedro Carchá broke down the door the ladinos took refuge in an anterior room. One of these men was Nicolás de Paz, who to defend himself fired his blunderbuss. It malfunctioned, exploded in his face, and blew off part of his head. He died immediately or shortly thereafter. It was probably at this time that Jacinto Zapatero also died. He had apparently tried to escape through the stable but did not make it. Cause of death was not mentioned in the records, but since the Indians used machetes and clubs in hand-to-hand combat, it is not hard to imagine.[39]

It is possible that the Indians of San Pedro Carchá would have killed more people at the Casas Reales had Friar Juan Asañón not intervened. The priest suddenly appeared carrying the Blessed Sacrament and called on the Indians in the names of God, St. John, and St. Peter (the latter two being the patron saints of the two villages near Cobán). He begged the Indians to kneel and pray. They did. Thus calmed down, these people of San Pedro Carchá killed no one else.[40]

At the Casas Reales the people of San Pedro Carchá did more than just attack human beings. They also broke up the household furnishings, let loose the mules and horses in the stable, and even freed the birds from their cage.[41] (Apparently it was the custom in Guatemala to keep pet birds, for this would also be reported in the revolt discussed in Chapter 7.)

Several Spaniards and ladinos were captured at the Casas Reales. Most were beaten and then tied up. The mulato barber Luis de Paz, however, managed to avoid capture and injury. He first tried to hide in the kitchen, but there an Indian from Cobán suggested that he hide on the roof. This he did, and his pursuers did not find him. When it became safe to come out, Paz got down from the roof, dressed himself as an Indian women, and went out into the street. He then went to the house of the Cobán Indian who had helped him find his hiding place and spent the night there.[42]

Several of the captured ladinos were then taken to the church and allowed to join the group taking refuge there. Those not freed were taken as prisoners to San Juan Chamelco. Some were freed there, but Juan Toc, the Cobán Indian who served as Barrueta's translator, after being captured, beaten, and taken to San Juan Chamelco, was forced to accompany the Indian magistrates of that village on a mission to Santiago. However, upon arrival in Tactic he was freed at the insistence of the parish priest.[43]

In all, some eighteen Spaniards and ladinos, as well as four Indian helpers or supporters of the high magistrate, were captured at the Casas Reales. Among them were Manuelito Ordóñez (son of Barrueta's lieutenant), the cook at the Casas Reales, and an Indian magistrate of Cobán who must have argued with the people from San Pedro Carchá. All were eventually freed, usually at the insistence of the priests, but some were deprived of food for as much as two days; others were robbed, and all were beaten up.

Some Spaniards and ladinos were not at the Casas Reales and escaped capture. The Spaniard Juan de Coto Mézquita heard the uproar resulting from the arrival of the people from San Pedro Carchá, went out to investigate, and was told by a fleeing mestizo to run for his life. He did—right to the church, where he took refuge with the others. The mulato Augustín Salvador de Guzmán, upon finding out about the arrival of the people from San Pedro Carchá, immediately went to the church for refuge and told a priest what was going on. The friar went out and talked with the Indians but apparently did not succeed in changing their minds. The Peruvian Spaniard Antonio López Morato simply hid in his house and did not emerge for several days.[44]

But other ladinos were less lucky. While some of the people from San Pedro Carchá upon entering Cobán headed for the Casas Reales, others—a group of between ten and twelve—were on a manhunt. They went to the house of former Indian magistrate Sebastián Bol and of other principales of Cobán. Upon leaving they were heard to say, "he gave us permission," although it was not clear who gave permission to do what. While walking past a few Indians from Cobán who were standing on the corner, the people from San Pedro Carchá ridiculed those of Cobán by telling them that they should watch out because their wives were the lovers of the ladinos. And in all the coming and going, someone told them where to find Juan Augustín de Sauza.[45]

Sauza had helped defend the high magistrate earlier in the day when the people from San Juan Chamelco had surrounded the Casas Reales. He had suffered a cut under his eyelid. At the time of the arrival of the people from San Pedro Carchá, he was at the house of Petrona Matamoros, a mulata, in the company of her brother Miguel and two other mulatoes. He saw the Indians coming toward the house, and yelled to Petrona Matamoros, "*Comadre*, let's lock the doors. They want to kill us." (He called her *comadre* because either she was the godmother of his child or he was the godfather of her child; Petrona Matamoros, in turn, would have called him *compadre*).

The Indians from San Pedro Carchá happened to have axes with them. They succeeded in breaking down the door, found Juan Augustín de Sauza, and yelled "this is the right house." They then set upon Sauza, first wounding him with a short lance or arrow, and after he had fallen to the ground they beat him to death. Then they beat Miguel Matamoros so badly that he died four days later. Juan Moto Torres, the brother-in-law of Miguel Matamoros, while fleeing tried to remind the Indians that they were Christians and therefore should not be doing such things, but he was shot with three arrows, captured, tied up, and beaten (although he lived to tell about it). He was taken to San Pedro Carchá, and then to San Juan Chamelco, where he was freed by the village priest.[46]

The only remaining person in the house, besides the owner, was Tomás Eusebio Esquivel, a mulato weaver. He tried to run and hide on the roof but the Indians found him, threw him down in the patio between the dead or dying Sauza and Matamoros, and shot arrows at him. One wounded him in the head. But then someone ordered the Indians to stop. Esquivel was tied up and taken to San Pedro Carchá, where he met up with a lot of other prisoners. From there he was taken to San Juan Chamelco, and then to Tactic, where the priest freed him.[47]

Many of the people who witnessed these events referred to them as a "revolution." And for a moment it was: Spanish authority was driven away and the Indians ran the village. Soon, even more humiliation, although not death, would be visited on the Spaniards.

Throughout the "revolution," the leaders of Cobán were once again conspicuous by their absence. But there were indications that some people from the provincial capital had joined in with those of San Pedro Carchá. The three mulatoes who survived the attack that killed Sauza and Matamoros all testified that they had heard that people from Cobán's barrios of Magdalena, San Marcos, San Bartolomé, and Cobán proper had participated. And people from Cobán were said to have joined with those of San Juan Chamelco in the first assault on the Casas Reales.

The village government of Cobán, however, held back. This was because, as Indian magistrate Domingo Putul later testified, Barrueta had given him no orders, and the arrival of the people of San Pedro Carchá in the afternoon had been so sudden and unexpected that he could do nothing. When he found out what was happening, it was too late, and even if he had gotten some of his people together, they would not have been as well armed as those from San Pedro Carchá and thus could not have accomplished anything other than to get themselves killed.

Nevertheless, some people from the provincial capital began to criticize Domingo Putul's lack of initiative and his failure to reestablish order. The wife of Augustín Salvador de Guzmán went out and scolded Putul, telling him that as Indian magistrate he should defend his village.[48] On the morning of the next day, Monday, Friar Asañón called together the village leaders and told them that they should be ashamed of themselves for letting excesses like those of Sunday take place in their village and allowing the high magistrate to be treated so badly. They responded by telling the priest that Barrueta had given them no orders. Asañón replied that at least they should do something to see that the people from San Pedro Carchá did not return and storm the church in order to kill the high magistrate.[49]

The Indian magistrates of Cobán eventually decided to act. At around 3:00 or 4:00 P.M. on Monday, January 31, they went to the church and told Barrueta that they would protect him and take him home. The high magistrate later regretted accepting the Indians' offer. Several days later he would write, "I was always careful not to be fooled by their well-known tricks," but this time, he believed, they fooled him. The high magistrate and the others in the church were taken not to their houses but to the jail. On the way, the people of Cobán were jeering and throwing stones at Barrueta and several others. The Indian magistrates of Cobán then put the lot of them in jail.

What happened next was of great symbolic significance. Colonialism required the systematic inequality of Spaniards and Indians, and this inequality extended to the realm of corporal and criminal punishment. For example, Indians were flogged for all sorts of offenses, even insolence, but it was thought inappropriate to whip Spaniards. For the same reason, in Indian villages like Cobán chains and irons were appropriate only for Indians. It therefore must have come as a quite a shock to everyone, Maya as well as Spaniard, when Domingo Putul and the other leaders of Cobán did the unimaginable: they put Barrueta, his assistant, and the other Spaniards in irons. They also had all the ladinos tied up.[50]

Once again the Kekchi Maya rejected the fundamental inequality between Spaniards and Indians. Even worse, from the Spaniards' point of view, they were turning the colonial order on its head. Indeed, putting Barrueta and the others in irons was not just subversive. It was revolutionary in its implications. No wonder that people in Cobán talked about the "revolution." Eventually the colonial authorities would have to punish this purely symbolic transgression by the Indians.

The shackled Spaniards and bound ladinos remained in that condition and in jail for several hours. Outside they could hear some activity, when in the early evening ("around prayer time," as Augustín Salvador de Guzmán put it) those who could understand Kekchi heard orders being given to the effect that the jail was to be guarded and protected from any further assault by the people of San Pedro Carchá. This heartened the bilingual prisoners, who told the others what was going on. Some Indians then provided the inmates with water and blankets for their comfort (for highland Guatemala is quite chilly in January). The high magistrate, however, was not optimistic about his chances. He told Guzmán that those who were shackled were going to die, and therefore he gave the mulato some objects of gold he had in his possession and asked that they be given to his wife.[51]

Then, at around 9:00 P.M., village magistrate Domingo Putul entered the jail. After giving everyone greetings, he asked Barrueta if he would like to have his shackles removed. The high magistrate was suspicious; pity, he thought, was foreign to the nature of Indians. Nevertheless, he replied in the affirmative, and as a result an Indian blacksmith went around and unchained everyone. The ladinos were untied. Barrueta was surprised, but later he found out that the relief column of Indian archers from Salamá had arrived on the outskirts of Cobán. Therefore, he reasoned, Indian magistrate Putul now found it convenient to start being nice to him again, for Spanish authority would soon be restored.

In fact the Nahua-speaking Salamá *flecheros* had arrived in Cobán at about seven or eight o'clock in the evening but were too wise and experienced to enter a potentially hostile village at night. Therefore they sent out scouts to reconnoiter the entrances and find food. They bought some tortillas from a woman at the village government building, and when asked why they were in Cobán they answered that they had come to rescue the high magistrate. The tortilla vendor immediately alerted the village.[52] It was possible then that Putul had been advised of the arrival of the relief force and therefore changed his behavior toward Barrueta.

The next morning, Tuesday, February 1, the Indian magistrate of Cobán returned to the jail. He asked Barrueta if he would like to inspect the damage done to the Casas Reales. All the prisoners were then released, and the high magistrate began to arrange for supplies for the archers from Salamá. The revolution was effectively over. The next day Juan de Coto Mézquita, a Spanish resident of Cobán, packed up his family and moved to Salamá because he feared for their lives. By Thursday Barrueta had also gone to Salamá. He too must have feared for his life.

It was from Salamá that the high magistrate wrote a brief report—in what was not the clearest of language—in which he gave his version of events in Verapaz. He blamed not only the people of San Juan Chamelco and San Pedro Carchá for their acts of violence and murder but also the Indians of Cobán. He argued that there must have been a conspiracy between the three villages, "because otherwise those of San Pedro and San Juan in no way could have had the fearless recklessness to enter Cobán with such undisguised daring and demolish houses belonging to the King and other people of the village, for they are small compared to Cobán and have always respected the people of the provincial capital."[53] The report was sent to the audiencia. Immediately the wheels of Spanish justice began to turn.

Repression or Pacification?

What happened in Cobán required an investigation and punishment. Four ladinos had died—one in an accident provoked by assault and the three others at the hands of Indians. The Casas Reales had been broken into and property destroyed. Finally, the representative of His Majesty had been publicly humiliated. On the other hand, there was no longer a grave threat to public order. Thus a show of force, but not the exercise of violence, was all that was necessary to reestablish Spanish rule.

The high magistrate's report was received by President Captain General Pedro de Rivera on February 6. Rivera passed it on to the Junta de Guerra, or War Council, which met the next day. The Junta, composed of the highest ranking military officers in the Kingdom of Guatemala, made several decisions. First, it ordered the provincial of the Dominicans to communicate with all the priests in the parishes under their control—which included all of Verapaz—and order them to use their influence to exhort the Indians to fulfill "their obligatory duty of fidelity, obedience, and submission, which they owe to the King Our Lord and to all his ministers and high magistrates," and to remind them of "the good that will thereby result and of the harm and punishment that will follow if they behave otherwise, as much from the hand of God as that of the King."[54]

Here, then, we see the familiar role of Christianity in Spanish America: to keep the people obedient, submissive, and in their place. And, of course, we have already seen the influence that the priests had in Verapaz: they helped calm the Indians down during the riot and encouraged the village authorities to reestablish order. Religion, therefore, while sometimes revolutionary in its implications, was also a useful weapon that the state could use to maintain the social order. As noted earlier, Christianity was a double-edged sword.

The Junta de Guerra's second decision was to recommend that the president dispatch to Cobán a military official "of science, experience, prudence, and practice in the handling of Indians." This was indirectly a criticism of Barrueta, for that high magistrate had not demonstrated that he possessed the virtues now required. The person chosen was to be accompanied by twenty-five men from the Palace Guard and 100 militiamen from the Valley of Urián (one of the few areas in Guatemala that had a non-Indian population of any size). The force was to be augmented in Salamá by 300 to 400 Indian archers, and then proceed to Cobán.

Third, once the show of force had been made, the War Council recommended that the audiencia appoint an attorney of that body to "investigate the causes of the uprising . . . and apprehend the principal ringleaders," who were to be punished "publicly and severely to serve as a warning to all the others and an example to the other provinces of the Kingdom." Here we have the first manifestation of the attitudes of the higher Spanish authorities. There would always be the desire to seek out and punish the ringleaders, for to the colonialist mentality there had to be a conspiracy behind every act of violence by the Indians. On the other hand, the emphasis on severe punishment is clearly the eighteenth-century military mind at work (for the War Council, after all, was made up of high-ranking soldiers). This view would not prevail.

After President Rivera and the audiencia had a chance to see Barrueta's report and the Junta de Guerra's recommendations, the documents were sent to the *fiscal* (attorney general) of the audiencia, Licenciate Don Isidro López de Ereiza. He reported on February 9, approving the appointment of an investigating judge, but also noting that the problem had begun because of complaints regarding the high magistrate's methods of tribute collection. Moreover, the attorney general brought to the audiencia's attention the important point relating to conflict of interest: Barrueta was the son-in-law of the senior audiencia judge. Fiscal López de Ereiza also recommended that the high magistrate be ordered to come to Santiago and stay there, presumably so that he would not be involved or interfere in the investigation in Verapaz.[55]

Later that day the audiencia responded, and put on record its displeasure over the appointment of a special judge because that would thereby exclude the high court from direct supervision of the case. Apparently the audiencia would have preferred that one of its own members be appointed to investigate. Nevertheless, it went along with what had now become a certainty: the appointment of an audiencia attorney—that is, someone with experience in presenting cases before the high court—as special investigating judge.[56]

By February 15 the president was ready to set matters in motion. On that date he appointed Joseph González de Rivera y Rancaño, *corregidor* (magistrate) of the province of Chiquimula de la Sierra (in eastern Guatemala) as the military official in charge of the show of force to be made in Verapaz. President Rivera described him as "a person who has my complete confidence."[57] We do not know if González de Rivera possessed all the virtues recommended by the War Council, but he did have more experience than Barrueta in "handling Indians." He had previously served as high magistrate of the province of Atitlán-Tecpanatitlán, located just to the northwest of the colonial capital. It was one of the wealthiest provinces in the kingdom, and González de Rivera apparently had done nothing to provoke the Indians under his jurisdiction to complain or rebel.

His instructions, however, did not reflect the attitude of the Junta de Guerra. The president ordered González de Rivera to restore order "without harm to the Indians or to any other person," and that he was to use "the most prudent means" consistent with "the gentleness, reflection, and zeal that a matter of such importance requires." In other words, severe repression was being ruled out. To make sure that González de Rivera did not use his position to his own advantage, he was forbidden to get involved in tribute collection. Finally, President Rivera went along with the fiscal's recommendation to have Barrueta leave Verapaz and come to the capital.[58]

González de Rivera received his orders, and after appointing someone to carry out his duties of magistrate in his absence, he set out for Cobán. He arrived on March 5. His very arrival signified a show of force, and in any case harsh measures were unnecessary. Eventually González de Rivera and his men were instructed to return to Salamá, where the expense of maintaining them was less, for most of the militiamen were from that village. In fact, the services of the military were no longer needed, and González de Rivera therefore played no further role in Verapaz.

On March 15 the audiencia resolved the problem of conflict of interest. It decided that Barrueta's father-in-law, senior judge Tomás de Arana, would be excluded from all business concerning his son-in-law, including the upcoming investigation. On matters concerning Barrueta, an audiencia attorney would substitute for Arana. Finally, on April 4 the president appointed the special investigating judge. Rivera named Licenciate Antonio de Paz y Salgado, an attorney of the audiencia.

The audiencia's instructions to Paz y Salgado, issued on April 5, are worthy of examination. As we have seen, the War Council had spoken in favor of "severe punishment," as might be expected of military men. But colonialism, like war, is much too important to be left to the generals. That is why the high court's instructions were so different. After specifying the kind of questions to be asked of the witnesses, the audiencia emphasized that "the principal end in observance of the laws of the Kingdom in cases like this" was "the quiescence of the province and the subjection of the Indians." Those goals could only be accomplished if the Indians could be convinced that the royal government would not impose "grave punishment." Therefore Paz y Salgado was ordered "to omit the rigor of laws and use prudence, which is what the state of the matter demands and what is ordered by His Majesty." After a preliminary inquest, the investigating judge was to make a report and wait for further orders. President Rivera approved these instructions, reiterating the need to use a combination of "zeal and prudence" to investigate the case.[59] Paz y Salgado left Santiago on April 18 and arrived in Cobán a week later.

Here then we have language that is quite different from that of the War Council. In effect, the civil authorities were making sure that the investigating judge did not do what the military had recommended. Instead, they clarified that the primary goal of the judge was to get the Indians to submit to authority. That would be best accomplished, they believed, by deemphasizing punishment, for if the Kekchi Maya thought that peaceful submission would do them no good, they might act differently. Once colonial rule had been reestablished and, most important, been *accepted* by the Indians, then punishment, tempered with prudence, could be administered. This was one of the most important principles of the colonial regime. It helps explain why Spain's rule in America lasted as long as it did (and why twentieth-century Guatemala's military governments, which so quickly resort to terrorist oppression, lack any sense of legitimacy).

Meanwhile, however, the Kekchi Maya had not been idle. They undoubtedly realized that the only alternatives to punishment were armed resistance or flight. Weighing their options, the leaders apparently decided those alternatives were impractical or undesirable, and therefore they readied themselves for punishment. But they realized that their behavior at this time could possibly mitigate the nature of that punishment.

Therefore they decided to cut their losses by pleading guilty and begging for mercy. This policy was put into effect even before González de Rivera had arrived in Cobán. Along the road he was met by the village governments of San Juan Chamelco and San Pedro Carchá. These Maya leaders "gave thanks to the Very Illustrious Lord President for the pity and commiseration with which he was looking after them by sending such a Christian minister to administer and attend to them as he would his own son." They "would obey him as their Father and Minister of His Majesty (God save the King)," and he in turn should inform the president of their "blind obedience and of the loyalty that they profess to their King and Lord and to his Ministers."[60]

This language of patriarchy appears throughout colonial documentation.[61] The Spanish state, like the Chinese and many others before it, chose to use the simile of the father-figure. It resonated in the culture of both Spain and America. The father ran the family—at least in theory—and thus patriarchal power was understood by all. The Spanish kings saw themselves, and wanted their subjects to see them, as fathers. But this was done not just to justify their power. It also established a family relationship between king and subjects and thus inspired loyalty beyond what could be expected by a nonpatriarchal leader such as the head of a representative assembly. Moreover, the familial relationship gave hope to those who had been naughty: punishment within the family is likely to differ from that carried out by impersonal authorities. Fathers do not kill or abuse their sons—again, at least not in theory—but rather punish them so they will behave better in the future.

Patriarchy therefore benefited the rulers, who used the patriarchal simile to their advantage. But by invoking the simile, the rulers also invoked a patterned response from the subjects. Rather than denying everything, the son can proclaim his guilt in the hope that the father will not be severe, will accept an act of contrition, and will administer punishment that balances the wrong done with the promise of future good behavior. The Kekchi Maya thus were pursuing their own interests. If the Spanish state wanted to play the role of father, then they would play the sons and thereby get better treatment. Both sides benefited by role-playing.

The welcome given González de Rivera was one example of the Indian appeal to patriarchy. Another was in the story they developed to explain their apparently naughty behavior. When they ultimately gave their own version of events, the villagers of San Juan Chamelco and San Pedro Carchá claimed that they had decided to send delegations to the colonial capital not merely to inquire about tribute but to thank the president for the good he had done by introducing the tribute reform. They were, then, like children thanking their father for his loving care. Even though this sounds like something they made up later, it is also likely that the delegates who did get to the capital actually thanked the president, because such an action could only have helped their cause. In any case, at the inquest, by stating this to be their goal, they were invoking and reinforcing the patriarchal relationship and, of course, hoping for the best.

Investigating judge Paz y Salgado wasted no time, for on April 26, the day after his arrival in Cobán, he began the proceedings and called witnesses to testify. The first people to appear were the Spaniards, ladinos, and indios ladinos. Between April 26 and May 2 the judge heard nine witness (four Spaniards, two mulatoes, a mestizo, and two Spanish-speaking Indians). All of these witnesses were male, and during the entire course of the investigation only one woman—the sister of one of the murdered ladinos—was called to testify. This was true even though the evidence clearly revealed significant participation by Indian women. Spanish law, like politics and ideology, was patriarchal in nature and did not give as much credence to female testimony as it did to male. If enough male witnesses were found, judges felt no need to call upon women.

Those called to testify first were the people who had come to the aid of the high magistrate when the Indians of San Juan Chamelco had come to town. Their version of events differed significantly from that given by Barrueta in his report, for several of them said that he had taunted the Indians. Moreover, although they were on Barrueta's side in the conflict, several stated that they had warned the high magistrate not to behave in that way. Barrueta, then, was clearly not a person "experienced in the handling of Indians," unlike the Spaniards and ladinos who lived in the village.[62]

One piece of information important for the criminal phase of the trial was revealed by Tomás Contreras, an indio ladino (Spanish-speaking Indian) from Cobán. His Hispanic surname suggests a possible mestizo ancestry, but he clearly was accepted as an Indian by the people of Cobán, for he had once served in the very important position of secretary of the village government. Yet it is rare to find a former secretary, for the position was almost always held for life. It is possible that Contreras had run into political problems and been forced from office. That would certainly explain his decision to cooperate with the Spanish authorities in the inquest. In his testimony, Contreras curried favor by claiming that he had talked one Indian out of throwing a rock at Barrueta and reminded him of how well the high magistrate had always treated them.

The important fact revealed by Contreras concerned Sebastián Bol, a former Indian magistrate of Cobán. The indio ladino testified that Bol was the person who had given the people of San Pedro Carchá permission to enter Cobán, and that he had even provided them with the rope used to tie up the high magistrate. Contreras then curried favor even more by lamenting the insults given to Barrueta, who had been kind enough to lend the village the money it needed to pay its tribute (thus getting the repartimiento system working, he should have added).[63] But now the Spaniards had the name of someone who could be blamed.

On May 4 Paz y Salgado began to question Indians. To do so, however, he needed interpreters, for it was very rare in Verapaz for a Kekchi Maya to speak Spanish. The investigating judge appointed Salvador Alibat and Marcos de la Cruz, natives of Cobán, who took an oath to translate fairly and "exactly." They also promised to keep the proceedings confidential, but that was easier said than done. Indeed, Paz y Salgado would soon be complaining about his interpreters, whose loyalty, it turned out, was to their fellow Indians first and to the Spaniards second. But he could find no one better to replace them.

On May 4 the judge, having sworn in the interpreters, ordered numerous Indians from San Juan Chamelco to appear. First to testify was Gaspar Butz, the senior Indian magistrate of San Juan Chamelco. This seventy-year-old village leader gave his side of the story of his disagreement with Barrueta over tribute, as well as of his flogging and incarceration. Butz also testified that his fellow village principales had set out for the capital to give thanks to the president for having lowered their tribute, but since he was in jail at the time he could not have known about that motivation until later. As noted, it is possible that the Indians made it up so as to disguise the fact that they were going to see the president to complain about Barrueta. Butz also explained that the people from his village who came to Cobán on Sunday morning, January 30, were carrying not clubs but walking staffs (bordones). When asked who the individuals were who had made the decision to come to Cobán, the senior Indian magistrate said that he did not know, because "all the people came when they found out" about what Barrueta had done to him and the other principales.[64]

After Butz, five more principales from San Juan Chamelco, including two former village magistrates, testified. The first of these, Juan de la Cruz Chuc, one of the former magistrates, used a word to describe what had happened that the interpreters translated as "revolution." Later witnesses would also refer to the events as a revolution. All these people stuck to Butz's story and refused to name names (of people in their village) but they also explained, as their senior Indian magistrate had not, that the people of San

Pedro Carchá had come to San Juan Chamelco's aid because of the friendship between the two villages.

On May 7 Paz y Salgado, having heard the testimony of some of the principales of San Juan Chamelco, acceded to a request from the people of that village and of San Pedro Carchá. They had pointed out to the judge that it was burdensome for them to go to Cobán to testify, and asked that he come to them instead. Paz y Salgado agreed, and left for San Juan Chamelco.

On May 10 and 11 the judge took the testimony of twelve people. They were all male Indians of the principal class, and included two former village magistrates. They usually identified themselves by which clan they belonged to. As a group, they were either middle-aged or old. Tomás Cam, for example, was eighty-one, while the above-mentioned Martín May was eighty-seven. The youngest, Domingo Tox, was thirty-four, and three other men were in their thirties. These witnesses claimed that after the village magistrates and principal delegates had been arrested, there was consternation in the village, and everyone—women and children, young and old, nobles and macehuales (or "plebeians," as one witness put it)—collectively decided to go to Cobán.

The people of San Juan Chamelco were thus closing ranks: neither these witnesses, nor those already questioned in Cobán, were willing to name names. In this way, they frustrated the Spanish effort to identify the ringleaders. So, just as the Spaniards had an agenda, the Indians had theirs. If anyone was going to get punished, it would be the whole village (a real-life example of the cinematic "I am Spartacus!").

The investigating judge next moved on to San Pedro Carchá and began to take testimony on May 12. Six witnesses, two of whom were former Indian magistrates, gave evidence. They all belonged to the principal class. In fact, during the entire investigation and trial the only Indian commoners who testified were those in the service of the Spanish high magistrate. Once again, the witnesses usually identified themselves by clan.

These people from San Pedro Carchá told the same story as those from San Juan Chamelco. They said that once they heard the rumor that the high magistrate and ladinos had killed their priest and many people from San Juan Chamelco, they all as a group decided to march on the provincial capital. When asked who had spread that rumor, they all proclaimed their ignorance. The people of San Pedro Carchá, like those of San Juan Chamelco, thus closed ranks. Once again, they refused to name names. They would therefore all share the punishment.

Here we might ask, Why did the people of San Juan Chamelco and San Pedro Carchá succeed in maintaining group solidarity while in Cobán someone—Tomás Contreras, the former village secretary—betrayed former village magistrate Sebastián Bol? In the latter case, it should be remembered, the witness was an indio ladino, someone who could speak Spanish. This allowed Paz y Salgado to interview him with no one else present except for the secretary, a Spaniard from the colonial capital of Santiago. If Contreras had wanted to betray someone in his village, therefore, he could get away with it, for in a matter of such importance both the investigating judge and the secretary could be expected to maintain confidentiality. Moreover, one other indio ladino was also called to testify, for Paz y Salgado was consciously calling on Spanish-speaking Indians precisely because he could speak to them directly and perhaps get them to implicate someone.

Cobán, however, was a large and important village, the provincial capital. It therefore had more Indians who could speak Spanish. San Juan Chamelco and San Pedro Carchá, on the other hand, were smaller and more isolated. They were less likely to have Spanish-speaking residents. Indeed, since no one but Kekchi speakers testified before the judge, it is almost certain that Paz y Salgado had been unable to find a single Spanish-speaking Indian in either village. This meant that everyone had to be questioned through an interpreter who could by no means be counted on to maintain confidentiality. The Kekchi language, therefore, was the linguistic equivalent of a wall that the Spaniards could not easily penetrate and behind which the Indians could take refuge and prepare their defenses. The very factor that placed the indigenous people in an unequal relationship with Spaniards under colonialism—their "Indian-ness"—also proved at times to be a fortress steep and mighty.

The people of San Pedro Carchá, of course, had the most to lose. They had killed the ladinos and therefore could receive the most severe punishment. Consequently, the village leaders, even while maintaining group solidarity and protecting their own people, tried to mitigate the severity of whatever was to be done with them. On May 13, just as Paz y Salgado was about to return to Cobán, the three Indian magistrates, together with the village's four *regidores* (councilmen), *escribano* (secretary), and three former village magistrates, made a statement before the investigating judge. They said, "truthfully knowing the error that their people had committed in going to Cobán on January 30, and knowing that for doing so they deserved grave punishment, for which they were at the disposition of his Lordship the President," they wanted to proclaim themselves to be "loyal vassals of His Majesty (God save the King), whose royal tribute they have never attempted to avoid fraudulently." It was only because of the rumor that their priest had been killed that the people became so passionate and angry that they the leaders could do nothing to contain them. They were making this official statement, they said, because the judge had told them that they must show respect for their high magistrates, and because "from the benign nature of the Lord President they could hope to be treated with the pity appropriate to their wretchedness and nature and to the subjection that they proclaim to the superior decisions of the said Lord."[65]

Here, then, we see the Indians putting their own strategy into effect. There was no point in denying their guilt, so they admitted it. But they also proclaimed their loyalty to the king, so that they would not be taken for rebels or traitors. Their behavior had been caused not by evil but by their Christianity, their love for their priest. Finally, they appealed to the president for mercy, for their behavior was the result of their "nature," that is, their "Indian-ness." As Indians, they were supposed to receive special treatment under the law because they were alleged to be less rational, more childlike, than Spaniards. In short, if the Spaniards were willing to be more lenient with Indians than with others, then the Indians would avail themselves of the opportunity. Colonialism, then, was characterized by role-playing. The people of San Pedro Carchá played the role of the Indians. It was in their interest to do so.[66]

On May 16 Paz y Salgado was back in Cobán. He had now finished his duties as investigating judge, and so he submitted all the documentation to the president. He also sent a cover letter, in which he explained that the proceedings had gone slower than he had hoped because of the "nature, rusticity, and state of the witnesses." In other words, the people were hard to deal with. Moreover, the need to rely on interpreters who themselves were Indians and belonged to the same "lineage" as the witnesses had made it difficult to find out the truth. He awaited further orders.[67]

President Rivera passed the documents on to the audiencia on May 23, and two days later the high court approved a resolution recommending that Paz y Salgado be ordered to continue the investigation. The audiencia judges wanted him to find out who had been in command of the violent Indians, and if at all possible identify some of the individuals who had been most notable among the masses of the people. This meant that the Spanish authorities were now willing to settle for the punishment of people other than the ringleaders. The high court also pointed out that if the leaders of Cobán knew of the "excesses" being committed in their village and did nothing to stop them, then they should be asked why they had failed to carry out their duties.

Moreover, the audiencia went on, those witnesses who clearly had been participants should be prosecuted. One of these was Esteban Siquiq, who had allegedly pushed the Spanish high magistrate. The judge should also try to identify and punish the person who had spread the false rumor of the priest's death. Finally, the participation of Sebastián Bol—betrayed by Tomás Contreras—should be investigated. On the other hand, the "mass of the people" should be left alone.

In order for Paz y Salgado to carry out these orders, he was appointed trial judge. Thus he now had the power to imprison, torture, and punish. His decisions, however, were to be reviewed by the audiencia before any sentence was carried out. Finally, Paz y Salgado was told that whatever he found out about the high magistrate would be reserved for the high court to resolve.[68]

Armed with these new powers, Paz y Salgado began the next stage of the proceedings, the criminal trial, on June 1. He immediately called the fifty-year-old mulata Petrona Matamoros to give testimony. She had witnessed the fatal beating of Juan Augustín de Sauza and of her brother Miguel Matamoros, which took place when the Indians broke into her house. As noted, she was the only woman called to testify during the entire proceedings. She provided details of the events, but did not know any of the individuals from San Pedro Carchá who did the killing. However, she said that she would recognize them if she saw them. Also, in response to a question, Petrona Matamoros said that she had heard hearsay to the effect that Sebastián Bol was the person who had spread the false rumor to the people of San Pedro Carchá. Her source of information was Joseph de los Angeles.[69]

The next person called therefore was Joseph de los Angeles, an indio ladino from Santiago married to an Indian from Cobán. His story differed from that of Petrona Matamoros, for according to him, Sebastián Bol was the person who gave the people of San Pedro Carchá permission to enter Cobán and commit their crimes. Bol was also identified as one of the Indians who helped shackle the high magistrate and his group in jail. The next three witnesses, all indios ladinos, confirmed this version of events. One of them also stated that Pedro Salá, a principal of Cobán, had been one of those most active in the "revolution." Once again, it was a Spanish speaker who betrayed an Indian from the village.[70]

Paz y Salgado then broke off the proceedings for a few days. He wanted to question some people mentioned in the most recent testimony in order to build a case against Bol, but they spoke only Kekchi, and the judge thought it was unwise to attempt an interrogation through interpreters. Therefore, he postponed the appearance of those witnesses.

On June 8 Paz y Salgado, either on his own or on the advice of others, came up with a scheme to identify individuals who could be blamed for committing or participating in acts of violence. Petrona Matamoros, who had said that she would recognize the people from San Pedro Carchá who had killed her brother, and Augustín Salvador de Guzmán, who had talked with people from San Juan Chamelco who were acting as that village's leaders, were told to attend the Corpus Christi festivities the next day and be on the lookout. Corpus Christi was a major religious feast and people from San Juan Chamelco and San Pedro Carchá always came to town to join in the festivities, and thus Paz y Salgado hoped that Guzmán and Matamoros might be able to identify the guilty parties. But this stratagem did not work. On June 10, the day after Corpus Christi, the spies reported that they had been unable to identify anyone.[71] Either the guilty people were too smart and stayed at home, or they blended into the large crowd of Kekchi Maya in Cobán. Thus was foiled one more effort to blame individuals.

Also on June 10, the judge took testimony from several more ladinos. The next day he changed the direction of the proceedings: for the first time he used his power to imprison. He ordered the arrest of Esteban Siquiq, the Indian from San Juan Chamelco who had pushed, or been pushed into, the high magistrate thus precipitating the scuffle at the Casas Reales. Paz y Salgado ordered that Siquiq be brought to Cobán and his property impounded.

The next day, June 11, the village *alguaciles* (constables) responsible for the arrest of Siquiq reported that they could not find him in San Juan Chamelco. That village's Indian magistrates informed them that he had disappeared ten days earlier. Obviously, the suspect had found out that he would be arrested and fled. Moreover, the constables reported that Siquiq had no property that could be impounded. Three days later Paz y Salgado declared Siquiq to be a fugitive, and issued an official proclamation threatening punishment—200 lashes and perpetual exile to a *presidio* (military outpost)—to anyone who helped hide Siquiq. Anyone who helped turn him in would be rewarded with exemption from tribute.[72]

On the same day, June 14, the judge ordered the arrest and imprisonment of the three men, all from Cobán, who were now the targets of Spanish justice: Domingo Putul (senior Indian magistrate), Sebastián Bol (former village magistrate), and Pedro Salá (a principal seen to be active in the "revolution"). The next day Pay y Salgado appointed legal council for the accused.[73] This was not a legal requirement, but since the judge's actions were going to be reviewed by the audiencia, he undoubtedly wanted to make sure that the higher court found nothing to criticize in his methods.

After issuing three more public proclamations regarding Esteban Siquiq, Paz y Salgado began to interrogate the prisoners on June 20. In all cases the judge had to speak to them through the interpreters. Domingo Putul, the fifty-three-year-old senior Indian magistrate, was the first to be questioned.[74] He denied that he had had prior knowledge that the people of San Juan Chamelco were marching on Cobán, and claimed to be surprised by their arrival. He also said that he had tried to help Barrueta, but the situation got out of control once the high magistrate had appeared at the doorway of the Casas Reales. He did identify Esteban Siquiq as the individual who had contact with Barrueta, although by now Siquiq's case was hopeless. Putul also denied prior knowledge of the plans of the people of San Pedro Carchá and claimed to have found out about them only after the killing had started. He said that the situation was confused, he had no orders from the high magistrate, and the invading Indians were better armed than his people would have been.

The judge then turned to the matter of the incarceration and shackling of Barrueta. Asked how his previous testimony could be true when it was public knowledge that he had participated in the "outrage" committed against the person of the Spanish high magistrate, Putul responded that Sebastián Bol and Pedro Salá were the ones who had recommended locking up and shackling Barrueta, but it was done because they were afraid that the people of San Pedro Carchá would return and try to kill him. When the judge pointed out that he had lied to Barrueta by telling him that he would be taken home, Putul answered that the people of Cobán began to stone the high magistrate and therefore he and the others changed their minds and took him to the safety of the jail.

Paz y Salgado then tried to get Putul to implicate more people. Asked to identify those throwing stones, he replied that he did not know, for practically everyone in the village was there at the time and he and his two companions —Bol and Salá—did all they could to save the high magistrate from being stoned to death. Asked how that could be true when shortly after he organized the same supposedly unruly and uncontrollable people of his village to guard the jail, he said that once the people had calmed down he regained control of the situation. The judge then argued that Putul's real intention was to humiliate Barrueta, for he freed the high magistrate only when he found out that the relief force from Salamá had arrived. Putul denied the allegation, claiming that he found out about the Indian archers after he had freed Barrueta, an action taken because the people of his own village had calmed down.

The judge thus succeeded in getting Putul to implicate his fellow prisoners in the "outrage" perpetrated against the high magistrate, but Bol and Salá were already implicated anyway. He named no new names, thereby making his village collectively guilty but less punishable. And he defended himself well by developing plausible explanations. He neither pled guilty nor begged for mercy.

The next day, June 21, was the turn of Sebastián Bol, sixty-two years old.[75] He claimed to know nothing of the intentions of the people of San Juan Chamelco and San Pedro Carchá, and when accused of giving permission to the latter to enter Cobán, he denied the accusation outright, claiming that he "didn't get involved in anything." Asked how he could lie when so many people had testified that the people of San Pedro Carchá had gone to his house, he responded by claiming that they had visited him to ask him if it was true that the ladinos had killed people from San Juan Chamelco, and that he had told them that he knew nothing about it. He also denied knowing anything about the rope that he allegedly gave the invaders, because he "didn't get involved in anything and didn't even know they wanted to tie somebody up."

The judge then turned to the outrage. How could his testimony be true when there were witnesses who saw him with the rope when they went to get the high magistrate out of the church? Bol admitted that he was there, but denied having a rope. Asked what his intentions were, he claimed that he was helping to save Barrueta's life. Why then was it necessary to put the ladinos in jail too and tie up and shackle some of them? He answered saying that he feared that the people of San Pedro Carchá might come back and kill them and therefore it was better to lock them up and guard them.

The next day featured the testimony of Pedro Salá, a forty-year-old principal of Cobán.[76] He also claimed to have known nothing of the intentions of the people of the other villages, and that he had participated in the incarceration and shackling of the high magistrate because that is how they saved his life. But Salá had also told the ladino Augustín Salvador de Guzmán that if he were not careful, they would have to say a prayer for him (that is, after his death). Salá explained this not as a threat but simply as a promise to pray for him if anything happened.

Bol and Salá thus succeeded in implicating no one else. Nevertheless, on important points they had to resort to little more than denials with no supporting evidence. Undoubtedly their explanations were not as good as those of Putul.

Paz y Salgado then issued several proclamations regarding Esteban Siquiq, and on June 23 he heard a petition from Don Juan Antonio de Pedrosa, the Spaniard who was the defender of Sebastián Bol and Pedro Salá. Pedrosa requested that his clients be released from jail on their own recognizance. The defender pointed out that neither of them had been accused of a specific crime, and that they would not run away because to do so would be the equivalent of perpetual exile from their home. Moreover, keeping them in jail was harmful to their families and was in any case the equivalent of a sentence to punishment that had no basis in justice. The judge acceded to the defender's request. However, he stated that his reasons for doing so were secret—although we shall soon see what they were—and would only be given to the president.[77]

That same day Luis de los Reyes, the defender of Domingo Putul, made the same request. He argued that his client also had committed no crime and in fact had tried to calm the people down. Moreover, Reyes added, because of Putul's "nature" (that is, his "Indian-ness"), and because his limited powers as Indian magistrate left him no alternative method of quieting the people, he should be treated leniently. Once again, Paz y Salgado acceded to the request.[78]

On June 25 the judge, having tried through proclamations and edicts to capture Esteban Siquiq, declared the fugitive to be guilty of the charge against him (pushing the high magistrate). He was declared to be an outlaw.

Paz y Salgado then tied up some loose ends. He took testimony, through the interpreters, from two Indians from Cobán who had heard the people of San Pedro Carchá say that they had received permission to enter the village upon speaking with Sebastián Bol. Next, on June 27, he called all the previous witnesses, read them their testimony, and had them swear that it was an accurate record of what had been said. In the middle of that tedious process he heard a petition from the defenders to be given twelve days to prepare their defenses. He gave them six.[79]

The defense began on July 6. Luis de los Reyes, defender of Domingo Putul, presented a list of five questions to be asked of the defense witnesses. The first two were about the witness's relations with Putul and knowledge of his character. The others concerned the motivation for jailing and shackling the high magistrate, the treatment given to Barrueta, and the time of arrival of the relief force from Salamá. Paz y Salgado approved the questions and defense witnesses began to appear the same day.

Putul's defender called four witnesses, one of whom was the junior village magistrate. All were of the principal class. They all testified to the good character of Putul, claimed that he had incarcerated and shackled the alcalde mayor to protect him, and that he had treated Barrueta well when he was in jail. Three of the four also stated that the arrival of the archers was not known until after Putul had freed the high magistrate.[80]

On July 11 Don Antonio de Pedrosa presented the defense of Sebastián Bol and Pedro Salá.[81] Rather than presenting witnesses, he simply argued the case. He pointed out that Bol could not have given permission to anyone because he was not a village magistrate at the time. (Presumably, had the people from San Pedro Carchá received permission, it would have been from Domingo Putul, the senior Indian magistrate). Second, Pedrosa argued that the various barrios—that is, the calpules—of Cobán had obviously given their permission, for without it the outsiders would not have entered in the first place. Third, the evidence of Bol's having provided the rope to tie up the high magistrate was the hearsay of partisan witnesses.

Pedrosa then turned to the case of Pedro Salá. He pointed out that although his client had helped remove Barrueta from the church and jail him, so had the whole village; Salá was no more guilty than anyone else. Regarding Salá's alleged threat to Augustín Salvador de Guzmán, the defender claimed that it was nothing more than the promise to pray for the ladino in case he died. Pedrosa ended by requesting that the judge declare both Bol and Salá not guilty.

Luis de los Reyes appeared the next day to argue for Domingo Putul. He pointed out that his client's only offense was to lock up and shackle the Spanish high magistrate and his people. His motives, initially misunderstood, had since then been clarified. He had acted to save Barrueta, and had also acted to defend the jail from further attack. Therefore, rather than be prosecuted, Putul should be rewarded for his behavior. Reyes asked the judge to find Putul not guilty.[82]

The verdict was announced on July 18.[83] Putul was absolved of guilt. Siquiq was found guilty and sentenced in absentia to death by hanging. The sentence was quite specific: Siquiq was to be placed on a beast of burden with a rope around his neck and shackles on his arms and feet, and led through the streets of the village while a muted trumpet was played (thereby attracting the people's attention) and the town crier proclaimed his crime. Then he was to be taken to the public plaza, where a gallows would be built (the village did not normally have one). He was then to be hanged until dead.

Sebastián Bol and Pedro Salá were also found guilty, although the judge did not state what they were guilty of. The former Indian magistrate was sentenced to 200 lashes, to be given throughout the streets of the village. In addition, all his property was to be confiscated. Finally, he would be sent to perpetual exile to serve in a frontier military outpost to be chosen by the president. Pedro Salá was also sentenced to 200 lashes, confiscation of his property, and perpetual exile to a location at least fifty leagues (200 to 250 miles) from Cobán.

The judge thus failed to make any individual from San Juan Chamelco (other than Esteban Siquiq) or San Pedro Carchá a target for punishment. Those villages had succeeded in forcing the Spaniards to punish them collectively. Paz y Salgado therefore had no choice but to do just that. He fined both of those villages and Cobán as well 500 pesos, to be paid annually for a period to be determined by the president. The guilt was not evenly shared: San Pedro Carchá, whose people had killed the ladinos, would pay 200 pesos; the other two would pay 150 pesos each.

The day the judge announced his verdict and sentence, he sent in his report to the president.[84] In this document, Paz y Salgado explained what did not appear in the record of the investigation and trial. Here he revealed what the Spaniards could not reveal to the Indians. The proceedings, he said, were conducted in a climate of insecurity and fear. The Kekchi Maya were not yet in a condition of subjection to authority and still manifested signs of disobedience, while in case of trouble help was not close at hand. Thus the judge had not yet attempted to begin the confiscation of property, and indeed during the entire proceedings he had had to move with great caution and circumspection for fear of provoking the Indians either to rebel or to run away and take refuge in the wild. Consequently, he confided, "I felt out the least noisy road to follow."

This climate of insecurity also explains Paz y Salgado's handling of the three prisoners. The latter had many sympathizers in the village, and the judge was afraid that if he moved too fast or made it look as if severe punishment were his goal, the Indians might rise up and break into the jail, "leaving me with no prisoners, and *perhaps more importantly without reputation* [emphasis added]." Appearances, in other words, are everything: the indigenous people had to accept Spanish authority but would do so only if they respected it. Once respect or reputation was gone, so was authority. Therefore, he asked the president to approve his decision, mentioned above, to free the prisoners on their own recognizance. No wonder that he did not dare to reveal his motives at the time!

The judge also defended his other actions. He had the power to use torture but chose not to use it. Why? Paz y Salgado said that it might have worked to identify accomplices and the author of the crimes committed, but "I did not dare to proceed with it." Indians, he said, while far from naive, are characterized by "imbecility." In this situation torture would be misunderstood. Instead of a method of getting at the truth, it would be seen as a means of getting them to say what they thought the Spaniards wanted to hear. As a result, they would all implicate each other and themselves, and it would then be necessary to lock up practically everyone in the village. The result would be the same: the whole village would be guilty.

Paz y Salgado also defended his sentences. He thought that Domingo Putul had cleared himself, while Esteban Siquiq had convicted himself, and thus his rulings regarding those two were beyond reproach. But he might be accused of being too lenient on Sebastián Bol and Pedro Salá. In reality, he argued, his sentences were quite severe, for "the harshest and most feared punishment and a warning that most impresses these people is the taking of their goods, expulsion from their huts, and exile away from the air of their homeland."

Regarding the fines imposed on the villages, he pointed out that masses of people cannot be punished the way individuals can. The sentences given to Siquiq, Bol, and Salá, however, served the purpose of instilling fear in all. He chose to castigate Bol and Salá because "these barbarous people are not permitted to punish using shackles," and therefore they must be punished for having done so. If the judge were to let them off, the Indians might mistake the kindness of the law for approval of the crime. On the other hand, the laws of Castile suggest that he should destroy the three villages because the "contagion might spread and cause harm elsewhere." But this was unreasonable on such a large scale.

The point, said Paz y Salgado, was that by doing things his way he had accomplished his main goal: the Indians had submitted to Spanish authority. This was done using "the gentlest of means, as well as the efficacious and powerful medicine of time." The indigenous people were not like sinners who escaped penance; on the contrary, he had them begging for pardon and genuinely promising not to do it again. Greater severity would surely have been counterproductive. On the other hand, the fines were heavy, and would certainly convince the Indians that they had indeed been punished.

Finally, in this very defensive report, Paz y Salgado felt it necessary to defend himself on the charge of being too weak—the kind of allegation the military might have made. This might, he thought, be the result of his "sedentary occupation"—his being a lawyer—and consequently of his need to rely on books. The military men might have imposed a different resolution of the case, but not a better one. Prudence, he said, "is to know how to fear," and it would do no good to fill his report with "happy thoughts and ridiculous speculations" (of how things would have been better had more severity and force been used).

This report and the records of the investigation and trial were received by President Pedro de Rivera on July 25 and then were passed on to the audiencia. It was now six months since the "revolution" in Verapaz. On August 9 the high court issued its verdict. The documents were to be put into the file to be used to judge Manuel Barrueta when his term of office was over. The audiencia also approved Antonio de Paz y Salgado's handling of the case. Prudence thus won out over severity. There was one exception, however: since Domingo Putul had put the Spanish high magistrate in irons and had failed to maintain order in the village as was his duty, he was to be punished. The high court fined him 200 pesos and sentenced him to perpetual deprivation of the right to hold office.[85]

Paz y Salgado's sentence had left several matters up to the discretion of the president, and on August 13 Rivera issued his ruling on the matters. He ordered Bol and Salá to serve out their exile in the *presidio* of the Petén, deep in the almost uninhabited tropical rainforest. Eventually the term of exile was limited to ten years. The president also ruled that the three villages should pay their fine for a period of two years.[86]

On September 12 the sentences were read to the principales of San Juan Chamelco and San Pedro Carchá. Those leaders promised to obey. On September 15 the principales of Cobán did the same. Domingo Putul was forced to hand over his staff of office (an object of great symbolic significance, as we shall see in a later chapter). However, Putul also proclaimed before the people that because he was poor he could not possibly pay his 200 peso fine. Paz y Salgado made inquiries, and as a result declared that Putul was telling the truth. The fine was never paid.[87]

That same day, sentence began to be served. Sebastián Bol and Pedro Salá were given 200 lashes. Their property was confiscated, to be sold later. On September 22 the two unfortunates were in jail in Salamá, on their way to their exile in the Petén.[88]

By October 4 most of the property of Bol and Salá had been sold. It turns out that the former was a man of means. He had loaned the villagers of Cobán 325 pesos so they could pay their tribute, and therefore the village had to raise that sum so that it could be delivered to the Royal Treasury. Bol also owned some raw cotton, in bales, worth 64 pesos, as well as some pepper, salt, tobacco, and a little cotton thread; his tile-roofed house was valued at 105 pesos, and the eleven urban plots he owned were sold for 55 pesos. It is likely that the real estate was worth more, but the need to sell immediately brought the price down. Pedro Salá, on the other hand, was poor. He owned some dishes, two horses, and two mules, but the animals were found to be "so old and badly treated as to be useless." His house plot was worth only 4 pesos.

The assets and property were worth a total of 524 pesos 7 reales, which were used to defray the costs of the investigation and trial. The latter (official paper and the salaries of the judge, secretary, legal defenders, scrivener, and interpreters) came to 1,958 pesos 4 reales. The deficit came to 1,453 pesos 5 reales. The fines were to be used to pay that debt.[89]

The only thing left to resolve was the desire of Paz y Salgado to get out of Cobán as fast as possible. On September 16, the day after the sentences began to be served, he wrote the president asking for permission to return to the colonial capital. He complained that his health had deteriorated because of his prolonged stay in a place of "such humidity." Indeed, three weeks earlier defense council Juan Antonio de Pedrosa had asked to be relieved of his position because he was sick "with so much rain and with the humidity of this country," and Paz y Salgado had allowed him to resign. The president acceded to the request.[90] The judge undoubtedly left Verapaz as soon as he could.

Ideology and Colonialism

In this history of the uprising in Verapaz in 1735, we see the importance of appearances, of maintaining what we call prestige or "face," what Spaniards then called respect and reputation. The latter is the word that appears over and over again in the correspondence of the Count-Duke Olivares, who led Spain to disaster in the Thirty Years War in order to defend Spain's "reputation." Without it, he felt, foreign powers would see Spain as weak and would act accordingly. Reputation was not only worth dying for; it was worth risking the ruin of the country.[91] Spanish rule in America rested on such intangibles. As long as the Spaniards were respected, they could rule. Whenever they lost respect or reputation, their position was precarious.

It was for this reason that the punishment to be given to Esteban Siquiq had to be special. It was not to be carried out behind the forbidding walls of a prison. It was rather to be trumpeted—quite literally—through the town. Moreover, not only would he have the rope that would kill him around his neck. He would also be shackled hand and foot. This symbolic punishment was, in this part of America, reserved for Indians. By putting Siquiq in irons, the Spaniards wanted to reassert the essential inequality between themselves and the Indians.

Nevertheless, this public spectacle and execution probably never had the impact the Spaniards desired. As far as we know, Esteban Siquiq was never found and brought to justice. The symbolism of the execution was significant, nonetheless, for the sentence was proclaimed in all three of the villages of Verapaz. The Spaniards did not reassert their superiority exactly as they wanted, but they did reassert it.

It was for the same reason that the high court, after approving the sentences given to Siquiq, Bol, and Salá, chose to overrule the trial judge and impose punishment on Domingo Putul. Like the others, he had violated the rules regarding roles. By placing the Spanish high magistrate in irons, they had reversed roles and called colonialism into question. For irons were reserved for Indians. Putting them on Manuel Barrueta therefore undermined the fundamental inequality that colonialism was based on. Appearances were important.

It is clear that the Kekchi Maya, as well as the Spaniards, understood this. What the Spaniards knew was that the shackling of Barrueta was not necessary to save his life. The Indians did it because they wanted to humiliate him by treating him like an Indian. What is more, they unquestionably enjoyed doing it. Such a reversal of roles had to be punished; otherwise, Spaniards would suffer a loss of reputation and colonial rule would be endangered. Statements like that of Martín May, who reminded the high magistrate that there is equality before God, could be ignored because the trial was not before God. It was before Spaniards who had to assert their superiority and before Indians who had to be made to accept their inequality. Colonialism, then, required not just punishment of the guilty but also the reestablishment of appearances. That could only be done carefully.

There is a postscript, as well as an epilogue, to this history of Verapaz in 1735. First the postscript: in 1738, when Manuel Barrueta faced the customary *residencia*—the inquest into his performance during his term in office—

the "revolution" was discussed but no charges were brought against the former high magistrate. The Dominicans of Verapaz even wrote letters of recommendation praising him. Barrueta was exonerated and even recommended for future offices.[92] However, as far as is known he never again held a position as important as that of provincial high magistrate.

Now, the epilogue: in November of 1736 the village governments of Cobán, San Juan Chamelco, and San Pedro Carchá petitioned the president through a procurator of the audiencia. They begged him to cancel their second year's fine of 500 pesos. They had already paid the money for 1735, but in the following year they said that the harvest was poor and they would find it hard to pay. Moreover, since the events of the previous year the villages were "in great serenity, quiescence, and obedience." The purpose of their punishment had already been accomplished.

The president ordered the head of the Dominicans and former trial judge Antonio de Paz y Salgado to investigate the claims. Both did so, and reported that the villages were telling the truth. The president therefore acceded to their request and the final payment of the fine was canceled.[93] At times even a colonial state could temper justice with mercy. In the long run, after all, it contributed to the maintenance of patriarchal authority.

3
Women's Power and Spanish Colonialism in Tecpán, 1759

*The Indian women should be condemned to receive the number
of lashes proportionate to their sex and weakness.*

—Attorney General Felipe Romana, 1759[1]

PARTICIPANTS

Maya

Francisco Bothz, senior village magistrate of Tecpán

Marcos Xicay, village magistrate of Pacicía

Juana Tomatle, woman interrogated at trial, alias the one-eyed; sentenced to be whipped

María Umul, woman interrogated at trial

María Ramos Cacrom, woman interrogated at trial

María Balam, woman interrogated at trial; had been struck by the high magistrate

Josepha López, woman interrogated at trial; an activist; sentenced to be whipped

Petronila López, woman interrogated at trial; an activist; sentenced to be whipped

Esteban Guibi, head of a calpul of Tecpán

Diego Mendoza, member of Guibi's calpul

Francisco Muchu, head of a calpul of Tecpán

Spaniards

Alonso Arcos y Moreno, captain general, president of the Audiencia of Guatemala

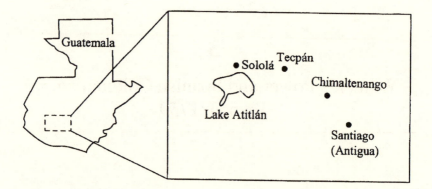

Map 3 **Tecpán and Vicinity**

Felipe de Romana, attorney general (fiscal)
Manuel de Plazaola, high magistrate of Chimaltenango
Valentín de la Lama, lieutenant of the high magistrate
Miguel de Argueta, militia squadron commander
Pedro Román, militia squadron commander
Juan Antonio Rodríguez Pardo, lawyer who represented the Indians

Ladinos

Gregorio Alemán, the hated scribe of Tecpán
Pedro Román, mestizo who gave evidence against the Indians

In the eighteenth century, males held a monopoly on political offices in Spanish America. It would be a mistake to conclude from this, however, that women had no political power. Officeholding, after all, is only part of the political process, for politics is a much broader concept than government. In fact, as has usually been true in history, women had influence over officeholders and by employing that influence they wielded real political power.

This truth is particularly clear in the case of the revolt that broke out in 1759 in Tecpán, a Cakchiquel Maya village in the central highlands of Guatemala. Women in fact played a leading role in instigating the events that constituted the revolt. Maya women took the lead in politics and led the men to temporary victory over their Spanish high magistrate. Then, because of their leadership, they were forced to suffer the consequences of ultimate political failure: they were whipped. Participation in politics therefore meant participation in punishment. Politics, for women as well as for men, was risky business.

The revolt in Tecpán is also important because it reveals quite clearly once again the efforts by the Maya to hold on to their social structure despite the attempts of colonialism to change it. The investigation into the revolt demonstrated that Tecpán was not a single community but rather eight different communities, all living in one small place. These clan-like communities, called *calpules* or *parcialidades* in the documents, had succeeded in maintaining their own separate identity and political structure after more than two centuries of colonialism—a testimony to the survival and continuity of Maya culture under Spanish rule. But this political survival of separateness eventually became a thorn in the Spaniards' side and therefore the colonial rulers took steps to eliminate the political power of the calpules. The Maya resisted, but the Spaniards were determined and eventually used enough force to get their way. Colonialism therefore gradually coerced the Maya of the village to become one community. Indigenous resistance, in short, failed, thereby demonstrating the ability of the colonial regime to force change onto the colonized people.

The events in Tecpán were significant for still another reason: the revolt got tangled up in the ongoing political conflict at the top levels of colonial society. Spaniards from Spain, called European Spaniards, were disputing political power with those born in America, called American Spaniards. The former, supported by the royal audiencia (composed mostly of Europeans), had recently gained control of the region around Tecpán by taking power away from the Americans, who were represented by the *ayuntamiento* (city council) of Santiago de Guatemala, the colonial capital. The latter in turn took advantage of the uproar at the local level to discredit the people who had deprived them of power in order to get the king to restore them to control over the region. Thus what were apparently minor local events could link up with politics at higher levels, thereby revealing both the issues of colonial politics and the links between the various levels of political conflict. Small events can be clues to bigger things.

Political Autonomy Versus Spanish Interference

Tecpán (called Tecpangoathemala in the colonial era) is one of the largest Maya villages in Guatemala. It is set on a rolling plateau in the central highlands, and is located some thirty-four kilometers northwest of the colonial capital of Santiago de Guatemala. The area's modern appearance is of a fertile valley, and in the colonial period the Cakchiquel Maya who inhabited the region were among the most prosperous Indians in Spanish America. In the late seventeenth century Francisco Antonio de Fuentes y Guzmán noted that the whole region was fertile and produced a variety of food crops and domestic animals, especially turkeys. He reported that Tecpán itself was a substantial village, having been an important city of the Cakchiquel empire.[2] Archbishop Pedro Cortés y Larraz visited the village in 1769, and although he was not impressed with most Guatemalan villages, he was with Tecpán. He reported that the land around the village was "very fertile with maize and wheat, which are harvested in great abundance." Moreover, he wrote, "the Indians are reputed to be rich, and this is well demonstrated by the adornment of their church, which was done at their expense." The dour archbishop, who rarely had much good to say about the Indians, was impressed by the people of Tecpán: "The truth is that I have not found Indians who work harder or who apply themselves so well to the cultivation of their land."[3]

In 1759 Tecpán belonged to the newly created *alcaldía mayor* (high magistracy) of Chimaltenango. The high magistrate was Manuel de Plazaola, a European Spaniard who had been appointed in 1754. Since Spain was at peace at the time and since the government did not sell offices during peacetime, Plazaola did not have to purchase the position. Nevertheless, the area included within the jurisdiction of the high magistracy of Chimaltenango was highly commercialized and densely populated, and therefore the post was certain to be quite lucrative. That, of course, meant that it was valuable. It therefore was a bone of contention for all those who wanted the benefits of office.

The minor revolt that broke out in Tecpán in 1759 resulted fundamentally from Spanish interference in Maya politics. American Spaniards would claim that the high magistrate's exploitative repartimientos were the cause, but the evidence suggests that exploitation was more of a secondary factor that became important only because of political conflict between European and American Spaniards.

It is likely that the uprising was the culmination of conflict that began over the appointment of a man named Gregorio Alemán to serve as the *escribano*, or official scribe, of the village government. The inquest following the disturbances does not reveal Alemán's exact identity. The people who made up the village government referred to the escribano as a "Christian of good conscience,"[4] but those words may have been put in their mouths by the Spanish high magistrate, Manuel de Plazaola. The rebellious Indians did not bother to identify the scribe by name, referring to him only as "the ladino escribano whom the high magistrate imposed on us."[5] Yet, as we have seen, at this time in history the word *ladino* did not have its modern meaning of someone who is not an Indian. Alemán's Hispanic surname suggests that he might have been a non-Indian, but that is by no means certain for many people with Hispanic surnames were Indians. It is possible that the scribe was an Indian who could speak both Maya and Spanish, that is, an *indio ladino*.

Whatever the case, Gregorio Alemán was not accepted as an Indian of Tecpán. The rebels made an allegation in Cakchiquel that was rather badly translated as meaning that they suffered "under the cruel yoke of an escribano foreign to our genealogy."[6] They probably said something like "he is not one of us." It is not clear what Alemán's "yoke" consisted of. The rebels made reference to his "acts and operations,"[7] and even defenders of the Spanish high magistrate testified that the scribe had been hiring Indians to work in his fields. They assured the authorities that Alemán paid good wages in cash,[8] but such statements were almost certainly made because other people thought differently about his "operations." It is likely, therefore, that Gregorio Alemán was using his political position to acquire laborers for his fields and either paid them badly or used coercion to get the labor in the first place.

The crux of the matter was this: High Magistrate Plazaola had appointed someone perceived to be an outsider as the village scribe. Escribano Alemán in turn was expected to do the high magistrate's bidding, and this he undoubtedly did. On the day of the revolt, for example, he happened to try to serve an arrest warrant at what proved to be an inopportune time. The revolt was breaking out at that very moment and the scribe either ran for his life or was run out of town.[9]

The high magistrate's intervention in the politics of Tecpán provoked resistance. There is no evidence of what was done, but it is very clear who did it: the fourteen people who were the heads of the village's eight calpules.[10] These parcialidades, it will be recalled, were the kin-based social units that served as the building blocks of Maya social organization. It is probable that those in Tecpán had originally occupied their own individual residential sites, and that the Spaniards relocated them all to one place during the *reducciones* (forced resettlement and concentration) of the sixteenth century. But this centralization and simplification was not completely successful, for in the middle of the eighteenth century the calpules, although residing in one settlement, kept their own separate identities and political structures. The village government, or *cabildo*, in turn, was not recognized as the only legitimate government in town; indeed, it may not have been seen as legitimate at all.

As a result, the resistance offered by the calpul heads to the pretensions of the Spanish high magistrate must have been significant, for eventually Alcalde Mayor Plazaola decided to take steps to limit or eliminate the power and authority that challenged that of the village cabildo. Therefore on April 20, 1759, he was presented with a letter from the village government requesting him to intervene in their village to suppress the calpules. The officials who signed the letter complained that the people of the village "pay us no attention," for the heads of the parcialidades usurped the powers of government and were even trying to force them to get rid of Escribano Alemán. The request also identified the person (a man named Nicolás Costop) who was most responsible for getting the calpul heads to oppose the village government.[11]

It is likely that Alcalde Mayor Plazaola himself had instigated the writing of this letter by pressuring the village government to request his aid formally. This is suggested by the behavior of Francisco Bothz, the senior Indian magistrate of Tecpán. Bothz's name did not appear among those found in the letter of April 20. Instead the name of one Francisco Guojos was in his place. Nevertheless, when called on April 26 by Plazaola to confirm under oath that he had participated in the formulation of the letter (he could not swear that he had signed it because he was illiterate and therefore could not sign anything), Bothz testified that his "voice" had indeed been included in the document.[12] But on May 4, when asked to ratify the validity of his previous testimony, Bothz must have had second thoughts. He stated that he did not remember testifying to the authenticity of the letter of April 20. Plazaola quickly "reminded" the Indian magistrate of his previous testimony, and Bothz in turn suddenly "remembered" what he had previously said and swore to it.[13] Five more Indians then followed suit, even though not all their names were on the original letter of April 20.[14] From this it is hard to avoid the conclusion that the letter from the village government to Plazaola was in fact instigated, or even dictated, by the high magistrate himself, and was drawn up to justify his armed intervention in Tecpán to enforce his will.

Plazaola then acted. He arranged for the detention of four calpul heads who happened to be in the nearby village of Jocotenango (located just north of Santiago de Guatemala and southeast of Chimaltenango), and sent his deputy, Valentín de la Lama, to Tecpán (northwest of Chimaltenango) accompanied by a squadron of twenty-five militiamen recruited from the Valley of Pacicía. Lama's orders were to arrest all the calpul heads and take them to Chimaltenango, where the high magistrate would deal with them. Lama's force arrived in Tecpán on Saturday, April 21.

Things did not go as planned. Heavy rain had delayed the soldiers' progress toward Tecpán, so that when they finally got to the village and arrested as many calpul heads as they could, the sun had already gone down. Lama therefore decided to put his prisoners in jail and spend the night in Tecpán. The soldiers occupied some rooms next to the jail, which was on the main plaza and therefore in close proximity to the church. They did not get much sleep, for the wives of the arrested men made a lot of noise outside. Lama decided that he should leave with his prisoners at four o'clock the next morning, but he and the squad leader (*cabo de escuadra*), Miguel de Argueta, over-slept, and as a result when they finally started their departure it was already after daylight.

When the soldiers stepped outside, a large number of people were in the plaza in front of the jail. It was now Sunday morning—Palm Sunday, April 22. If someone wanted to find a lot of Maya people together at one time, Sunday morning would be the time, for most of the villagers had to go to Mass. When the wives of the arrested men appealed to the churchgoers, they received considerable support, especially from the village women. Eventually there were so many females in front of the jail that the soldiers suspected that some men must have put on shawls and pretended to be women.[15] The militiamen (mestizos and Spaniards from other villages) undoubtedly under-estimated the powers of Maya women.

Valentín de la Lama, Plazaola's deputy and commander of the soldiers, found himself in a serious predicament. He decided to get out of Tecpán as soon as possible, and therefore ordered his men to saddle up. As they left the house, swords drawn, mayhem broke out. Screaming, furious Maya women attacked the militiamen. Lama himself was unhorsed, as was squadron leader Pedro Román. The hated village scribe, Gregorio Alemán, then appeared to serve a warrant, discovered that he had chosen the wrong time for such an endeavor, and ran for his life. He managed to get on his horse, but Indian women chased him, knocked him off his horse, and dragged him back to the plaza. In all the commotion, someone broke the lock on the jailhouse door and let the prisoners out.[16]

Meanwhile, apparently on the very same day, a less spectacular jailbreak was occurring in Jocotenango, just a few miles from the colonial capital. There, four calpul heads, detained on Plazaola's orders, asked permission of the jailer to go to the village fountain to wash their clothes. They were let out and immediately took off. It is not known if the jailer was an accomplice of the calpul leaders. No investigation of the jailbreak in Jocotenango was ordered, so it is possible that he was simply duped.[17]

Back in Tecpán, Lama and the men under his command were saved by the intercession of the village priest (whose name was never identified in the proceedings). The cleric called the people to the church, and they obeyed him. As a result, neither Lama nor any of the soldiers suffered bodily harm. The priest was said to have promised the Indians that he would write a letter to set things right with the Spaniards. Lama in turn wrote a message to Plazaola informing him of events in Tecpán.[18]

Lama's note arrived in Chimaltenango on the same day as the riot, April 22. Plazaola immediately wrote a hysterical letter to the president, Alonso Arcos y Moreno, informing him of the rebellion in Tecpán. The high magistrate blamed the calpul leaders, who by exercising the powers of government were usurping royal authority. He also warned that the "cancer" of rebellion might spread and therefore quick action should be taken.[19] Plazaola's letter was sent to the attorney general (fiscal) of the audiencia, Felipe Romana.

Two days later Fiscal Romana dealt with the case. The attorney general, a native of Bogotá, Colombia, was new to his job and apparently had not yet learned the ropes. Eventually he would learn more about the Mayas and the magistrates who ruled them (as we shall see in later chapters), but, still somewhat of a neophyte in 1759, Romana believed all that Plazaola reported without question. He informed the audiencia that "the daring of the principal Indians, called heads of the fourteen parcialidades of the village" was sedition and must be punished right away. Otherwise, "bad consequences" would result from unpunished disobedience. Romana recommended that Plazaola be sent to Tecpán to carry out a thorough investigation. His brief, dated April 24, was approved by the audiencia the same day.[20]

The high magistrate of Chimaltenango received his orders on April 25 and immediately acted. He did not march on Tecpán yet, however. Rather, he appointed interpreters and began to question the members of Tecpán's village government who happened to be in Chimaltenango, having fled their own village two days after the riot. These men swore that they had requested the high magistrate's intervention against the calpul leaders.[21] Plazaola did this to protect himself from possible criticism. Among the witnesses was Valentín de la Lama, safe and sound in Chimaltenango after his misfortune in Tecpán.

Plazaola meanwhile was gathering a large military force. He mobilized the militia of the villages of San Martín, Sierra del Agua, Valle de Pacicía, and Izapán. Once 180 men were assembled, the high magistrate on April 27 marched on Tecpán and arrived in the village later in the day.

In the meantime the people of Tecpán had not been idle. The village government having fled, the calpul leaders began to gather money to pay for legal aid in the appeals that they were planning to make to the president and the audiencia. This was hardly the act of a revolutionary, or even rebellious, village. On the other hand, it did occur to someone to seek the help of other Cakchiquel Maya. A man and a women, either on their own or in response to orders, went to Pacicía and Izapán and requested the support of the Indian magistrates of those villages.

It is notable that persons unknown in Tecpán thought that other Cakchiquels might help them. Perhaps in other circumstances help would have been forthcoming, but it was not this time. Marcos Xicay, Indian magistrate of Pacicía, met with the emissaries from Tecpán. He knew where they were from by their distinctive dress (which means that the villagers of highland Guatemala had by then developed the modern practice of using distinctive clothing to identify themselves as people from particular villages). But he refused to get involved, and under questioning said that he reminded his people of what had happened in Cancuc. Knowledge of the village that had led the great Tzeltal Maya revolt in Chiapas in 1712 was apparently quite alive in Guatemala in 1759. The memory of history thus affected the making of history. The village leader of Izapán also refused to risk the destruction of his people to help those of other villages.[22]

The people of Tecpán were more successful in their other endeavor, that is, their appeal to the president in Santiago de Guatemala. An unidentified group of individuals met in the capital with an audiencia lawyer named Juan Antonio Rodríguez Pardo, who presented on their behalf an appeal to the president on April 30. It was made in the name of "the calpules and other tributaries" of Tecpán—in other words, in the name of the people. They complained about the riot, provoked, they said, by the unwanted scribe, and asked for the president's protection from their high magistrate, who would surely be angry that they were bringing these matters to the attention of higher authorities. They requested the president to uphold their right to defend themselves in a legal way, and stated that without his help they would be afraid to return to their village. President Arcos y Moreno was absent at the time, so the audiencia acted without him. It ordered Plazaola to refrain from punishing the supplicants for making their appeal. The high magistrate received the order in Tecpán the next day, May 1, and he promised to obey.[23]

But by that time Plazaola had been quite active in Tecpán. Arriving on April 27—Good Friday, the Friday following the Palm Sunday riot—he discovered that there was no uprising to put down, but to make sure that all remained calm he ordered all Indians, except those who wanted to testify at the proceedings, to stay in their houses. Nevertheless, resistance of a sort did take place. A Spanish squad leader, Miguel de Argueta, later testified that "shortly after the arrival of the said [high magistrate] in the said village, the Indian women began a commotion and caused a commotion among the Indian men as well by threatening them and exchanging furious words with them." Argueta informed Plazaola of what was happening, and the high magistrate responded by ordering the arrest of known troublemakers.[24] With that, he probably thought that he had put an end to the commotion in Tecpán. He was soon to discover otherwise.

Plazaola immediately began to call witnesses to the events of the previous Sunday. The people called to testify were the two squad leaders and a few of the soldiers who were present when the jailbreak took place. For the most part they agreed among themselves as to what had happened (although not about whether one of the squad leaders had fallen asleep and overslept).

Since they were not natives of Tecpán, they could not identify any of the Indians involved. They did agree, however, that the Maya women were particularly aggressive and insolent, and that one of the females was *tuerta* (one-eyed).[25] The search would now be on for a one-eyed Maya woman.

The questioning of the militiamen lasted until Saturday, April 28. The high magistrate then called the local *vecinos* (non-Indian residents of the village) to testify, which they did on Easter Sunday. Most of the non-Indians were careful not to injure their Indian neighbors in any way. They claimed for the most part to have been at home when the jailbreak and riot took place, and refused to name names.[26]

There was one exception, however. This was Pedro Román (not to be confused with the squad leader of the same name), a thirty-six-year-old mestizo. On the Saturday night before the jailbreak he had helped identify the calpul leaders to be arrested. He then went home to bed, but was awakened by his wife on early Sunday morning. Informed that there was something going on in the plaza, he hurried to see what was happening and witnessed the Indians threatening the soldiers as they tried to leave. He also followed the women chasing the scribe Gregorio Alemán and witnessed what happened to him. He recognized and identified by name four women.[27] Plazaola now had more people to pursue.

The high magistrate then tried to prove that the calpul leaders had been usurping royal jurisdiction by exercising powers supposed entrusted exclusively to the village government. On Monday, April 30, he sent out a group of soldiers to inspect the houses of the calpul heads and report back. Either Plazaola knew what they would find or the soldiers knew what to report. In the houses of the calpul leaders were found whips and pillories with leather straps to hold in place those who were to be punished. These were always found next to the altars that each calpul leader maintained in his house.[28] Whether or not the pillories were used, they were, like Roman fasces, symbols of authority to punish, authority that only the official village government had. Plazaola had found his proof. He was less interested in the altars, which manifested a close connection in Maya culture between religious and political authority. The same, after all, was true to a point in Spanish culture.

On Tuesday, May 1, Plazaola received the unwanted order from the audiencia to refrain from taking reprisals against those who had made their appeal to the president in the capital. He announced his compliance with the order, but then had to act quickly on another matter. He was informed of the emissaries sent by Tecpán to other Cakchiquel villages and he immediately ordered an investigation. The three people with the information were quickly sworn in. Their testimony having been taken, Plazaola got the Indian magistrates of Pacicía and Izapán to testify.[29] He now had more ammunition to use against his enemies in Tecpán.

By May 2 the high magistrate must have thought that his job was almost over. On that Wednesday he drew up an official act (*auto*) in which he stated that he had finished taking all the testimony and that it was time to have the witnesses ratify under oath the authenticity of their testimony. One by one they did so, and although Francisco Bothz, the senior Indian magistrate of Tecpán, did not follow the script, he was eventually convinced to do so, and none of the other village government members caused any problems. Plazaola then stayed in the village a few more days, and on Saturday, May 5, he drew up another *auto*. He declared that he had finished the proceedings, and that he would be leaving the next day. He must have been aware that the villagers of Tecpán were unhappy, however, for he noted, albeit in an offhanded sort of way, that the eighty militiamen who had accompanied him were being withdrawn and that he would have to leave too because without this "escort" he could not remain in Tecpán. Finally, he ordered the fourteen calpul heads to be ready to leave with him the next day, Sunday, May 6.[30]

Once again, things did not go as planned. Plazaola had apparently not learned that Sundays were bad days to do anything unpopular in Maya villages, and so it proved once again in Tecpán. The Indians, as the high magistrate put it, "having resisted on infinite occasions," had to be coerced to form a line. Then, although only fourteen calpul heads were supposed to be transported out of Tecpán, a mass of individuals insisted on joining them, and eventually the group of prisoners numbered not fourteen but over 100. Among them were four women, whom Plazaola identified as "the ones who were at hand among all those who had fomented the sedition." Later he would claim that some of them were important ringleaders. Meanwhile a mob surrounded the Spaniards and subjected them to insults and obscenities. Once again, Maya women were in the forefront of the tumult. Soon rocks as well as insults were being hurled at Plazaola and his men. One woman was particularly aggressive and insulting, and the high magistrate lost his temper and struck her with his rod of office. There would eventually be a discussion over where he hit her, how many times he did so, and what red liquid it was that she spat from her mouth. Finally, a squad leader informed Plazaola of the approach of numerous Indians armed with bows and arrows. The high magistrate, realizing that haste was necessary, ordered an immediate departure.[31] He and his men fled, hurrying along the more than one hundred prisoners in their custody. In all the confusion, however, some of those detained managed to escape. It was hardly a dignified end to the high magistrate's proceedings in Tecpán.

Plazaola was so convinced of the need to make haste that he later claimed that his column and the prisoners made it from Tecpán to Chimaltenango, a distance, he said, of seven leagues (about twenty-eight miles), in eight hours.[32] The modern road, which undoubtedly follows that of the eighteenth century, covers 32 kilometers, so clearly the high magistrate led his men and his prisoners on a rapid forced march. This must have been hard on the Maya, for in the group were many elderly people.

On the next day, May 7, Plazaola sent in a report to the president.[33] Noting that he had been ordered on April 24 to carry out an investigation of what he called the "resistance, sedition, riot, and flight [from justice] that took place in the said village," the high magistrate declared that he had proved the responsibility of the fourteen calpul heads. Nevertheless, even the presence of eighty militiamen in Tecpán had not deterred "the said Indian men and Indian women, particularly the latter," from perpetrating sedition and riot again when he tried to imprison the leaders of the parcialidades. He had asked anyone mistreated by the justice of those heads to come forward during the proceedings, but "not even that measure was enough to get anyone to do so." Rather, the villagers manifested "a single and total renunciation and lack of respect for justice." He had found evidence that the leaders of the parcialidades "not only administer justice and punishment in their houses but also raise funds in the village using official town criers." Moreover, they dispatched emissaries to get other villages to join them.

Plazaola warned the president not to be misled by the villagers' dislike for the scribe. The high magistrate had thought that the original riot might have been caused by the escribano's attempts "to tie up and whip one or two of them," but the second riot had nothing to do with the scribe, who was absent from the village at the time. In this way the high magistrate sought to direct the attention of the president and audiencia away from his appointed crony and toward the illegal acts of the Indians themselves.

The Indians, however, resisted Plazaola's designs by using legal channels. On May 9, two days after the high magistrate's report, some of the prisoners in the Chimaltenango jail, working through their lawyer, Rodríguez Pardo, directed a petition to the president. They identified themselves as "the fourteen guilds [gremios] or calpules of the village of Tecpán."[34] They declared that their high magistrate had imprisoned them on a false pretext, for Plazaola, they knew, was alleging that they had rebelled against royal authority. The Indians denied that categorically, claiming that they "had never tried such a thing nor even made the slightest move in that direction, but only acted because of the harassment of the ladino escribano whom the high magistrate imposed on us." Furthermore, "if it had been our intention to rebel in a premeditated fashion, as our high magistrate alleges, we would not have turned to this Supreme Tribunal [that is, the audiencia] to help us." They claimed that Plazaola "wanted through the use of force and against the very laws of the kingdom to make us put up with" a scribe who was an outsider. They therefore requested that the unwanted escribano be removed from his post.

The heads of the calpules also drew attention to how this state of affairs was damaging to the king. The people under arrest would be unable to care for the wheat in their fields, and so many were in detention that royal taxes could not be paid. Their province would be ruined "and will never return to its old self because many tributaries are afraid of such harsh rule" and because the high magistrate tried to attribute "unthinkable crimes" to them. There would be harm not only to royal revenues but also to the capital city of Santiago de Guatemala, which would find itself short of wheat for bread.

The imprisoned Indians of Tecpán did not merely defend themselves, however. They also began their own counterattack against the high magistrate by bringing up the matter of his physical mistreatment of a Maya woman on the day of the second riot. They informed the president that "the said high magistrate, ignoring the fact that Polonia Pocon, an Indian woman of the said village, was several months pregnant, gave her so many blows on Sunday May 7 that she is still very gravely ill." This was a significant charge, for if true, Plazaola had surely overstepped the bounds of acceptable behavior. Gentlemen did not beat women, and if the woman were pregnant the offense would be even greater and more disreputable. Thus the Indians were attempting to use the Spanish code of conduct against their own Spanish magistrate.

The calpul leaders ended their appeal almost defiantly. After claiming that their high magistrate had subjected the villages of their province to "excesses and violence," and after requesting that they be freed from jail, they concluded by saying that "we affirm our rights, and even will reaffirm them as long as we need and against whomever." The next stage of the proceedings then began.

Defiance and Punishment

The revolt was now over, and the Spanish justice system had to address the matter. It took a little more than a week for Fiscal Felipe Romana to get through the papers and submit a brief, which he issued on May 18.[35] He pointed out that the documentation thus far assembled was insufficient as evidence because very few individuals were named. The high magistrate's reports and investigation had failed to identify the calpul heads who escaped during the jailbreak of April 22, the people who assaulted the soldiers and freed the prisoners, the emissaries sent to Pacicía and Izapán, and the person or persons who wrote the note that they carried. The only people mentioned by name in the proceedings were Nicolás Costop (denounced by the village government in its letter of April 20) and the four women identified by Pedro Román as having participated in the second riot.

Nevertheless, it was clear to the attorney general that the leaders of the parcialidades were at fault. They, he said, were "the ones who induced the first and second outbreak of mayhem," and therefore he recommended that the prisoners be questioned to identify the calpul heads. The audiencia agreed, and on May 23, presumably after consulting with Romana, the judges made a crucial decision: they appointed High Magistrate Manuel de Plazaola as the person to question the prisoners and other witnesses.[36] The guilt of the Indians thus became a foregone conclusion. As we shall see in later chapters, Fiscal Felipe Romana would learn from his mistake and act differently in the future.

It was then decided to move the prisoners from Chimaltenango to Santiago de Guatemala and carry out the rest of the proceedings there. The men—ninety-nine in all—were transported and jailed in the capital. The four women in the group were put in the Casa de Recogidas, a place usually used to detain women guilty of various forms of bad behavior.[37]

Five days after receiving his orders, Plazaola was ready to begin the questioning of the prisoners. However, he must have been busy in the days before the opening of the formal proceedings, for the first people he chose to question were not the Maya prisoners but six Spanish or mestizo soldiers who proved to be well rehearsed. The high magistrate in fact had prepared his own defense, and would succeed in defending himself before the judge because he was his own judge.

The six soldiers included all five of those whom Plazaola had questioned in Tecpán about the first riot.[38] The first four even appeared in the same order. Spanish squad leader Miguel de Argueta testified first, repeated what he had said regarding the first riot, claimed that the one-eyed Maya woman who had caused so much trouble was among those under detention, and said that when Plazaola had tried to leave with his prisoners the day of the second riot, the Indian women made "indecent demonstrations that infuriated the said" high magistrate. The other soldiers told the same story regarding the riot, and all added that the women in detention were among the most aggressive and insolent of the group that had caused all the mayhem. One soldier added the rather unsoldierly comment that he and his companions were so frightened that the only thing they wanted "was to get out of the said village as fast as possible, which is what [we] did."

Three of these witnesses added a detail of great importance to Plazaola. They claimed to have witnessed the altercation between the high magistrate and the Maya woman that ended in violence. All three witnesses told the same story: Plazaola had hit the woman with his rod only once, on the legs, and the woman was probably chewing annatto (*achiote*) at the time, which caused her to spit a red liquid from her mouth. This, then, was the story that the high magistrate tried to use to exonerate himself on the charge of abusing a woman. Since Plazaola did all the questioning, the responses were the same, and no damaging information was revealed. It paid to be prosecutor as well as judge and jury.

Having finished with the Spanish and mestizo witnesses who provided an explanation, however far-fetched, of whatever had happened between the high magistrate and the Maya woman, and after finding and swearing in interpreters, on May 29 Plazaola began the interrogation of the Indians. The first to be called were the women, who numbered not four, as had originally been reported, but six. In practice it was very rare to call any women at all as witnesses in civil or criminal proceedings, and in fact these were the only Maya women interrogated as a result of the revolts discussed in this book. But the case of the rebellion or riot in Tecpán was special. Women had been in the forefront of the two disturbances and had perpetrated most of the illegal acts carried out by the Indians. Moreover, the women in detention in the Casa de Recogidas had been identified as perpetrators of mayhem, and several others had been named. To exclude the Maya women from interrogation would make it legally difficult to punish them. So, Plazaola had them brought forward.

The testimony of the six Maya women is one of the few examples in the historical record of indigenous females being given the opportunity to express themselves. To be sure, the circumstances of their appearance—as accused criminals and speaking through interpreters in the third person—hardly allow us to hear what they wanted to say. Nevertheless, their testimony, used carefully, tells us much.

First to appear was a women whose name the Spaniards recorded, probably somewhat inaccurately, as Juana Tomatle.[39] She was undoubtedly chosen to be first because she had been identified as the one-eyed troublemaker.[40] Like virtually all Indian witnesses, male as well as female, in all the proceedings, she did not know her age.[41] The Spaniards judged her to be about fifty-five years old. After swearing her in, Plazaola asked, "what her motive was in provoking riot and sedition" in Tecpán, to which Tomatle responded that she was not involved in any riot. The high magistrate then pressed her, asking "how could she betray the religion of her oath, when the proceedings prove that she was one of the principal motors of the sedition, and that she had infuriated and provoked the soldiers and the deputy." Unflinchingly, Tomatle "repeated that there was no such thing and reiterates what she testified, saying that on that day she was at home."

Plazaola thought he had her. He pointed out that the day of the riot was Sunday, and if she had not left her house then she would have missed Mass (and thereby have committed a mortal sin). Tomatle, apparently unfazed, responded that "it was true that she had gone to Mass, and when she went to the church the prisoners from the jail were already there," (in other words, they had already escaped), "and regarding the riot, she heard that everyone had participated, but she neither knows nor can testify who the participants were, and everything she has said and declared is the truth under oath." The high magistrate, after duly noting that the witness was illiterate and therefore could not sign her testimony, gave up and ended the interrogation.

The second Maya woman to appear was María Umul, thought to be around twenty-five years old. She was the youngest women interrogated. Plazaola asked her if she knew why she had been brought to the city, and Umul replied that "she did not know why, since she had only been going to get water when the soldiers took her, and later brought her to the city." The high magistrate pressed her, asking how she could not know the cause of her arrest "when the very same soldiers had given notice of the riot which the witness and the others had provoked, screaming thousands of shameful words at them and threatening them." Umul apparently was scared and therefore tried to make a deal: she denied having participated, but gave the names of three women who had. The three identified, however, were not among those detained in the Casa de Recogidas and were never brought in. Plazaola then ended the interrogation. María Umul, perhaps as a reward for naming names, went unpunished.[42]

The next to be questioned was María Ramos Cacrom, about forty years old. Like the previous witness, she was not perceived as a ringleader of the women. Also like the previous witness, she claimed not to know why she had been arrested, and that she had gone to the plaza with her jug to get water. She claimed to have seen, but not to have participated in, the disorder. She did testify, however, that the mayhem was caused by the Indian women, although she claimed that she could not identify anyone by name. The high magistrate did not choose to pursue the point, the interrogation was ended, and María Ramos Cacrom, like María Umul, escaped punishment.[43]

The fourth female witness, like the first, was more important. This was María Balam, estimated to be about thirty-five years old. She also claimed to have gone to the plaza to get water from the fountain, but admitted that she had yelled and screamed at the militiamen. That, however, was because her husband was among the group in the plaza about to be taken away as prisoners. Plazaola then pressed the point, for María Balam was the very person he had struck with his rod of office. He asked her why she had not obeyed his orders (to shut up) but instead kept arguing with him "in a raised voice."

She refused to answer the question. The high magistrate then asked her why she had pretended to spit blood and about the blow she had received. María Balam answered by telling Plazaola what he wanted to hear: "she said that she had been hit only once, on the legs, and the mouthful of blood resulted from something that she had had for a long time." Plazaola then ended the interrogation, and perhaps for her cooperation, María Balam went unpunished.[44]

The last two female witness were already perceived to be ringleaders. The fifth Maya woman to be interrogated was Josepha López, estimated to be about thirty-five years old. Plazaola possibly recognized her, for he asked "how is it that she did not obey his mercy the said high magistrate when he ordered her on an infinite number of occasions to go back to her village and stop mistreating the soldiers with bad words, as she was doing when she left with the others in pursuit of his men until way outside" the village? López responded curtly that "she had gone out to bring tortillas to her father, and since she saw the others screaming and creating riot, she joined in." Plazaola next asked her "for what purpose had she picked up a rock and held it in her hand when his mercy [the high magistrate] was admonishing her to go back to her village?" Josepha López replied that "she tried to run and fell down, but she did not pick up any rock and hold it in her hand."

Finally Plazaola asked her if she had any complaints or charges to make against anyone. López responded with a statement that must have angered the interrogator. She said, "that his mercy [the high magistrate] had caused her no harm, and only was immediately harmed by the Indian governor of her village, the other village government officials, and the escribano, who put her in jail, the escribano pushing her in and then hitting her, injuring her hand. But then that was over, and she has no complaints to make nor charges to bring against anyone." She thus cast aspersions on the village government that served Plazaola's interests, and had this put into the official record, all the while claiming that she had no reason to complain.[45] For this act of defiance and bravado, Josepha López would pay with her blood.

The final Maya female witness called was Petronila López, about fifty years old. She was one of the women identified by a vecino of Tecpán back on April 29 as having been involved in the first riot, and the questions were to that effect. Plazaola asked her to "tell what the motive or cause was that moved her to join in the mayhem that took place in the said village last April 22 and for having knocked squad leader Pedro Román off his horse the day of the riot." López simply denied all involvement, saying that "she was not involved in the riot because she was sick in her house as a result of a blow to her arm given her by her husband, and others went to tell her that Pedro Román had been dragged around. After that she went to take tortillas to her husband who was working in his corn fields [milpas], and she didn't see anything."

By now Plazaola must have been frustrated with all the Maya women, but he still pressed his point, although by now, one suspects, half-heartedly. How, he asked, could her testimony be true, when the day of the riot was Sunday? That would mean that she had missed Mass and her husband was working on the Sabbath. Petronila López answered that "she went first to Mass and then left to catch up with her husband and bring him the tortillas, and that she didn't see anything." Finally the high magistrate asked her if she were involved in the riot the day that he was leaving with the prisoners. López responded "that it is true that she was in the plaza because her son Manuel Espansay was among the prisoners, but she did not get involved in anything." The interrogation ended.[46]

We have gone into such detail regarding the testimony of the female witnesses because there are so few examples in the historical record of women, especially Maya women, being given the opportunity to speak. Of course, their "voice" was very much affected by their status as prisoners accused of crimes and interrogated through interpreters by a hostile adversary. Despite these circumstances, we can still hear—almost—some of what they said. Although three of the women seem to have made a deal in order to lessen their punishment, it is clear that all six denied under oath that they had committed any crime. The Spanish system of justice did not awe them or terrify them into submission. Some even responded defiantly, surely knowing that they would pay for their bravery. They were tough people.

We can almost see them living certain aspects of their lives. Women carried jugs and went to the fountain in the plaza for water. They made tortillas and took them to their men in the fields. They argued with their husbands and occasionally were beaten as a result. They were frequently sick, and went to Mass on Sundays. And they jumped to the defense of their children. They are true ancestors of the modern Cakchiquel Maya.

The women certainly appear to have been just as tough as the Maya men whom Plazaola started to interrogate as May 31, once again by means of interpreters. But by then it must have been clear to the men that their cause was lost, and therefore they tried to cut their losses, undoubtedly in hopes that Spanish justice—or at least the high magistrate—would show mercy.

The first person to testify was Esteban Guibi (Wibi), a calpul head who was estimated to be around eighty years old. Perhaps because of his age he was believed when he swore that he had not participated in the riot because he was at home sick. He said that he had heard that the Indian women had been involved in mayhem, and although he did not give any of the women's names, he did identify three people of his calpul who came to see him to get him to authorize making the legal appeal in the capital. They were Nicolás Jiat, Francisco Guaxan (Waxan), and Diego Mendoza. These men were also said to have raised money to pay for the legal appeal, although the witness said that he had not gone to the capital "because of his elderly condition and illness." On the other hand, he denied that the calpul heads administered justice in their houses, although he did admit that they used to.[47] Perhaps because of his age, or because Plazaola was really done with him, the high magistrate ended the interrogation.

In two days of questioning Plazaola interrogated a total of twelve individuals, as well as two groups that included sixteen people, who were questioned en masse—a most unusual procedure that the high magistrate got away with.[48] The twelve men had all been in jail, eight in Tecpán and four in Jocotenango, the day of the first riot. The ages of these leaders is significant. The youngest was thirty-five; the oldest—Esteban Guibi—was eighty; the median age was fifty. Since life expectancy was of course low, the leaders were people of advanced age. Among the Cakchiquel Maya, seniority and experience counted. Indeed, a purely hereditary, dynastic-like leadership would have produced younger men.

Plazaola asked each of the witnesses how he got out of jail and why he did not turn himself in later. They all responded that their village priest had told them to go home after the riot and that he would try to take care of things. They all did what they were told. Plazaola also wanted to know if they administered justice in their houses, and they all said no. The high magistrate, however, had found out that one of the calpul heads, Francisco Muchu, had recently punished the daughter of a villager named Juan de la Cruz Choc, so Muchu had to admit that he had administered punishment, but he had done so, he claimed, on the father's request.[49]

The high magistrate also questioned the witnesses about the raising of money by the calpul heads. This would have been an illegal tax and therefore a usurpation of royal authority. All the witnesses denied having done so, but the first witness had already implicated two of those interrogated. The first of the two, Francisco Guaxan, simply denied it, and claimed to have been out in the fields at the time.[50] Plazaola did not pursue the point further in the case of Guaxan, but he did press the other man implicated, Diego Mendoza. Mendoza first claimed that he and the others who had gone to the capital to make the appeal had used their own money for their expenses, but the high magistrate pointed out that Esteban Guibi had testified that Mendoza and the other two had raised the money in the village as a tax. To prove it, Plazaola brought Guibi in and had him repeat his testimony in front of Mendoza. The latter then changed his story and stated that Guibi's version was the truth.

The high magistrate tried very hard to find individuals to blame, which is what the attorney general had ordered him to do. Over and over again he asked the witnesses who had been the person or persons who had organized the riots, and just as persistently all the Indians, with one exception, responded that no one had, that the whole village was responsible. The one exception was Thomás Saxuin, who blamed it all on an Indian woman named Andrea Pablo, who conveniently happened to be dead.[51] Plazaola also tried to find out who had written the notes to the Indian leaders of Pacicía and Izapán, but no one seemed to know anything about that.

The high magistrate did accomplish some of his goals in his interrogations. Probably in hopes of getting diminished punishment, the Indians all denied that they had anything to do with any petition sent under their names to the president, that is, the petition in which they had alleged that Plazaola had beaten a pregnant Indian woman. A few people testified that the high magistrate had hit a woman once, but that was it. Most of those interrogated denied that they knew anything about the matter, and one of the two groups of men questioned supposedly said, "may God punish whoever wrote such a thing in their name." They also claimed that the Plazaola had always treated them well.

Finally, the high magistrate tried to answer what was for him a puzzling question. When he had ordered the detention of the fourteen calpul heads, why did so many other people—numbering over 100—come forward and insist on being arrested too? Everyone questioned had the same answer: all for one, one for all. If anyone was to get punished, then they would all get punished. (Once again we see the Maya equivalent of "I am Spartacus!") This show of solidarity undoubtedly did not please the Spanish authorities. As a result, although the Indians may have hoped that they would all escape by sticking together, the Spaniards felt compelled to punish them all just to prove that they could and would do it.

The interrogations were now over, and the next day, June 1, Plazaola was ready with his summation.[52] It was not completely triumphant. The high magistrate reported that he had been unable to identify by name those who had broken into the jail to free the prisoners, and although he had been able to get the names of some of the principal Indian women who participated in the riot, he could not identify any man involved. Nor could he find out who the male ringleaders were, for he assumed that men must have organized the mayhem. He also failed to find out who wrote and sent the messages requesting aid from the other Maya villages; once again he assumed the authors to be men, for all the women were illiterate.

The high magistrate nevertheless did accomplish some of his goals. He reported that the testimony demonstrated that the people in jail had never written the petition to the president in which it was alleged that he had beaten a pregnant Indian woman so bad as to leave her gravely ill. All the witnesses disowned the document, and most claimed to know nothing about any altercation between him and a female Indian. The petition, he concluded, had been written by someone who wanted "by any means possible denigrate my honor." This effort did not succeed. To prevent such things from happening in the future, Plazaola recommended that the government accept petitions from no one but from single individuals or the duly constituted village government. Whatever the parcialidades say should be ignored, for otherwise "there will always be produced an accumulation of fantasies that will be inextinguishable and unverifiable, because normally those who produce or foment such fantasies—who never show their faces—are those who are poor and do so hoping to gain financially and to support themselves in this way."[53]

Only four days after receiving Plazola's summation, Fiscal Felipe Romana submitted his brief on the case.[54] It was short and to the point: his first sentence reads "the Indian women who participated in the riot, even though they deny having caused it, should be condemned to receive the number of lashes proportionate to their sex and weakness." Moreover, "to provide an example to all the rest of the women, it would be useful for the punishment to be carried out in the public streets of the village of Tecpán, especially in the case of Josepha López." She had to pay for her defiance. The Indian men who were heads of the parcialidades should also be whipped, either in the capital or in the village, whichever should be judged best. On the other hand, the others in jail, whose participation in the riot was not proved, should be released but warned that in the future they should obey their high magistrate. Very importantly, the attorney general recommended that the government take steps to ensure that justice in the village be administered only by the recognized village government, not by the heads of the calpules. Finally, Romana politely but firmly rejected the high magistrate's recommendation regarding petitions from Indians. The government, he argued, should continue to accept any and all petition made by individuals or groups as long as they were signed, as this one was, by the petitioners. (The Spanish government, it should be noted, did not accept or act on anonymous denunciations.)

The full audiencia, composed of four judges, made the final ruling on the case on June 20, 1759.[55] Its sentence was harsher than that recommended by the attorney general. The nine calpul heads who had been identified were sentenced to 100 lashes each. The audiencia also sentenced seven women— including Juana Tomatle alias "the one-eyed," Petronila López, and Josepha López, as well as two or perhaps three others identified by Pedro Román, the vecino of Tecpán—to fifty lashes. These men and women were judged to be guilty "of being the principal prisoners involved in the sedition, riot, usurpation of royal authority, and lack of respect for their high magistrate and village officials." Their sentence was to be publicly proclaimed throughout Tecpán. All the other prisoners in the jail, whom Fiscal Romana had recommended releasing with no more than a warning, were sentenced to twenty-five lashes, in the case of the men, and twelve in that of the women. The latter sentences were to be carried out in the capital city by the public executioner (*verdugo*), whose name, as always, was kept secret. On the other hand, the high magistrate, who was supposed to be present when sentencing was carried out, was instructed to use his judgment and moderate the punishment "in recognition of the age and strength of the prisoners" if he saw fit. Finally, the audiencia forbade the calpul heads to carry out justice, and a warning to that effect was to be issued to them annually. Anyone found violating the order would be given 200 lashes and ten years of exile to the presidio of San Fernando de Omoa (on the disease-ridden coast of Honduras).

The audiencia's ruling thus went beyond that recommended by the attorney general. Perhaps this had to do with the friendship that high magistrate Plazaola had with the judges (of which more below). Both the judges and the attorney general did agree, however, on the need to make the punishment fit not the crime but the criminal: the elderly were to receive less than the young, and women half has much as men. Age and sex counted in colonial Guatemala.

Some of the sentences were carried out that very same day. First the high magistrate, accompanied by an interpreter, went to the jail to inform the prisoners. Then he went to the Casa de Recogidas to inform the women. Next, the men, with the exception of those specifically named in the sentence, were led out two by two and given their floggings, probably twenty-five lashes each. No women were punished that day.[56]

Six days later Plazaola and some prisoners were back in Tecpán for the punishment of those specifically mentioned by the audiencia. The sentences were publically proclaimed, and the high magistrate announced that they would be carried out the next day. So, on June 27, 1759, Plazaola ordered the prisoners to be brought forward. The sentences were read, and the executioner, brought in from the capital for just this purpose, got ready to do his work. But the high magistrate now showed some mercy. The elderly men were spared the whip. Seven men received not 100 but thirty-five lashes. Three women—Juana Tomatle "the one-eyed," Petronila López, and Josepha López—were given not fifty but twenty-five lashes. The punishment was carried out, according to Plazaola, before the village government officials and "an infinite number of other persons." Several of those supposed to be whipped were not to be found at the moment, and the high magistrate therefore ordered the village government to arrest them when they appeared so they could receive their punishment. But here the paper trail ends, and we do not know whether the missing people ever showed up.

Spaniards Versus Spaniards

What happened in Tecpán did not go unnoticed in the rest of Guatemala. In fact, it soon became a bone of contention in politics. Indeed, it provoked conflict among the colonial elites, that is, between the European and American Spaniards.

Tecpán was in the High Magistracy of Chimaltenango, created in 1752. Before that time the district had been under the direct jurisdiction of the city magistrates of Santiago de Guatemala. Such a situation was normal in Spanish America, for all cities had some jurisdiction in the surrounding region in order to facilitate control over the urban food supply. The city council of Santiago de Guatemala, which was always dominated by American-born Spaniards, appointed special magistrates—called corregidores of the Valley—to exercise control over the Indians. They did so by administering justice, by organizing labor services benefitting the urban elite, and by carrying out the same repartimiento business that royal high magistrates carried out in their districts. It was estimated in the 1740s that each corregidor of the Valley earned as much as 12,000 pesos per year in business activities with the Indians.[57]

The audiencia, always dominated by European Spaniards, came to have an interest in the administration of the valley surrounding the capital. Since the corregidors of the Valley were city, not royal, officials, they could not take charge of tribute collection and census taking, as would royal high magistrates. The audiencia complained that the Indians were not paying enough tribute, but because the area was under the city's direct jurisdiction little could be done to solve the problem. The audiencia therefore, beginning as early as the 1690s, had tried to take jurisdiction away from the city and put it in the hands of two new high magistrates who as royal officials would be responsible for tribute and would be under the control of the audiencia. But to give to one side, of course, was to take away from the other, and therefore, as was to be expected, the city council strenuously objected to the proposed high magistracies every time the issue came up.[58]

The crown finally gave in to the audiencia and allowed the creation of the new high magistracies in 1752. The first person to occupy the post died after only three months in office, and the president at the time immediately appointed Manuel de Plazaola, a European Spaniard, to fill the vacancy. He did so, the president reported, despite candidate's inexperience "because of his intelligence, activity, and complete independence."[59] That is hard to believe, especially in light of what followed.

The city council of Santiago de Guatemala of course protested vigorously against its loss of power and of the opportunity to exploit the Indians of the

Valley. The events in Tecpán gave the American Spaniards on the city council a golden opportunity and new ammunition in their struggle to regain control of the Valley. They claimed that the rebellion had been caused by Manuel
de Plazaola's "excessive" repartimientos. He was said to have invested over
30,000 pesos in the business, forced the Indians to carry bales of cotton all
the way from the Pacific coast to the highlands, and even monopolized the
supply of quetzal feathers that the Indians needed for their ceremonial clothing.[60] And indeed, the high magistrate's business activities were undoubtedly a factor causing the revolt in Tecpán, for that is why Plazaola met
resistance from the calpul leaders and why he had to impose his own crony
as the village scribe.

But Plazaola was a European Spaniard and had friends in high places.
The European Spaniards on the audiencia were his friends, for the high magistrate, like all people in his position, provided the judges with gifts (sugar,
cacao, and meat), threw good parties, and helped find jobs for the judges'
sons. (The gifts were openly admitted by the judges, who did not give up
what were called their "table gifts" from the magistrates until 1798.[61]) Consequently, even though the city council took its case to the Council of the
Indies and the king in Spain, the audiencia backed Plazaola all the way. To
do otherwise would possibly have meant restoring control of the Valley to
the city council and the reduction of the audiencia's power of patronage. In
fact, Plazaola was even reappointed later in the year to serve a second term
as high magistrate of Chimaltenango, at a time when reappointments were
virtually unheard of. Eventually the crown chose to maintain the new high
magistracies, thereby approving not only the audiencia's position but also
Manuel de Plazaola's performance in the post.[62] The European Spaniards
thus got their way in the short run. But the price was the further antagonism
of the American Spaniards, and in the long run that would prove fatal to the
Spanish empire in America.

The little stories of supposedly unimportant people in reality tell us about
important things in history. First, the events in Tecpán in 1759 reveal significant details about the historical process of change and continuity among the
Maya. We can see the survival of the calpules as the basic building block of
Maya society. The Spaniards were able to gather together the people scattered in the countryside and bring them in to a concentrated settlement. But
that resettlement did not by itself make the people members of a single community. Rather, in Tecpán, there were at least eight different communities in
residence. Their survival after 200 years of colonialism speaks volumes for
the continuity of Maya social organization. The Spaniards, of course, were
not blind to such contraventions of their goals, but since, as we saw in the

previous chapter, the Maya had to be encouraged, not just forced, to accept Spanish rule, the colonial regime was willing to turn a blind eye to most of what did not interfere with the accomplishment of their major goals.

On the other hand, the survival of Maya social and cultural structures sometimes did interfere with Spanish goals. The calpules of Tecpán ended up exercising too much power, and interfered with a government official's ability to earn the money that allowed him to rule at little cost to the crown. Open resistance could not be tolerated, and therefore the colonial regime acted. It could not abolish the calpules overnight, but it could undermine them by stripping them of their political power. In the long run that worked. Without political power the calpules lost what must have been one of their most important functions, and many of them eventually disappeared.[63] In short, the calpules of Tecpán are a story of change as well as of continuity.

Even so, the power of the Spaniards was definitely limited. Sometimes it was limited by the Indians themselves. In this chapter, we have seen how the royal high magistrate wanted to accomplish certain goals during his interrogations but could not achieve complete success. The Maya resisted his efforts and limited the damage that could be done. In the face of such determined resistance, Plazaola had to admit political defeat. His power was restricted by his need to stick to forms, because without them the colonial regime would have been a naked dictatorship based on brute force. Of course, repression existed, but even that was restricted. Eventually the militia had to be withdrawn from the village, and the high magistrate had to withdraw too. Once again, we see that colonialism, unlike modern military dictatorship, worked best when combining coercion with conciliation. The Maya, in turn, combined their resistance with resignation.

Once again, then, we see the process of maintaining Spanish authority in America. Both sides had to give and take. Note, for example, that the Maya people of Tecpán, even while resisting their high magistrate, did not overtly challenge the legitimacy of the king of Spain. On the contrary, they appealed to Spanish justice and worked through colonial institutions to mitigate repression. In their words, they exercised their rights. Moreover, they did this even before they had been arrested. They believed, in other words, that it was worth the effort to use colonial institutions to their own advantage. True, by doing so they helped legitimize the very colonial system that oppressed them. But from the Maya point of view that was better than romantic but futile rebellion. By giving up their political independence they gained a lessening of punishment and a significant degree of local autonomy.

The events in Tecpán also help us understand the nature of local politics and the place of women in the structure of power. What happened demonstrates clearly that while women may be excluded from political office, they are not thereby excluded from politics. It must be emphasized that politics is not limited to government and governmental elites. The latter are important, of course, but in fact they are the apex of a pyramid of politics. The local people play their role too, and when women got events going and kept them going, they were exercising real political power. The soldiers who were unhorsed undoubtedly got the point. So too did Manuel Plazaola, who was so angered by the women insulting him that he lost his temper and struck out at María Balam in rage. He later had to play down what had happened, for he had overstepped the bounds of acceptable Spanish male behavior, and he must have known that. The higher authorities, in turn, let him get away with it. The punishment of a royal official for beating an Indian woman would not have been good for the Spaniards' reputation—as much in their own eyes as in the eyes of the Indians.

Finally, the events in Tecpán spilled over into another arena of politics. It allows us to see what was taking place at the apex of power, where a struggle had already begun that would culminate, in Guatemala as elsewhere, in national independence. Unfortunately, the American Spaniards who ruled Guatemala in the nineteenth century would have violent disagreements over just how the country should be run. Moreover, the collapse of the tributary system as a result of the Independence movement meant that governments no longer got their revenues directly from the Indians. Customs duties, only a minor source of colonial state revenues, were crucial after Independence. This might have lightened the tax burden on the indigenous people, but it also meant that governments no longer had to show restraint when dealing with Indians because their revenues no longer depended on them as taxpayers. The Maya would learn that as bad as colonial rule was, their condition could get worse. And it soon did.

4

Renegotiation, Injustice, and Persistence: Santa Lucía Utatlán, 1760–1763

> *He has nothing but his body.*
> *They should sell his soul.*
> *He has nothing to give; they should sell him, his wife,*
> *and his children.*

> —Juan Ebange, Francisco Queg, and Antonio Yac,
> Villagers of Santa Lucía Utatlán[1]

PARTICIPANTS

Maya

Antonio Ixcol, junior Indian magistrate (second alcalde) of Santa Lucía Utatlán
The people of Santa Lucía Utatlán

Spaniards

Joseph Ventura Manso de Velasco, high magistrate of Atitlán-Tecpanatitlán
Alonso Arcos y Moreno, captain general, president of the Audiencia of Guatemala
Felipe Romana, attorney general (fiscal)
Juan de Carrascosa, local landowner, owner of Hacienda Argueta
Domingo López de Urrelo, oidor (judge) of the audiencia, president's asesor (legal council)
Alonso Fernández de Heredia, captain general, president of the Audiencia of Guatemala (succeeded Arcos y Moreno)

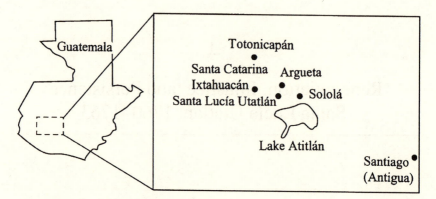

Map 4 **Santa Lucía Utatlán and Vicinity**

Juan Rodríguez Pardo, lawyer of the audiencia
Juan Antonio Bosque, procurator of the audiencia
Licenciado Domingo de Oliva, lawyer of the audiencia

The colonial regime rested on the balance of give and take. The conquered Indians had accepted exploitation (which in any case they had known before) in return for autonomy and for limits on that exploitation. When Spaniards were perceived to go beyond those limits, the Indians defended themselves by claiming their rights.

It would be wrong, however, to see the actions of indigenous people simply as a reaction to what Europeans were doing to them. They also acted on their own and manifested considerable autonomy in doing so. This is what we will see in this chapter, which concerns the events in the village of Santa Lucía Utatlán. There, the Maya carried out a plan designed to diminish what the Spaniards could get away with at their expense. In other words, in this case the first step did not consist of Spanish aggression followed by Maya self-defense. Rather, the Indians first went on the offensive themselves and demanded the end to a long-established colonial practice. In short, they tried to renegotiate the conditions of their domination and tried to put greater limits on colonial exploitation.

At the same time, events in Santa Lucía Utatlán would once again reveal the difficulty of maintaining Spanish hegemony in the face of determined Maya resistance. At one point the people of the village challenged the Spaniards by offering to sell their own bodies—an action that would certainly have undermined the Spanish belief in the benevolence of their rule. Eventually the government had to give in and back off. The Indians were punished, but not in the way the Spaniards had wanted.

Finally, the violence in Santa Lucía Utatlán once again reveals the cleavages within the power structure. The attorney general, previously neutral in the struggle between European and American Spaniards, felt compelled to take sides. Fiscal Felipe Romana, a native of Colombia, in this case began to side against the Europeans and therefore with the Guatemala-born Americans. One suspects, then, that it was only a matter of time before such disputes at the apex of the political structure would eventually lead to irreconcilable differences. Independence from Spain was in fact just around the corner.

The Burden of Colonialism

Santa Lucía Utatlán is a small village located four kilometers northwest of Lake Atitlán in the highlands of central Guatemala. It was in the jurisdiction of the High Magistracy of Atitlán-Tecpanatitlán, which eventually became known as Sololá, after the large village that served as the capital of the district. Despite the very rugged terrain, in the eighteenth century the population of the region was large, agriculture was well developed, and considerable commerce took place between the numerous villages, as well as between the Atitlán district and the capital of Santiago de Guatemala, some eighty-nine kilometers to the southeast of Sololá. Santa Lucía Utatlán was one of the smallest villages of the region. Fuentes y Guzmán reported a population of only 308 people (seventy-seven tributaries) in the 1690s.[2] Archbishop Cortés y Larraz, while noting Santa Lucía Utatlán's existence, was sick when he visited the area in 1769 and apparently did not get around to determining the village's population.[3] Nevertheless, there must have been considerable population growth in the eighteenth century, for in the early 1760s it was reported that there were between 330 and 600 tributaries in Santa Lucía Utatlán.[4] This would have meant a population of between 1,320 and 2,400 people.

The people of the village were of mixed Maya ethnicity. Santa Lucía Utatlán is right on the border between the Quiché- and Cakchiquel-speaking regions, and the village included people from both those linguistic groups.[5] Cakchiquel was certainly the language of the majority of the population, and it was undoubtedly for that reason that Santa Lucía Utatlán belonged to the parish of the large Cakchiquel village of Sololá (about twelve kilometers to the east). The village was also close to the Tzutujil people who lived on the southern shore of Lake Atitlán, but no one from the latter group was found in Santa Lucía Utatlán. It is not known how the ethnic differences among the residents were manifested, or whether they were historically important. The villagers of Santa Lucía Utatlán were somewhat unified economically, for they belonged to a complex commercial system oriented around the market held every Friday, then as now, in nearby Sololá. They also marketed goods in Santiago de Guatemala, and to carry goods both to the capital and to Sololá, the villagers owned a considerable number of mules. The profession of muleteer must have been extremely common in Santa Lucía Utatlán.[6]

The Atitlán region to which Santa Lucía Utatlán belonged was one of the most prosperous in colonial Guatemala. The High Magistracy of Atitlán-Tecpanatitlán was judged by those in the know to be one of the "juiciest" ("*más pingües*") posts to buy in the whole Kingdom of Guatemala.[7] In the 1740s the post sold for 4,600 pesos, but in 1758, when Spain was at peace with the world and there was no desperate need for hard cash, the crown, as part of a policy of ending the practice of selling offices, granted the post free of charge. It was given to a European Spaniard, Infantry Captain Joseph Ventura Manso de Velasco, who received the post as a reward for his military service to the crown.[8] Nevertheless, the new high magistrate undoubtedly expected to make money from his office, and indeed in the 1760s it was estimated that the post could yield in profits between 8,000 and 20,000 pesos a year if the repartimiento business there were well managed.[9] We do not know if Manso de Velasco made that much, but we do know that the post caused him numerous headaches because Santa Lucía Utatlán was under his jurisdiction.

Since the time of the Spanish conquest the Indians of Guatemala were subjected to forced labor. After initial brutal exploitation by the first generation of Spanish conquistadors and colonists, the royal government in Guatemala, as elsewhere, eventually succeeded in imposing limits on forced labor.[10] Most importantly, the crown authorized the allotment of draft labor—called a repartimiento (not to be confused with the commercial repartimiento carried out by government officials in alliance with merchant backers)—that consisted of a certain proportion of the able-bodied male population. Every year, that proportion had to work a certain number of days for specific Spanish landowners. The workers were paid for their services at low wages, which helps explain why coercion was required to make people work. The draft was authorized because of the alleged social utility of food production, for the workers were supposed to be assigned to work in wheat fields, wheat bread being considered the staff of life and culinary manifestation of civilization by the Spanish, although not the Indian, population.

In Mexico the labor draft for landed estates producing wheat was abolished in 1632 because it was considered abusive.[11] But just because it was abolished in Mexico does not mean that it ceased to exist everywhere else. Indeed, in Guatemala it lasted until the very end of the colonial period and was even revived for coffee production in the late nineteenth century.[12] Forced labor, therefore, is one of the most enduring, and infamous, features of the history of Guatemala.

Santa Lucía Utatlán apparently had a history of resisting overexploitation. During the inquest into the disturbances of 1760, one ladino resident of the village testified that the villagers had once burned the thread owed to a previous high magistrate as a result of that official's repartimiento business.[13] Another witness said he could remember no fewer than five uprisings that took place in his lifetime in Santa Lucía Utatlán.[14] Don Miguel de Cuéllar, a Spaniard who was the former owner of nearby Hacienda Argueta and who had served as the lieutenant of a previous high magistrate, said that the villagers in the past had received presidential dispatches limiting their forced labor obligations, and that they kept these documents in a strongbox, which was placed next to idols and was incensed with copal. The same witness also said that when as owner of the hacienda he had delivered to the villagers a presidential dispatch favoring him and ordering the people of Santa Lucía Utatlán to work for him, the villagers first asked to borrow the document to have it translated and then claimed to have lost it and refused to obey. Cuéllar tried to take action against them for this "infamy," but finally gave up and sold the hacienda.[15]

A factor that helped lead to the disturbances of 1760 was the election of Antonio Ixcol as junior Indian magistrate of the village. Ixcol had already served as church warden (*fiscal de la Iglesia*), and he stands out from almost all the rest of the Maya because he knew his exact age: fifty-three and a half years old in May 1760. He was also one of the very few people identified as an Indian who could speak Spanish. Perhaps his contact with a wider world of non-Indians explains why he knew his age. He was the father of at least three sons and two daughters, and had suffered an accident many years before 1760, as a result of which he had a crippled shoulder. The Spaniards later tried to claim that Ixcol had always been a troublemaker, and he may have been one, but we would expect the Spaniards to say that. They were always looking for someone to blame for revolts. As President Alonso de Arcos y Moreno put it at the time, "it is natural to find that these things begin with a troublemaker."[16]

Shortly after taking power as Indian magistrate, Ixcol, either on his own or with the encouragement of others, took steps to reduce the demands being placed on his village. For years the people of Santa Lucía Utatlán had been required to provide workers for the nearby Hacienda Argueta (seven kilometers to the northeast of the village). According to High Magistrate Manso de Velasco, this labor had been performed "since time immemorial" but "always with repugnance," even though in addition to their pay the workers were allowed to graze their horses, mules, and sheep on hacienda land and to take firewood and fodder back home with them for their own use.[17] This "repugnance" led Ixcol to try to challenge the labor draft. He and a group of other leaders went to the capital and hired a lawyer, Juan Rodríguez Pardo (who appeared in the previous chapter as the legal representative of the people of Tecpán), who presented a petition to the president in the name of the people of Santa Lucía Utatlán on April 15, 1760. They requested that they be relieved of the obligation to provide workers for the hacienda because the distance from their village to the estate was greater than the legal limit, as a result of which the labor service had "caused and causes very grave injury to our own harvest." In addition, they claimed that the owner of Hacienda Argueta, Juan de Carrascosa, was requiring them to transport his wheat to the capital, a distance of eighty kilometers, not on their mules, as was permitted, but on their backs, which was not.[18]

This petition was passed on to the attorney general, once again Felipe Romana, who reported on April 16. Romana pointed out that any order requiring Indians to carry grain on their backs would be illegal, and that the high magistrate should be so informed. He also requested that an inquiry determine the distance between the village and the hacienda, for without the facts he could make no ruling. President Arcos y Moreno therefore ordered Manso de Velasco to determine the distance and report back. Since the Indians of Santa Lucía Utatlán had made the original petition that resulted in the order, the government entrusted Antonio Ixcol with delivery of the message. Ixcol informed the people of his village that he planned to deliver the document to the high magistrate in Sololá on Friday morning, April 18.[19]

While these events were taking place, others, which would also culminate on April 18, had already been in preparation. First, back in March the city council of Santiago de Guatemala had informed the president that the quantity of grain arriving in the city was insufficient and that a grain shortage could result. It recommended that the president take steps to facilitate the transport of food from surrounding provinces. Arcos y Moreno quickly responded by ordering the high magistrates of several provinces, including Manso de Velasco of Atitlán-Tecpanatitlán, to require all owners of mules to make their animals available to transport grain to the city. As was always the case when such measures were taken, the owners were to be paid the normal transport fees.[20]

Second, and ominously, there had been a tax increase. Indian women had always been exempt from tribute, but in 1759 the crown decided to impose a special impost of four reales, called the *tostón de servicio* (1 tostón = four reales) on each adult female. Unfortunately, there was confusion over the implementation of the tax, and it was not clear when the officials should start to collect. Since high magistrates were legally liable for all royal tax revenues, they were naturally afraid that if they did not start collecting immediately they might be held responsible for uncollected revenue.

In Atitlán-Tecpanatitlán, Manso de Velasco in March 1760 wrote to President Arcos y Moreno asking for an explanation of the new tax and clarification of when it should be implemented. He had been on the job only for six months and was concerned because, not knowing when the tax was to go into effect, he had not collected the *tostón de servicio* in December 1759 and was afraid he might be held responsible. But then, pending clarification, Manso de Velasco decided to collect the tax from the women just to be on the safe side. He was guided, he said, by his own principle that "with Indians it is always better to have to return something than not to collect at all." He informed the president of his decision and requested that his action be approved. It was not, but the decision by the attorney general to that effect was not made until April 18—too late to help Manso de Velasco, who had already encountered fierce resistance not only from Santa Lucía Utatlán but also from the Cakchiquel Maya village of Santa Catalina Ixtahuacán. To avoid further problems, therefore, and perhaps fearing that he had made a mistake, the high magistrate returned the funds to the village government of Santa Lucía Utatlán.[21]

Thus many events were leading up to what happened on April 18. The money returned by Manso de Velasco never got back to the women of Santa Lucía Utatlán, for Indian magistrate Ixcol combined it with some money paid by the owner of Hacienda Argueta for the workers, and used it all to hire the lawyer in the capital. By the time this was done, he had a lot of good complaints to make about the high magistrate. First, Ixcol was convinced that the new tax was not an official tax at all but rather an effort by Manso de Velasco to extort more money from his people in an illegal manner. As we have seen elsewhere, the Maya could always be counted on to resist any arbitrary change of the rules of exploitation, and this time, true to form, they resisted. Ixcol's resolve was possibly strengthened by the knowledge that the nearby village of Santa Catalina Ixtahuacán was also resisting the new impost.

It also happened that Manso de Velasco, to carry out his orders regarding grain for the capital, ordered the mule owners of Santa Lucía Utatlán to transport the very wheat they were being forced to harvest on Hacienda Argueta, owned by Juan de Carrascosa. That added insult to injury, and therefore Ixcol or one of his associates came up with an ingenious way of bringing the matter to the attention of the higher authorities. Rather than use the villagers' mules, as the high magistrate had ordered, he had half of the grain carried on the backs of the Indians and claimed that his people had been forced to transport the wheat that way for lack of mules.

Ixcol's plan, as we have seen, succeeded. When the government received his village's petition of April 15, Fiscal Romana immediately acted to stop such abuse by pointing out the illegal nature of such an order. The president then sent a message to that effect to the high magistrate, and this was the order that would arrive on the morning of April 18.

Having gotten a quick ruling from the audiencia, although not one abolishing the labor draft for the hacienda, Ixcol then prepared his people for the delivery of the order to the high magistrate in the district capital of Sololá. He sent word to Santa Lucía Utatlán for as many people as possible—young and old, men and women—to be in Sololá on Friday morning, April 18. That happened to be market day in the chief village, as surely everyone knew, and therefore there would be throngs of people in the village from all over the area around Lake Atitlán. An extra-large contingent from Santa Lucía Utatlán would not be noticed. The Spaniards later claimed that Ixcol ordered his people to come armed with machetes and rocks, but the Indians firmly denied that, and indeed it is unlikely. No one actually saw an Indian from Santa Lucía Utatlán armed with a machete, and as for rocks, there were more than enough of those on hand in Sololá; there was no need to carry any all the way from Santa Lucía Utatlán. But very importantly, Ixcol did tell his people that the dispatch to be delivered to the high magistrate would free them from exploitation.[22]

High Magistrate Joseph Ventura Manso de Velasco therefore had a big surprise on Friday morning, April 18. The market day is still held in Sololá, and is one of the best examples of the famous regional marketing systems of the highland Maya. People from all over the area, some coming by boat across Lake Atitlán, assemble there to sell their specialties and buy other people's goods. In 1760, at 9:00 A.M., Manso de Velasco was sitting at a table in his office in the Casas Reales, located, as was always the case, on the main plaza. He permitted a delegation from Santa Lucía Utatlán, led by Ixcol, to come in and talk to him. Outside, waiting in the corridor, were scores of men and women of the village.

What happened next is not entirely clear, because accounts are conflicting.[23] What is certain is that the high magistrate and the Indian magistrate of Santa Lucía Utatlán had a disagreement over the degree of exploitation that would be permitted. Manso de Velasco also demanded to know why Ixcol had failed to return the tax money taken from the Indian women, and the Indian magistrate responded that the money would be used to pay the salary of the village's new schoolteacher. Eventually Manso de Velasco angrily demanded that Ixcol surrender his staff of office. Ixcol later claimed that he voluntarily did so, while the Spanish witnesses stated that they had to take it away from the Indian magistrate. The high magistrate then ordered his men to arrest Ixcol.

At that point the people outside the Casas Reales started yelling, screaming, and throwing rocks, and then broke down the door and pulled Ixcol away from the Spaniards, asserting that "they would not let him be captured because he is the father of his village, the one who defends them."[24] Others were heard to say that Ixcol was "the father of the fatherland."[25] Manso de Velasco later claimed that he distinctly heard people say in a loud voice, "kill the high magistrate and then kill the priest!" but since he spoke no Cakchiquel or Quiché and they spoke no Spanish, at best what he got was a rough translation of what was said. The Indians rescued their village magistrate and removed him from the Casas Reales, while in the building and in the corridor the high magistrate's bodyguards, drawing their sabers, fought with the people. No one was seriously hurt, for the soldiers claimed to have struck only with the flat of the blade.

Ixcol and the people of Santa Lucía Utatlán then went back to their village. Manso de Velasco acted with pen and sword. He sent off a message to President Arcos y Moreno, informing him of what had happened. He also sent an order to the village government of Santa Lucía Utatlán to appear before him the following Monday morning, April 21. He began mobilizing the local militia. One of his messengers, the village constable of Sololá, however, never got through. On his way to the village of San Andrés, with orders to call up the militia, he ran into people from Santa Lucía Utatlán. They tore up his papers and for good measure beat him up with his own staff of office.

It is not clear whether Manso de Velasco began to organize the militia before or after he received permission to do so. In any case, on April 20 President Arcos y Moreno, responding to the high magistrate's initial report on the events of April 18, wrote Manso de Velasco that "It seems to me to be wise to take the step of calling up the militia of the chief village [i.e., Sololá] and of whatever others you deem necessary."[26] This certainly suggested to the high magistrate that he was correct in mobilizing the militia, although later there would be disagreement over just how large a force had been authorized.

The village government of Santa Lucía Utatlán, minus junior magistrate Antonio Ixcol, appeared before Manso de Velasco as ordered. Many other citizens of the village also showed up. All told between fifty and sixty Indians met with the high magistrate. They all asserted that the uproar had been caused by their junior magistrate. They blamed him for interpreting the new tax as just a trick of the high magistrate to extort more money from them. When Manso de Velasco showed them the president's order regarding the use of mules, they then blamed Ixcol for coming up with the idea of carrying the grain on their backs in order to get the high magistrate in trouble. They even claimed that Ixcol had ordered the people to go to Sololá on

April 18 armed with machetes and rocks. All this information was taken down in front of witnesses, namely, practically all the Franciscans of the province of Atitlán-Tecpanatitlán, who had been invited the day before to the baptism of Manso de Velasco's newborn baby girl. They later testified in his behalf.

The high magistrate then wrote another report to the president, to keep him abreast of the what was happening.[27] Next, he turned to the matter of the allegations that Ixcol had made about him in the capital. He drew up a defense, pointing out that the petition in the name of Santa Lucía Utatlán was filled with half-truth and untruth. It was true that he had ordered the people to transport grain to Santiago de Guatemala, but he had done so in response to a presidential order, and he had told the Indians to use mules and promised to pay them the customary freight charge. Since the villagers had, he claimed, more than 250 beasts of burden, the use of twenty-five mules to carry fifty fanegas of wheat would not have been burdensome. The decision to carry the grain on their backs was made without his knowledge and was clearly done to embarrass him. He also pointed out that the labor draft for Hacienda Argueta was not a new burden he had imposed but an old custom the legality of which the government had recently upheld by ordering Santa Lucía Utatlán to provide one-quarter of the able-bodied men as weekly workers at the regular wage. Yet despite this order, which would have required 150 men to work (the village having, he claimed, 600 able-bodied men), only twenty-five showed up—a clear act of disobedience. Finally, he stated that the hacienda in question was only a "short league" (perhaps three or four kilometers) from the village and thus was within the legal limits of the labor draft. Because of all these "calumnies," however, the high magistrate complained that his honor had been besmirched.[28]

Manso de Velasco undoubtedly defended himself well in his statement of April 21. But that very same day he made a very serious error in judgment. Having used his pen a lot that day, he also tried to use his sword. To assert his authority he decided to send a force of fifty-four militiamen to arrest Antonio Ixcol. By itself that might not have been a mistake, but in command of the column the high magistrate named Juan de Carrascosa. He did so, he said, because the latter was "a person of my Satisfaction and of Experience."[29] That may have been true, but Carrascosa was also the owner of Hacienda Argueta, the labor draft for which was so disliked in Santa Lucía Utatlán. His appointment to command was one more insult added to injury. Moreover, Carrascosa could not speak the language of the villagers, and to make things worse, his column arrived in the village at 11:00 P.M. Since in most peasant villages people retire shortly after nightfall, the arrival of the column took place in the middle of the night and must have been disturbing and confusing, for any outsiders would have been suspected of being bandits. For all these reasons, as the attorney general pointed out later, Manso de Velasco had not acted wisely.

What happened next must have been especially confusing because it took place in the dark. Having arrived in Santa Lucía Utatlán at 11:00 P.M., Carrascosa told someone in the village that he had come to arrest Ixcol. Because of language difficulties, it was not known if the people understood. In any case, Indian women—once again an active group—began to insult the soldiers and their commander. A large mob of men and women assembled, and soon the villagers were throwing stones. Carrascosa decided to get out of town without his prisoner and ordered his men to withdraw. This they did, but when they entered a nearby ravine, they discovered that the high ground was occupied by Indians, and when they tried to pass through the ravine the Indians hurled stones at them. Panic ensued, and the militiamen ran for their lives. In the darkness many got lost. Eventually Carrascosa and most of his men made it back to Sololá and reported to Manso de Velasco.

The high magistrate quickly fired off still another report to President Arcos y Moreno. He claimed that the column had been attacked in the ravine by a force of between 1,000 and 2,500 Indians. Moreover, some soldiers had been killed, although since their bodies had been left behind he did not yet know how many. Carrascosa had received four wounds from rocks, but was not seriously hurt. Manso de Velasco ended his report by requesting that a supply of guns and ammunition be sent to him so that he could crush the rebellion.[30]

The president acted quickly. He authorized the dispatch of fifty rifles with bayonets and ten rounds each to the high magistrate in Sololá.[31] The quantity is significant, for it suggests that Arcos y Moreno did not quite believe that he had as many as 2,500 rebellious Indians on his hands. The reason for his skepticism is probably some information that he now possessed that the high magistrate did not: Antonio Ixcol and several of his supporters were in the capital apparently trying to make another appeal to the president. These were hardly the actions of committed rebels. In any case, Arcos y Moreno took advantage of the situation. He had the people from Santa Lucía Utatlán locked up pending an investigation.

That same day President Arcos y Moreno, who was dying at the time, sent a letter to Manso de Velasco and tried to calm him down.[32] He informed the high magistrate that Ixcol and some of his associates had been arrested in Santiago de Guatemala, and advised once again that the high magistrate act with prudence so that "these wretches [the Indians] not be made more criminal; and just as illness is inevitable, so it is to proceed with caution." Arcos y Moreno then suggested that maybe Manso de Velasco had overreacted: he hinted that it had not been a good idea to send Carrascosa so suddenly, and with soldiers, to the village. Had he wanted Ixcol detained, he should have sent an order to the village government to that effect. He closed by emphasizing that "since malice and ignorance, which usually go hand in hand, are prominent here, our knowledge must be used to correct rather than injure." This advice may have helped avoid further violence, but did not succeed in checking the high magistrate's tendency to overreact.

Meanwhile, back in Sololá, Manso de Velasco continued to make mistakes. He called for help from surrounding provinces and soon had a force of over 500 men assembled in Sololá. On April 27 he sent another panicky report to President Arcos y Moreno, warning of the danger of the revolt spreading. He had been told that Ixcol was trying to get the villages of Santa Catalina Ixtahuacán and Santa Clara to join Santa Lucía Utatlán, and that "a multitude of Indians from different villages, with machetes and axes" had been seen coming down the road toward Sololá.[33] Yet nothing happened, and the large military force was never used, not even against Santa Lucía Utatlán. Messengers from that village went to see the high magistrate and begged for mercy, and several priests served as peacemakers to make further violence unnecessary.[34] For all intents and purposes the revolt was over.

Nevertheless, the large military force was kept in Sololá for a month. Since the soldiers and their forces had to be fed, and since the militiamen received a salary when on active duty, the high magistrate had to spend all the tribute revenue he had already collected. He was not authorized to do so, but he felt he had no other choice, for the government sent him no money. However, at the same time, in his reports to the president Manso de Velasco failed to update his panicky report of April 22 regarding the "battle of the ravine." What he forgot, or chose not to report, was the following crucial piece of information: all of the militiamen lost in the battle had turned up alive. They had either gotten lost in the dark or had lagged behind as stragglers and were late in arriving at Sololá. This meant that not a single person had been killed or even seriously injured during the entire revolt. When the higher authorities found this out, and thought about the large militia force kept mobilized for a full month, they would not be happy.

The revolt was over. Now someone had to pay.

Investigation

High Magistrate Joseph Manso de Velasco was new on the job and was not always certain of what to do. Therefore, in his very first letter to President Arcos y Moreno, informing his superior of events in Sololá on April 18, he requested that a special judge be appointed to investigate what had happened. The president responded by informing the high magistrate that "such a step is not yet appropriate at this moment, since the legitimate judge of the case is Your Mercy," that is, Manso de Velasco himself. On the other hand, Arcos y Moreno advised the high magistrate that "Your Mercy should apply yourself with great care and circumspection in carrying out the proceedings that prove the facts."[35]

Even before he received this sage advice, Manso de Velasco had begun to "prove the facts." On April 19, the day after the mayhem in the high magistrate's office, he questioned three "prisoners" from Santa Lucía Utatlán, two of whom had been captured in other villages and one in Sololá itself. They told Manso de Velasco that their village magistrate Antonio Ixcol had told them to come to Sololá on Friday morning to find out about the dispatches from the president, in which, they were assured, Arcos y Moreno would relieve them of the obligation to work on Hacienda Argueta.[36] Moreover, even before the battle of the ravine, the high magistrate drew up a long questionnaire to be used to take the testimony of those people who had witnessed the mayhem in Sololá on April 18. One of the questions referred to the power that the calpul heads exercised in Santa Lucía Utatlán, revealing again the continued importance of those basic elements of Maya social organization. In this case, however, the role that calpules played was never clarified, although it is possible that Ixcol was the leader of only one parcialidad and that those who would betray him were of another. In all, there were a total of ten questions, all designed to get the witnesses to claim that Santa Lucía Utatlán had always been a troublesome village, that Antonio Ixcol was a troublemaker, that the high magistrate had done nothing wrong to the Indians, and that he had been assaulted in the Casas Reales by a mob of Indians.[37]

The first witnesses began to give statements on April 22.[38] That was the day after the battle of the ravine, but it is likely that the high magistrate had not yet found out about the disaster suffered by Carrascosa's column. Only two people testified that day, the small number probably explained by the return of the panicky and scared soldiers. With all the subsequent writing of reports and mobilizing of troops, only six witnesses appeared in the next four days. All of those who testified were non-Indians, and six had been in the Casas Reales when the confrontation between Ixcol and Manso de Velasco took place. Several could speak Cakchiquel and thus claimed to have understood what the Indians were saying.

Many of the witnesses managed to add details about which they had not been asked. Several mentioned the box in which the Indians of Santa Lucía Utatlán supposedly kept their important papers, and referred to the idols and incense associated with that box. Several noted that Santa Catalina Ixtahuacán was also famous, in their opinion, for being a troublemaking village.

Soon all fear of a serious uprising was gone, and therefore the high magistrate prepared to take evidence from the Indians. On May 1 he ordered thirty-eight specific individuals from Santa Lucía Utatlán—including the three sons of Antonio Ixcol—to come to Sololá to give evidence. Most simply failed to show up. The high magistrate interrogated thirteen people over a three-day period beginning on May 2. Manso de Velasco was so inexperienced in interviewing potentially hostile witnesses that at first he asked very general questions that allowed the Indians to wander from the point and add things that they, but not he, thought to be relevant. Therefore, after the first day's testimony, having heard from four people, including two of Ixcol's sons, the high magistrate finally drew up the typical list of leading questions designed to prove the guilt of Antonio Ixcol.

As was usual in this form of procedure, the interrogator got some, but not all, of what he wanted, and the Maya managed to get things into the record that were not sought.[39] Most of the witnesses dutifully blamed Ixcol for what had happened, but most also added that he was supported by practically everyone in the village because they did not believe that there was a presidential dispatch ordering them to work on Hacienda Argueta or to transport the grain to the capital. Nor did anyone believe that the new tax was anything but an attempt by the high magistrate to extort money from them. As Juan Choox put it, Ixcol "told them that it was infamous that all the time they had new burdens to bear."[40] The sons of the village magistrate complained bitterly that when their father was standing up for the people, they all said "that they would lay down their lives in his defense," but now that he was a prisoner facing punishment, "those who encouraged him . . . are hiding in the bush, having taken from their houses the food and other things they need, and although his father has called on them to defend him, they pay him no attention, which makes it look like all they wanted was to put him over a fire."[41]

A few other details were also revealed. When Ixcol and his group went to Santiago de Guatemala to deliver the grain, some of which was carried on their backs, they also took with them mules loaded with their own wheat to sell on the market.[42] It was through these market activities, of course, that the people earned the money to pay their taxes and to buy machetes and other desired goods. More important for purposes of the revolt, however, is the information to the effect that before the revolt the leaders of Santa Lucía Utatlán had met with those of Santa Catalina Ixtahuacán and Santa Clara in order to resist the new extortion that they believed the high magistrate was inventing.[43] Thus, although no other village joined Santa Lucía Utatlán in the revolt, the Maya once again showed their propensity to try to work together against the Spaniards. The hoped-for solidarity never materialized, but the attempt to accomplish it meant that to the Maya it was at least within the realm of the possible.

Having finished with the available witnesses on May 4, Manso de Velasco ordered the arrest of all those who had been called to testify at the inquest but who had failed to show up. He claimed that their noncompliance with his previous order demonstrated that they were either "extremely stupid or extremely malicious."[44] He also declared that the calpul heads had been found guilty. Orders for the arrest of all these people were sent to Santa Lucía Utatlán. Noting that he could not interrogate Antonio Ixcol because the junior magistrate was being held in the capital, the high magistrate sent all the papers to the audiencia on May 6.[45]

The attorney general therefore got the materials on the case by the time that it had become clear that no major revolt had taken place. Moreover, Fiscal Felipe Romana was more experienced than he had been the year before when he had dealt with the revolt in Tecpán. Therefore, in his first brief on the revolt, based on the reports from Manso de Velasco, the attorney general manifested a skepticism not demonstrated the year before.[46] Throughout his brief, dated May 10, he used phrases like "if proved" and "if demonstrated" when referring to the report by Manso de Velasco. When discussing the events of April 18, he immediately noted that the high magistrate had not been authorized to collect the new tax, and since Indian women had always been tax-exempt, any collection from them would be such a novelty that it should have been attempted only after the people had been informed of the official nature of the tax. That way, they would realize that it was the king's decision, and would not interpret it as extortion by their high magistrate. Moreover, regarding the transport of Juan Carrascosa's grain from his hacienda to Santiago de Guatemala using mules owned by the people of Santa Lucía Utatlán, Romana recalled dealing with an appeal by the Indians regarding the hacienda, and therefore again Manso de Velasco should have waited until the Indians had been informed that the order in question was presidential in nature. Otherwise, he noted, the people of Santa Lucía Utatlán would probably have understood it as a favor that the high magistrate was doing for Carrascosa. (Indeed, that is exactly how the Indians saw it.)

The attorney general also found fault with Manso de Velasco's actions on April 18, the day of the riot. Although Romana stated that any effort to kill the high magistrate or the priest should receive "severe punishment," he noted that the uproar began only when Manso de Velasco had tried to take away Ixcol's staff of office, yet the high magistrate chose to leave that detail out of his report. Moreover, in the ensuing struggle between the ladino guards and the Indians, only the latter were hurt.

Turning to Manso de Velasco's report of April 21, in which the high magistrate informed the president of his appointment of Juan Carrascosa, a person of his "Satisfaction and of Experience," to lead the fifty-four soldiers to

Santa Lucía Utatlán to arrest Ixcol, Fiscal Romana was again critical of the high magistrate's actions. Manso de Velasco failed to mention that Carrascosa had been involved in a dispute with the Indians over forced labor and therefore must have been detested in Santa Lucía Utatlán. Moreover, he could not speak the language of the people, yet supposedly he was to tell the villagers that he had not come to hurt them but only to apprehend their junior magistrate. The soldiers arrived late at night. The Indians' response was natural: they stoned the intruders. Moreover, although the high magistrate's letter reported the death of many soldiers, his later correspondence failed to confirm how many, if any, had died.

Finally, turning to Manso de Velasco's letter of April 27, in which he reported the participation of other villages in the revolt, Romana argued that the Indians "are worthy of severe punishment, for although superior authority can necessitate complaints, lack of respect is never justified." But such punishment should be meted out only "if the truthfulness of the facts are verified." In other words, the attorney general was not making the same mistake as a year earlier, when he had accepted High Magistrate Manuel de Plazaola's initial reports on the Tecpán case at face value.

Romana ended up recommending that the president order an investigation of the events in Sololá and Santa Lucía Utatlán. President Arcos y Moreno agreed, and on May 21 he appointed Licenciado Domingo de Oliva, a lawyer of the audiencia, to question the Indian prisoners being held in the capital.[47]

Meanwhile, those prisoners had not been inactive. They had begun to receive legal aid from audiencia procurator Juan Antonio Bosque, who on May 13 submitted an appeal to the president asking that Antonio Ixcol be freed from his chains. He was being held not only in irons but also with what was called a "Mary chain" (which probably went around his neck). Since Ixcol was not an able-bodied man, such confinement, said Bosque, was harmful and unnecessary. President Arcos y Moreno, however, ruled that "for now, the petition is out of place." Ixcol stayed in chains.[48]

Licenciado Oliva, after swearing in interpreters, began to question the prisoners on May 23.[49] There were six at first, and then, at the end, Antonio Ixcol himself. Oliva asked the first people the usual leading questions, which were designed to get the Indians from Santa Lucía Utatlán to confess their guilt. Thus they were asked to confirm that Ixcol was a troublemaker, that on Ixcol's orders they had gone to Sololá on April 18 armed with machetes and rocks, that they had been paid properly for their labor on Hacienda Argueta and for transporting grain to the capital, that they had maliciously carried the grain on their backs to get the high magistrate in trouble, and that they had beat up the messenger sent by the high magistrate to the village of San Andrés with orders to mobilize the militia. They were also asked a general question about what had happened in the Casas Reales in Sololá on April 18 (when Ixcol had been rescued from arrest), since most of them were eyewitnesses. On the other hand, Licenciado Oliva also tried to find out what had happened during the night of April 21 during the battle of the ravine, but he soon gave up upon discovering that all the witnesses were with Ixcol in the capital at the time, which was why they were detained. Interestingly, the interrogator tried to get the prisoners to admit that in their village the heads of calpules were more important and respected than their official village government. The ghost of Tecpán was hanging over the proceedings involving Santa Lucía Utatlán.

As was usually the case in such interrogations, the Spaniards got some of what they wanted, while the Indians succeeded in preventing their interrogator from getting too much. Although two people did admit that Ixcol was a troublemaker, the others did not. Only one person agreed with the leading question to the effect that the calpul heads were more important than the official government, while the rest either denied it or claimed not to know. Several of them even claimed that no malice had been intended by carrying the grain on their backs; it was done, they said, because the available mules were already worn out from such work and there were not enough fresh ones on hand. Very importantly, they all denied going to Sololá armed with machetes or rocks or that Ixcol had given them orders to carry such weapons. When asked where the rocks thrown in Sololá came from, one witness answered that they "picked up the rocks right there."[50] It must have seemed a stupid question. On the other hand, on the Spanish side of the ledger went admissions that they had beaten up the messenger, and some witnesses revealed the names of six women present in the Casas Reales in Sololá the day of the riot. However, their explanations of what had taken place were by no means an admission of guilt.

The last prisoner interrogated was Antonio Ixcol. Oliva questioned him on May 30, three days after completing his interrogation of the others.[51] In the meantime, a special set of questions had been prepared. This was because Ixcol's case was special; indeed, his testimony was referred to as a "confession," while the statements of the others had been called "declarations." He was the only one put into a "Mary chain," which was removed during his questioning. He was the only one who knew his age. And he was the only one who claimed to be able to speak Spanish; no interpreter was necessary.

Of all the Maya people questioned during the revolts and revolutions of the eighteenth century discussed in this book, Antonio Ixcol was possibly the most defiant. His defiance started no sooner had he identified himself. Asked if he understood why he had been arrested, he answered "for having come to get the president to issue a dispatch in our favor." Oliva immediately went on the attack: how, he asked, could that be, when such a request was insufficient grounds for arrest and therefore he must have been arrested for some other reason? Ixcol said that he did not know what that other reason might be.

Oliva then got to the matter of the correspondence between Ixcol and the villagers of Santa Lucía Utatlán after the president had issued a dispatch and entrusted him with delivering it. Asked if he had sent a missive (*correo*) from the capital to the village, he said no. The interrogator pressed him: surely he sent a message (*recado*). The Indian magistrate of Santa Lucía Utatlán again said no. But when questioned further, he did admit to sending a message, not from the capital but from the village of Panajachel, a lakefront town just to the east of Sololá. Ixcol denied, however, that he had ordered that his message be announced by town criers, and if that were done it was because the village officials were very "officious"; those who claimed that he gave such an order "are not telling the truth."[52] He did admit to having ordered the people to go to Sololá on the morning of April 18. But he was not even asked if he had instructed them to carry weapons; by now the Spaniards had abandoned their attempt to prove that.

Oliva then asked Ixcol about events in the Casas Reales in Sololá on the morning of April 18. Did you not refuse to surrender your staff of office to the high magistrate and as a result of your refusal did not the plebeian people riot? asked the interrogator. The Indian magistrate responded that he "did not refuse to surrender his staff of office and does not know about the rest" suggested in the question. When informed that witnesses (Oliva did not mention that they were all either ladinos or Spaniards) had sworn that he had refused to give up his staff of office, Ixcol replied that "the witnesses are not telling the truth."[53]

The interrogator then turned to the riot in and around the Casas Reales on April 18. After the incident with the staff of office, the high magistrate ordered his arrest, and was that not what started the riot? Ixcol said that after the order to arrest him was given, "some women and some men grabbed him and rioted, throwing stones, and then the high magistrate ordered the door to be closed and seven soldiers entered." Asked how he could have escaped if the door was closed, the witness stated that "the people who were outside pushed open the door, which is why he could escape." Asked next if in the riot some people were injured, Ixcol revealed, or claimed, that he could not explain because he himself had been wounded, possible by a rock, although he did not know if he was injured by the soldiers or by his own people. (He may have been lying about his injury, but it would explain why one witness had testified that Ixcol, upon being rescued, was "dragged away" by his people.)[54]

Oliva then turned to other matters. Was it not true, he demanded to know, that before going to the capital to get a presidential dispatch he had assembled the villagers to tell them that his goal was "to lighten their burdens"? Yes, said Ixcol, that is exactly what he had done.[55] He did not have to add that his actions were entirely legal.

The interrogator then turned to the money used to pay for the lawyer in the capital. This concerned the funds returned to them by the high magistrate, and use of that money had been discussed at a village meeting. Asked if some people had suggested saving the funds to pay tribute, Ixcol answered that it was true that some people had made that suggestion. Asked how he had responded to the suggestion, he said that "he did not respond at all." He did reveal the origin of the money actually used to hire the lawyer: 12 pesos were the wages paid by the hacienda for the weekly workers of the labor draft, and the other 10 pesos were from a fund set up by previous village magistrates "so that one day the money could be used to free them from their burdens." Oliva then asked if it were not true that Ixcol had used coercion against those who tried to avoid the labor draft, but the prisoner found the question to be unintelligible "no matter how many times it was explained to him and how well he understood Castilian."[56] Asked if it was true that he had ordered the Indians to enter the Casas Reales in Sololá with him "so that if the high magistrate wanted to punish him all would die where he died," he answered that such a statement was false.

The interrogator next wanted to know if Ixcol had not said that the new tax was not for the king but rather for the high magistrate. The witness denied saying that, and when Oliva told him that there were witnesses to what he had said, Ixcol once again said that those people were "not telling the truth." He also claimed that the villagers, not he, had wanted to use the money collected from the women to pay the schoolteacher.[57]

Oliva then brought up the beating of the messenger sent by Manso de Velasco. Ixcol admitted that the incident took place, but denied that the messenger had been beaten with his own staff of office. He also claimed that the injury he had suffered prevented him from remembering the names of the people who had administered the beating to the messenger: "because since his head had been broken, he was confused."[58] The interrogator finally asked if it was true that during the scuffle in the Casas Reales people had yelled "kill the high magistrate and then do the same to the priest," to which Ixcol replied that such a charge was "contrary to the truth." And although Oliva tried to get the Indian magistrate to admit that he had lied under oath, as proved by other witnesses, Ixcol refused to admit to perjury, saying that "the witnesses are lying."[59]

The testimony of the number one suspect thus yielded very little. The interrogation completed, Ixcol was returned to his cell—and to his "Mary chain." He had been forced to make a statement, but it was hardly the "confession" that the Spanish authorities had wanted.

Shortly after the interrogation of the prisoners held in the jail in Santiago de Guatemala, some people of Santa Lucía Utatlán took steps to try to diminish the suffering of their village and the punishment believed to be in store for them. First, the village government—with a newly elected junior magistrate—in jail in Sololá wrote a petition to Manso de Velasco. After noting that their village was doing all it could do to provide the militia troops with maize, they begged, "for the love of God feel sorry for us and give us liberty to get out of this jail." They claimed to be innocent of any wrongdoing, and blamed everything on Antonio Ixcol. They informed the high magistrate that several *regidores* (members of the village governmental council) had in fact resisted their former junior Indian magistrate's plan to challenge Spanish authority, but Ixcol had "ordered us all to follow him, and [told them] that he wanted to remain in their eternal memory for having liberated them from all work, and whoever failed to follow him would be whipped." When the regidores continued to object, he told them that "he knew what he was doing, and even if he were to lose his head by defending his village, he had to do what he was trying to do, and what he ordered had to be done."[60]

The non-Indians of Santa Lucía Utatlán were also concerned about the future. The squadron commander of the militiamen from the village therefore wrote a letter to the high magistrate on behalf of his men and asked Manso de Velasco to order the village leaders to stop the Indians from insulting them. He was especially worried by a threat: the indigenous people of the village were telling his men that they would be cut into fillets and eaten. The non-Indians were clearly worried about what such hatred augured for their future in the village.[61]

All of the documentation in the case reached the attorney general on June 9. Romana submitted a brief ten days later.[62] In his opinion the cause of the disturbances was the collection of the new tax, which concerned other villages besides Santa Lucía Utatlán. In fact, Santa Catalina Ixtahuacán made an official complaint against the tax, which caused the audiencia to rule on the subject. But, Romana noted, the high magistrate had already gone ahead and collected money from the Indian women. The attorney general concluded that although Santa Lucía Utatlán's decision to embarrass Manso de Velasco by carrying grain on their backs when mules were available was indeed due to the Indians' "malice," their seeking of a ruling in their favor regarding the tax was not. Moreover, the calling together of the people of the village to hear the presidential dispatch was customary among Indians; it was a response to their notorious "weakness and natural lack of confidence" regarding anything Spaniards do and was not due to "a spirit of sedition," as the high magistrate had alleged. In short, the people of Santa Lucía Utatlán did not plan to revolt, nor were they motivated by a desire to overthrow the social order.

Romana also examined some of the specific charges that had been made, and found some of them wanting in proof. There was no evidence that the Indians of Santa Lucía Utatlán carried weapons to Sololá or that they wanted to kill their high magistrate and priest, as Manso de Velasco had claimed. Moreover, the high magistrate had accused them of killing militiamen, but that did not take place either. Even in the matter of the staff of office Manso de Velasco had not acted properly, for in order to deprive Ixcol of his post as Indian magistrate he first had to draw up a written order to that effect and provide reasons for doing so; otherwise Indians would have nothing on which to make an appeal, and deprivation of office—that is, punishment—would be administered before any legal steps had been taken. The attorney general concluded regarding the matter that the high magistrate's decision to deprive Ixcol of his staff under the circumstances—that is, with lots of Indians from Santa Lucía Utatlán present—was made at a "bad conjuncture" of events.

Regarding events in Santa Lucía Utatlán on the night of April 21 and at the battle of the ravine, Romana found no one to accuse. Carrascosa had entered the village in the middle of the night and without an interpreter. The Indians could have had no reason to believe that Carrascosa's orders should be obeyed. The people naturally threw rocks at the intruders. No one was killed or seriously hurt. Ixcol and his companions in jail could not have had anything to do with the matter anyway, since they were in Santiago de Guatemala at the time.

Nevertheless, according to the attorney general, Ixcol and some of his associates were guilty of crimes. First, they lied to the president when they claimed that their high magistrate had ordered them to transport grain on their backs. The Indian magistrate had also acted illegally by retaining the money taken from the Indian women rather than returning it. He also disobeyed the high magistrate's order to surrender his staff of office. Finally, he was responsible for beating up the constable of Sololá who had been sent to San Andrés carrying an official order from the high magistrate.

For these offenses Fiscal Romana recommended punishment, as the law specified. Ixcol should be condemned to flogging, deprivation of office, and one year's exile from his province. His associates in jail in the capital, with the exception of two clearly not guilty (they were in the village of Quezaltenango on the day of the riot), should be given 200 lashes and freed. The four women identified in the testimony, including the wife of Ixcol, should each receive twenty-five lashes. Finally, eleven of the Indians interviewed by Manso de Velasco in Sololá should be given twenty-five lashes.

Regarding the high magistrate, the attorney general recommended that Manso de Velasco should answer charges for his conduct; how that would be done was left up to the discretion of the president.

As was the normal procedure, the president passed the attorney general's brief to one of the judges of the audiencia appointed to serve as legal council (*asesor*). The oidor chosen was Domingo López de Urrelo, a European Spaniard, who reported back to the president on June 27.[63] The asesor agreed with Romana that Ixcol was guilty of the enumerated offenses and should be punished. He also agreed that the other people found guilty by the attorney general should likewise be punished in the manner recommended by Romana. But López de Urrelo took a much harder line on punishment. The legal council recommended that Ixcol's punishment include not one but four years of exile. Moreover, the two men in jail in the capital found to be innocent by Romana because they were in Quezaltenango should be presumed guilty because they had accompanied Ixcol to the capital, and should be given twenty-five lashes.

The president's legal council also was more specific regarding the punishment to be meted out. The flogging of Ixcol and four of his companions should be done "through the accustomed streets of this city" of Santiago de Guatemala; it was to be, once again, a public ceremony with a clear message to the people. The other two jailed men—the ones whom Romana had recommended releasing because they had been in Quezaltenango—were to be whipped by the public executioner at the pillar just outside the jail. The four women and all the others found guilty were to be flogged "throughout the public streets of the village of Sololá signaled by war drum." Once again punishment was to have a social as well as personal meaning. Finally, all the guilty parties were to be required to pay the financial cost of mobilizing the militia—an issue unmentioned in the attorney general's brief. López de Urrelo added, before knowing what those costs were, that the whole village of Santa Lucía Utatlán should pay whatever else was owed, "the great majority having joined in and failed to stop [the riot] as was their obligation." The asesor had nothing critical at all to say about the high magistrate.

Why would Judge López de Urrelo take this hard line in the case? First, he may have been genuinely fearful of how a lenient sentence would be interpreted by the Indians throughout Guatemala. Therefore he felt that the punishment should be such that "it serve as an example and as a check on the other villages of this kingdom as a notorious case and a means of good government, and that it promise similar measures in the administration of justice." On the other hand, it is possible that Oidor Domingo López de Urrelo, a European Spaniard, was already an enemy of the American-born Fiscal Felipe Romana. What is certain is that if they were not yet hostile to each other, they would soon become so.

On June 28 President Arcos y Moreno ruled on the case.[64] He accepted the judgment of his legal council López de Urrelo and ordered that punishment to be given. He also decided that Ixcol's four years of exile would be spent in the Presidio of Omoa, on the Honduran coast. For an Indian from the highlands, four years in the disease-ridden tropics was virtually a death sentence. On June 30 the secretary of the audiencia certified that Ixcol and four others had been given 200 lashes each, "through the public streets of the city and announced by town crier." Two other men received twenty-five lashes each, presumably at the pillar outside the jail. On July 5 all the prisoners were finally released from jail.[65]

Meanwhile, on July 1, President Arcos y Moreno ordered the high magistrate of Atitlán-Tecpanatitlán to arrest the other Indians sentenced to a flogging and to administer the punishment. He also order Manso de Velasco to hand in a detailed report of the expenses incurred in the revolt. The high magistrate carried out the punishment in Sololá on July 4, when an unspecified number of men and women—probably eleven men and four women—were each given twenty-five lashes throughout the public streets and plaza of the village. Guarding Sololá during the spectacle were soldiers armed with rifles.[66]

Shortly after the whipping of those found guilty, the issue of Ixcol's exile was brought up by his legal aid, Juan Antonio Bosque.[67] The former Indian magistrate of Santa Lucía Utatlán was reported to be a semi-invalid, not because of the 200 lashes that he had just been given, but because of a permanently dislocated shoulder. He would thus be useless in the Presidio of Omoa, and Bosque therefore requested that the place of exile be changed to the district of Totonicapán, just to the north of Atitlán-Tecpanatitlán. The lawyer stated that his claim regarding Ixcol's physical condition could be verified by surgeons. The president ordered an examination of the prisoner, and when the surgeon reported that Ixcol's shoulder had been dislocated for around eleven years and as a result he was a semi-invalid, Fiscal Romana submitted a brief recommending approval of the change in destination of exile. He noted that the law required Indians to be exiled no further than the next province, and added that sending a native from a cold climate to the tropics would be "a notorious danger to life." The asesor and the president went along, and the former Indian magistrate of Santa Lucía Utatlán was sentenced to four years of exile from his home province—a decision that probably saved his life.[68]

A Spaniard with a Conscience and a Village that Dared

What followed was a political struggle, not between Indians and Spaniards, but between the European-born and American-born Spaniards. The records of the inquest into the revolt give us no clue as to what was in fact going on, but other sources reveal that the events involving Santa Lucía Utatlán uncovered old wounds. The high magistrate, the asesor, and the president were all European-born Spaniards, while the fiscal was American-born. It also turns out that High Magistrate Manso de Velasco's wife was a relative of President Arcos y Moreno.[69] In these circumstances, Fiscal Romana, by trying to blame the high magistrate, was attacking the Europeans who dominated the political structure of the kingdom, and the Europeans in turn defended their power by sticking together. This was true even though earlier in the year Arcos y Moreno had been involved in a dispute with several of the European-born judges, as a result of which a good deal of mutual recriminations had taken place.[70] The former enemies were now allies, and the president, for his part, was at the same time supporting his in-law, for kinship was an essential element tying together political alliances. Once again, then, a supposedly unimportant local event revealed the nature of politics at the apex of power.

The process began on July 12, 1760, when High Magistrate Manso de Velasco submitted a report to the president about the cost of mobilizing the militia for one month.[71] The price was high: 3,066 pesos 4 1/2 reales. Since the government had sent him no money, he had used tribute revenues to defray expenses and had not been authorized to do so. The audiencia had ruled that the guilty parties and the village of Santa Lucía Utatlán should be forced to pay for the cost of the revolt, but the village was small and poor. How could it possibly pay such a large sum? The high magistrate thought it impractical to force the villagers to sell their land, cattle, or mules (for how could they pay their tribute if they possessed no means of production?). Moreover, the disturbances, combined with the threat of severe punishment, had caused many people to give up on next year's crops or to abandon the village altogether and start life anew elsewhere. Unless something were done, royal revenues, for which Manso de Velasco would be held responsible, would decline even further.

The high magistrate therefore recommended a solution suggested by the senior Indian magistrate of Santa Lucía Utatlán: the principales (the native upper class) would pay as much of the debt as they could because they were more guilty than everyone else, and what was still owed would be paid over time by the macehuales (the common people). This plan was then sent by the president to Fiscal Romana and Asesor López de Urrelo for their opinion.

Attorney General Romana, in a brief dated July 29, used the opportunity to comment on several aspects of the case.[72] He expressed his great displeasure over the sentences already carried out, for the two men who had been in Quezaltenango at the time of the riot had been flogged on the asesor's recommendation, even though they had not been implicated in any criminal act. The punishment, he lamented, had been carried out "against the request of the Fiscal [that is, himself] who reflected on the matter in a rather prolix manner and still found no cause" for such action. Now he reiterated his position regarding the culpability of the entire village: not guilty. Nowhere in the documents, he noted, was there evidence that even the majority of the people participated in the events in Sololá on April 18, yet if the high magistrate's recommendation were approved, innocent people would be punished by being forced to pay for the expenses of the revolt. The whole village could be held responsible for tribute debts but not for a fine to pay for the salaries and even meals of militiamen and the fodder for their horses. Furthermore, money could not be taken from the village treasury, for community funds were likewise exempt by law from such use. The fiscal therefore "protests, as is his duty, in accordance with the law," against Manso de Velasco's proposal. He argued that the person who should be held responsible for the cost of the revolt was the high magistrate himself.

As was by now to be expected, Asesor López de Urrelo disagreed emphatically. Writing his opinion on August 5, he recommended accepting the high magistrate's proposal because it was "in accordance with fairness and with the wretchedness of the Indians." The legal council saw nothing wrong therefore with blaming all the villagers, and even said that Santa Lucía Utatlán was "a tumult-causing village." Two days later President Arcos y Moreno sided once again with the asesor and against the fiscal.[73]

The president's legal council fanned the flames of political conflict by submitting a second report on August 5. This was a public rebuke to the fiscal. It was of course rare for a judge of an audiencia to criticize openly an attorney general of the same institution, but López de Urrelo obviously felt that he had to respond to Romana's arguments to the effect that an injustice had been done.

The asesor defended the sentences using several arguments.[74] First, they were necessary. The nature of rebellion requires prompt action in the administration of justice to prevent other revolts from taking place, as was the case in all of the four or five such cases with which he had experience. Second, López de Urrelo noted that the previous year's revolt in Tecpán had been "identical" to that in Santa Lucía Utatlán but at the time the fiscal went along with prompt punishment; if he had a change of mind regarding the case now before him, then he should have appealed the sentences immediately, "not now, a month later, alternating his duties from that of Fiscal to that of Protector of the Indians." Moreover, the president's legal council noted, the leaders of Santa Lucía Utatlán had agreed to the high magistrate's plan for repayment.

Then López de Urrelo struck hard at Romana: "if the said lord attorney general had examined, as His Majesty has ordered, and as he who writes this brief has practiced, the identity and truth of the allegations made by Antonio Ixcol, he would not have written the dispatch [sent by the president] that caused the already mentioned uprising." The Europeans were thus blaming an American Spaniard for the revolt.

Regarding the attempt to make the village pay the costs, the legal council argued that this was perfectly acceptable, considering that in cases of rebellion "even the death penalty can be applied." With respect to the two men allegedly flogged unjustly, the asesor argued that "there will always be found more proof of guilt in the case of prisoners than in that of innocent people." People under arrest, in short, should be presumed guilty until proved innocent, for if these men had been in Quezaltenango, 12 leagues (60 kilometers) further away from the capital than Sololá, as was alleged, then how could they have accompanied Ixcol to Santiago de Guatemala? Finally, wrote López de Urrelo, the village should pay, and if any charges should be made against the high magistrate they should be made at his *residencia* (trial for conduct in office), that is, after he had left office. Then, having made his points, López de Urrelo deliberately fanned the flames of discord: he submitted his brief as a public document, ensuring that anyone who wanted to could read his criticism of the attorney general.

Fiscal Romana wasted no time in replying, for on August 8 he submitted a defense of his actions that filled five full folios.[75] (The asesor's had comprised less than two.) He got right to the point: the cause of the revolt in Santa Lucía Utatlán was not the presidential dispatch regarding mules and the transport of grain but "the lack of confidence that caused the Indians to assume that a royal order was the work of the high magistrate." His brief that served as the president's dispatch was only a warning that it was illegal to force Indians to transport grain on their backs, not an assumption that the magistrate was guilty of such an offense, and in any case "it is hardly necessary for the Lord Asesor to advise the Fiscal because without regard to partisanship . . . and with notable purity he knows how to carry out the obligations of his office, as he knows the same Lord Asesor knows how to carry out his." That was why he could not ignore the attempt to fine the whole village, and he would have done his duty "not only if one month had passed, but even if twenty-five had passed," because justice was the issue involved. Since the legal council had ignored what the law specifies regarding the use of village community property and also failed to recommend the appointment of a legal defender of the Indians, the fiscal acted; they both should therefore "report to the sovereign so that he declare if the lord asesor can and should advise the fiscal as to what is his obligation and whether he has carried it out."

Romana also defended his action in the case regarding Tecpán the year before. The difference with Santa Lucía Utatlán was the recourse being made to community funds, which violated the law. He felt compelled to act because no one else could, and he did so now again and protested against the plan to force the whole village to pay the costs of the mobilization. To impeach his motives, as the president's legal council did, was to show disrespect to the fiscal.

The attorney general insisted that protection of the Indians was his duty. The asesor had suggested that the fiscal was confusing his job by trying to carry out the duties of two contradictory offices. But in Guatemala, unlike Mexico, there was no position of Protector of the Indians, and as a result the duties of that position had been included in those of the fiscal. As Protector of the Indians he was therefore completely justified in getting involved in a case in which Indians would be punished and deprived of office, and as fiscal he was required to intervene regarding an illegal decision with respect to village community property that would, if implemented, result in a significant change in the law. It was also his duty to listen to the Indian complaints regarding forced labor on Hacienda Argueta, especially since it could be legally argued that such labor drafts should be abolished. They had been originally justified on the grounds that the Indians needed money to pay their tribute, which was no longer the case. Moreover, since it was the Indians' right to use legal procurators to present their case, as fiscal he was obliged listen to them. It was up to the procurator to find out if their accusations were valid.

Next, Romana dealt with the insult that the legal council's release of his criticism to the public represented. It was, the attorney general noted, forbidden by law even for viceroys and presidents to reprimand publicly anyone as high-ranking as a fiscal. Even in cases of public scandal, any criticism or reprimand was supposed to be made in secret before the whole audiencia, and in case of a minor offense before the president and the senior judge (*oidor decano*). Any charge that the fiscal was not carrying out his duties should not have been made public, for punishment could be administered only by the king or a specially appointed investigating judge. Anything else would harm the office of the fiscal; the attorney general had the right to communicate directly with the king, and any attempt to restrict that right would be "to put chains on his mouth to prevent him from pursuing justice with innocent Christian liberty."

The attorney general reiterated his position regarding the two Indians who had been whipped despite his finding that there was no evidence against them. These people, he said, had been punished because they had been presumed, not found, guilty. His interest in their case was his duty as fiscal, and

the same was true of his concern for "the unhappy people whose rural nature, semi-nakedness, and wretchedness cannot be seen without compassion."
Romana then claimed to have traveled all over the Kingdom of Guatemala,
seeing the Indians' world with his own eyes and always declining the gifts
he was offered, paying for all his needs in cash. To accuse someone like him
of inattention to his duties was "an injury that cannot be passed over in si-
lence without abandoning his honor and his privileges as [the king's] minister." Romana then closed his lengthy statement reiterating that the high
magistrate should be the one to pay the costs of the mobilization of the militia. Consequently, on October 26 he formally recommended that the government move to impound the property of Manso de Velasco in order to ensure
the payment of the debt.[76]

The attorney general may have succeeded in defending his reputation, but
he was unsuccessful in stopping the plan to make the whole village of Santa
Lucía Utatlán pay the 3,066 pesos 4 1/2 reales owed to the royal treasury.
The village leaders agreed to pay 200 pesos per month until the debt was
paid. Meanwhile, López de Urrelo chose to have less to do with the case, and
when informed that Fiscal Romana was going to serve him with a warrant to
provide documentation to aid him in bringing charges against the asesor, he
declared that he was no longer involved in the case, and "if the Lord Attorney General imagined himself injured, he knew not why."[77] Romana in the
end did not bring charges against the president's legal council.

The plan to pay the debt, however, soon fell through. On September 28
Manso de Velasco reported that the Indians of Santa Lucía Utatlán had
changed their minds and were now claiming that they would not be able to
pay what they had promised. President Arcos y Moreno, noting that the villagers seemed to know their guilt, warned the high magistrate to beware of
another "trouble-making spirit like the Indian Ixcol" who might be behind
the change of attitude. He should also make sure that the former Indian magistrate in fact was obeying the order exiling him from the province.[78]

On October 4, when the first payment was due, the leaders of Santa Lucía
Utatlán went to Sololá. There they informed Manso de Velasco that "they
had taken all possible measures to collect the money," but because tribute
collection was running behind as a result of the abandonment of the village
by so many people, they did not succeed in collecting anything. When the
high magistrate reminded them that only a month previously they had said
that it would be possible to pay, the Indians looked at each other and started
to smile. Manso de Velasco concluded from their attitude that they were
refusing to pay, and soon found out why: Ixcol had recently passed through
the village, thereby violating his exile, and although he had then moved on
to a village in the province of either Quezaltenango or Totonicapán, he was

continuing to direct affairs in Santa Lucía Utatlán. The high magistrate then investigated and found to his satisfaction that Ixcol had indeed been in the village. No witnesses had actually seen him, but four people reported that they had heard he had been there. Ixcol was said to have taken an Indian girl (*indizuela*) with him when he left to go into exile.[79]

The high magistrate passed this information on to the president, warning that "from a delinquent Indian new distress and problems must be expected." Moreover, should Ixcol go unpunished, this would set a bad example to all the other Indians.[80] However, nothing was done, probably because of the lack of eyewitnesses to his presence in the village.

Because of the problem of collection, the case then went back to Fiscal Romana. The attorney general wrote another brief on November 26, repeating once more the injustice of forcing the whole village to pay. This time, however, he was more explicit in his criticism of the high magistrate. Considering the total lack of resistance by the Indians during the revolt, why, the attorney general asked, "was it necessary to mobilize so many armed people against a few half-naked Indians" when that many soldiers "would be enough, and indeed were enough, to conquer entire provinces in the past"? Furthermore, he argued that the consent of the village government to have the whole village pay the debt was invalid, because that body had no right to punish the innocent. Finally, the expenditure of tribute funds to pay for the mobilization would not have been allowed by the Treasury Council, but since that body was never convened, the high magistrate got away with it. Therefore, the high magistrate should pay.[81]

By then the high magistrate had already begun to defend himself. From the very beginning of the revolt he had sought the help of the local priests, and once they had received permission from their superiors they wrote letters certifying that Joseph Ventura Manso de Velasco had been a good man, a good servant of His Majesty, and a good Christian gentleman. A total of ten such letters written by Franciscans were composed between September 1 and October 30, most of them alleging that the Indians of Santa Lucía Utatlán were mischievous, perfidious troublemakers who had provoked the problem in order to avoid work.[82] Manso de Velasco also got himself a lawyer, none other than Procurator Juan Antonio Rodríguez Pardo, who had represented Ixcol and his supporters back in April in their appeal against forced labor, and who the previous year had served as legal aid to the people of Tecpán. In January 1761 Rodríguez Pardo began to act in behalf of his client by asking for copies of all the documents in the case.[83]

By early 1761 the high magistrate found himself in trouble. He had used tribute revenues already collected to pay for the troops and was having difficulty collecting what the Indians were supposed to pay him as reimbursement. He therefore owed the royal treasury 3,066 pesos 4 1/2 reales. On February 11 Fiscal Romana recommended that the treasury officials take steps to collect the debt owed by the high magistrate.[84] A week later Manso de Velasco's lawyer requested a writ from the acting president, Juan Antonio Velarde y Cienfuegos (the previous president, Alonso Arcos y Moreno, having died), extending the time period for the Indians of Santa Lucía Utatlán to pay off the debt. Velarde and the audiencia agreed, and gave the high magistrate an entire year to collect the money from the villagers.[85]

But Fiscal Romana went forward relentlessly. On April 18—the first anniversary of the riot in Sololá—he presented a brief to the president arguing once again that the high magistrate should not have mobilized so many troops and paid for them with tribute revenues before receiving authorization to do so. After all, the attorney general noted, Manso de Velasco had been confronted by only "wretched, half-naked Indians whose leaders . . . were being held prisoner in this city while others were in jail in Sololá." Romana reiterated that tribute funds could not legally be used in the way that the high magistrate had used them.[86]

Manso de Velasco's lawyer, Rodríguez Pardo, responded with a statement on May 2, 1761.[87] He noted first that President Arcos y Moreno himself had authorized the mobilization of the militia. Had Manso de Velasco not acted, the revolt could easily have spread, "for the Lord Attorney General knows perfectly well that it is notorious throughout the Indies, and these proceedings prove, that when a village rebels it has already secretly conspired with many others." Had a half-hearted mobilization taken place, the rebellion could have grown to become one like "that of the Tzeltal of Cancuc." Once again the specter of 1712 was haunting Guatemala. Once again, memory of history was making history.

Rodríguez Pardo defended the original decision to make the Indians pay. The high magistrate had had no choice in the matter of the funds to be spent: since he had just arrived from Spain, and since his trip had cost so much, he had no money of his own on hand. Had he not spent the tribute revenues, the militia either could not have been mobilized or would have had to resort to pillaging in order to eat. And finally, he pointed out, "regarding what the Lord Attorney General has argued that the militia were mobilized against [the threat of] some half-naked Indians and people already in jail, we must be careful for others even more naked have caused us plenty to regret." He suggested that money be taken from the community funds of Santa Lucía Utatlán and returned gradually over time.

Eventually the case was heard in Spain and considered by the Council of the Indies. That body recommended, for reasons not specified, that the government revert to its original position, that is, that the Indians pay. A royal order to that effect, signed by King Charles III, was received and certified in Santiago de Guatemala on August 16, 1761.[88]

Manso de Velasco was thus authorized, as before, to collect the money from the Indians within a year. And as before, it proved impossible to force the people of Santa Lucía Utatlán to pay up. On November 11 a group of village leaders informed the government of their inability to collect what was owed, explaining that "what they earn from their personal labor is very limited and is used to pay their tribute and religious brotherhood dues and to maintain their families."[89] In December, therefore, the high magistrate's lawyer had to request that his client not have to collect the money and that the government authorize the use of the village's community funds instead.[90] This undoubtedly meant using the property of the religious brotherhood, or *cofradías*. Fiscal Romana, however, once again objected and recommended going back to his idea of forcing the high magistrate to pay.[91] The case had now dragged on into 1762. And it still had a year to go.

In January 1762 the Franciscan priest in Santa Lucía Utatlán, Friar Manuel Joseph Zaldívar, got involved in the dispute. He certified that the people under his pastoral care were suffering "extreme necessity," and of the 400 or so tributaries (adult males) in the village, only about twenty were able to pay their tribute and other taxes. The cause was two successive bad harvests.[92] This letter was presented along with a petition by the village government of Santa Lucía Utatlán in which the Indian leaders claimed that they could not pay what was being demanded "because of physical and moral impossibility [caused by] extreme poverty." Probably sensing that the Spaniards had their eyes on the properties of their cofradías, they pointed out their poverty had caused a decline in economic support for the religious brotherhood and thus their annual religious festivals had been canceled. They therefore requested the cancellation of their debt to the royal treasury.[93] The attorney general, however, recommended on February 10 against the request (probably hoping that the high magistrate could still be made to pay), and the new president, Alonso Fernández de Heredia (who had replaced the acting president), agreed two days later.[94] As a result, in March Manso de Velasco's lawyer, Rodríguez Pardo, had to request postponement of collection of the village's debt for still another year. Once again, Romana recommended against the request, but the president and the audiencia granted it anyway on March 29.[95]

In June 1762 an old problem reemerged: Antonio Ixcol was back in town, having violated his sentence to exile. He showed up in Sololá on June 4 at the office of Manso de Velasco and told the high magistrate that he wanted to go back to his village to live "because his wife did not want to live in [the provinces of] Quezaltenango or Totonicapán, which caused him great and overwhelming public shame." A wife who defied her husband's will was humiliating to a Maya man, especially to a leader like Ixcol. He pointed out that he had not killed anyone, and therefore asked that he not be required to live out the rest of his exile. Manso de Velasco reminded the former Indian magistrate of Santa Lucía Utatlán that he had been warned not to come back until he had served his exile, and that his punishment had been specifically chosen and ordered by the kingdom's highest tribunal, the audiencia. Yet, noted the high magistrate, "without any fear at all and with complete insolence, here he was, coming to sell cloth in the public plaza." Ixcol was jailed and put in irons.[96]

Manso de Velasco immediately informed the president of the exile's return. He reported that the former Indian magistrate requested permission to attend the annual festival of Santa Lucía in his village and promised to leave afterward to serve out his exile. The high magistrate would have none of that. Declaring him to be "made wicked by his trouble-making and despotism with which he dominates those Indians" and noting the "submissiveness with which he is obeyed," Manso de Velasco sent Ixcol to the capital where the case would be handled thereafter. There the attorney general submitted a brief on July 1, ruling that Ixcol had violated his exile and therefore, in accordance with the law, his time to be served in exile should be doubled.[97]

The former Indian magistrate of Santa Lucía Utatlán now broke down and begged for forgiveness. In a letter to the president (written for him) he stated that he had already served twenty-two months of exile when he received news that his wife was gravely ill, leaving no one to take care of their two maiden daughters. As a result he returned to his village to help care for his wife and children. He threw himself at the feet of Manso de Velasco to seek mercy, but the high magistrate, a bitter enemy, had him arrested "with no pity at all."[98] Nevertheless, the government rejected his petition and doubled his sentence of exile.

Ixcol, still in jail in Santiago de Guatemala, tried again in September. This time, however, he identified himself as Juan Antonio *Gómez* Ixcol, "indio principal." Previously he had refused to use his Hispanic surname, perhaps because he did not think it important, or perhaps because in his village it was better to use Maya names. Indeed, of all the Indians who testified or were convicted, all but one had nothing but Maya names, and the only one who had a Spanish surname—Gaspar Cristóbal Chávez Tzul—like Ixcol had a Maya one as well. In his second letter the former Indian magistrate tried to downplay what had happened in Santa Lucía Utatlán, referring to it as "some tumult said to have occurred in my village." As a result of that he had been punished, and his exile had forced him to "leave my wife and family, absenting myself in other territories, which being foreign cause me hardship and discomfort" for lack of a domestic environment. When he found that his wife was sick he had to return, because his family was helpless and his two maiden daughters were "exposed to danger." He went immediately to Sololá to talk to the high magistrate, and went accompanied by an interpreter (either Ixcol did not really speak Spanish well or else he could not understand the Castilian spoken by peninsular Spaniards). But he was put into jail, and remained there for two months while his case was being considered and had no news of his wife and family. He asked the president to allow him to go back to his village or at least to free him from prison so he could live somewhere else. In jail, he lamented, he was dying from hunger. Nevertheless, the government, sensing a lack of remorse on Ixcol's part, once again refused to change its mind, and even added 200 lashes to his sentence.[99]

In November, with the help of a lawyer, once again Juan Antonio Bosque, Ixcol tried once more. He was still in jail but his new sentence of 200 lashes had not yet been administered. Once again he identified himself as Gómez Ixcol, but instead of "indio principal" he was just "native of the village of Santa Lucía Utatlán." He also referred to himself humbly as "a poor man, a tributary, of advanced age and burdened with a large family and the few goods I once owned have been exhausted during my absence living out my exile." He was, he said, at the end of his tether: "Necessity and the inability to work motivated me to throw myself back to the place where I was born so that my family could care for me more easily." Because of his many altercations with the high magistrate, he was now desperate, and to the president he begged, "I hope that your compassionate heart will provide me with relief from such misfortunes that surround me, although my days are about to run out, and therefore I ask you and plead that you dispose of this wretch as you see fit."[100]

As usual, the president passed the request on to the fiscal. Romana replied on November 25, arguing regarding Ixcol this time that "no other resolution can be reached than to free him [from prison] as he requested, after such a long imprisonment that the poor wretch has suffered without any [legal] defense and without anyone giving him any relief." The attorney general reminded the president, however, that in the Kingdom of Guatemala, unlike the Kingdoms of New Spain and Peru, there was no General Indian Court and Defender of Indians, and that "this is what happens to the poor when the fiscal has so many duties that he cannot defend them properly."[101] The asesor who had replaced Romana's nemesis López de Urrelo agreed with the fiscal, noting that the actions of Juan Antonio Bosque, the defendant's legal advisor, had helped resolve the matter.[102] Ixcol was released on November 27, 1762, and presumably went home.

The only loose end to be tied up now was payment of the money spent on the mobilization of the militia. Manso de Velasco still could not collect it from the Indians, and so in September 1762 the king gave him yet another year to do so.[103] The grateful high magistrate asked, however, that the Indians be informed of the king's decision "so that they are not convinced that [the collection] is all my doing, since their ignorance of the resolution has stopped the effort [to collect]."[104] The people of Santa Lucía Utatlán obviously still did not trust their high magistrate.

Manso de Velasco had been politically weakened by the death of President Arcos y Moreno, his wife's relative, and therefore in September 1762 he appealed to the highest authority. He wrote a letter to the king in which he blamed his problems not on the Indians but on the American-born Spaniards in Guatemala. Merchants from the latter group, he said, were owed money by his predecessor as high magistrate of Atitlán-Tecpanatitlán, and they had made it difficult for him to assume his post until those debts had been collected from the Indians. They refused to loan him the money necessary to fund the repartimiento business, and since that was necessary to get the Indians to pay their tribute, tax revenues were falling. The American merchants had even moved in on the business that traditionally was reserved for the high magistrate, leaving him only a little in wheat and textiles. (These allegations required Manso de Velasco to admit that he was carrying out the repartimiento, which was in fact illegal. He therefore pointed out to the king that the business with the Indians "has been practiced, and is practiced, by all the high magistrates and magistrates of the Kingdom since the time of the conquest.") Manso de Velasco further complained that the royal treasury officials of the Kingdom of Guatemala always took the side of the Americans in disputes because of their economic interests, and as a result European Spaniards serving as high magistrates had recently been deposed from their offices in El Salvador and Nicaragua. The Americans always harassed the Europeans to discourage them from coming to America, thereby leaving the Americans to rule the country as they want. According to Manso de Velasco, all this explained why the Indians of Santa Lucía Utatlán rebelled against him.[105]

The high magistrate of Atitlán-Tecpanatitlán then returned to the matter of getting the Indians to pay up. He called the leaders of the village to come before him to be informed of the king's decision. But no sooner had he informed the Indians than they informed him that they could not pay. Some said they could sell their houses, while "those who have none may sell themselves," but there was just no way the money could be raised. They even drew up a document in Maya to prove their assertions.[106]

On October 14, Manso de Velasco informed the president of his predicament. He reported that he had even tried to make the people plant extra crops on their community lands, but they insisted that they had none. He knew they did, however, so he considered their conduct to be further proof of their refusal to accept the ruling of the audiencia. He sent along the document in Maya drawn up by the villagers so that it could be translated.[107]

On November 27 a translation was ready and placed into the record. It consisted of a survey of the people of the village, in which each person questioned was asked to disclose how he could be made to pay off the debt. The first person on the list was Sebastián Pian, who reported that "he has no money, he is poor, he has no more than his house, if you want he could sell it, if there is anyone who would buy it." Several people said the same thing as Isidro Basque: "I have no children, only my house, sell it and I will take to the road." Diego Esqul's statement was also echoed by many: "I have no house, I am poor, sell me and my wife." Marcos Escah stated that "he has children; sell them." Francisco Joh said that he would like to know "where he was going to get any money, he does not know, he has nothing he can give, if they want they can send him somewhere else or he can go where he chooses, but what can he do?" Diego Pol: "sell his children, they are of God and of the king, and he has no money." Juan Ebange: "he has no way of earning money to give, he has nothing but his body." Esteban Golon: "he hasn't earned any money, he will leave with his wife, or else they should kill him, that would end it." Francisco Queg: "they should sell his soul, and he has nothing else to say." Juan Colpere offered to sell one of his sons to pay the debt. Juan Gaspar reported that "he has nothing to say, that he only has his soul and nothing else." Antonio Yac: "he has nothing to give, they should sell him, his wife, and his children." Pedro Chir: "he has a house, they should sell it, he has nowhere to go to earn money, they should take him and his wife." A total of ninety-five men—and no women—made statements.[108]

Attorney General Romana commented on January 18, 1763. The case had now dragged on into another year. The fiscal noted that the testimony of the ninety-five villagers from Santa Lucía Utatlán proved "the impossibility of the Indians paying" as well as their "repugnance" to any attempt to make them pay. He drew attention once more to the lack of foresight on the part of the person who spent the money in the first place (in other words, Manso de Velasco). Moreover, he recommended that the matter be brought up in the residencia of the late President Arcos y Moreno, for he had authorized the high magistrate to mobilize some, but not all, of the militia. Bringing charges against a former president, argued Romana, would "serve as an example and put a check on the despotism with which superior authority manifested itself in the abuse of power." In other words, he was placing some of the blame squarely on the former chief executive.[109]

And there the trial record ends. Fortunately other documents allow us to see the final resolution of the problem of paying the cost of mobilizing the militia to crush a revolt that never was.[110] As might be expected, neither High Magistrate Manso de Velasco nor the estate of President Arcos y Moreno was required to pay. The Council of the Indies in fact ruled in their favor and against Fiscal Romana, who was criticized for failing to carry out an investigation before writing the first presidential dispatch in the matter of the transport of grain to the capital. The attorney general, who had been denounced by Manso de Velasco for being anti-European, also failed in his efforts to get the crown to authorize the creation of a special office of Protector of the Indians in order to relieve the fiscal of that time-consuming task; the government thought it was too expensive.

The Council of the Indies ordered that the whole village of Santa Lucía Utatlán be taxed until the money was paid. Attorney General Romana had thought that such a resolution would be unjust, and it undoubtedly was. On the other hand, the debt was not paid the way that the high magistrate, the president, and the audiencia had wanted. Instead of paying 200 pesos per month, as originally ordered, the villagers paid 200 pesos per year—a much lighter burden. To raise the money, each adult male was required to pay an extra four reales (1/2 peso) every six months. Even that decision was disputed by the people of Santa Lucía Utatlán, but to no avail. Their debt of 3,066 pesos 4 1/2 reales was finally paid off in 1777—a full seventeen years after the revolt.[111]

The resolution of the case demonstrates not merely colonial injustice. It also shows the extent to which the persistent resistance of the Maya was effective. The villagers simply refused to pay the way the Spaniards demanded. The Spaniards, in turn, did not even consider forcing the Indians to sell their mules and land, for without them they would have been unable to pay tribute and thus there would be even more diminution of royal revenues. The villagers' statement to the effect that taking the money from them could only be done by destroying the village and selling the inhabitants into slavery had an effect. It was the need to have the Indians pay their future taxes that forced the colonial regime to moderate its demands. Once again, the fiscal restraints of the political system gave the indigenous people some leverage over the Spaniards. State formation was a two-way street.

The revolt of Santa Lucía Utatlán thus demonstrates important details in the process of indigenous resistance to colonialism. Once again, we see the Maya using the law, lawyers, and the courts to advance their cause and to defend their interests. Their frequent, even customary, willingness to follow this course of action demonstrates that they did not expect to lose all the time in the Spanish courts. Of course, it also signifies that the indigenous people helped legitimize Spanish rule, and demonstrates the Spaniards' success in institutionalizing their hegemony. This does not mean that violence, rebellion, or even revolution never occurred. But it does mean that the Maya usually did not see those courses as their first resort. Rather, they usually tried to take advantage of a system that for all its faults provided them with either the forum for presenting their side of the story or the promise of lenient treatment in return for recognition of Spanish authority and their own caste-like status of second-class subjects of the Spanish king.

To be sure, the villagers of Santa Lucía Utatlán were poorer at the end of their ordeal than at the beginning. Their taxes were raised for the next fourteen years or so. Moreover, several people had received what by modern standards would be considered severe corporal punishment. Antonio Ixcol suffered not only a flogging but also almost two years of exile and many months languishing in jail. He and his supporters paid a price for their attempt to renegotiate, roll back, and limit the terms of exploitation. Moreover, their efforts failed. But in the long run they also succeeded in their own small way. They outright refused to pay what the Spaniards demanded, and they dared the Spaniards to do something about it. Their utilization of delaying tactics reveals how so often in history those dominated by the powerful nevertheless negotiate and renegotiate the conditions of their acceptance of domination and thereby contribute to the very structure of the state. They frequently do so by resorting to the "weapons of the weak," a topic that will be discussed further in a later chapter.

5

The Yucatec Maya in 1761,
Part I: The Origins of Revolution

It was said that he would come, and he came, from the East.[1]

—Tomás Balam, scribe of Tixméuac

PARTICIPANTS

+ = executed after the trial

Maya

+Jacinto Uc (Canek), Canek King Montezuma
Joseph Chan, teniente, chief political official in Cisteíl
Joaquín Xix, senior Indian magistrate of Cisteíl
+Pedro Chan, junior Indian magistrate of Cisteíl
Pedro Chan, fiscal de doctrina (church warden) of Cisteíl
+Felipe Chan, cantor of Cisteíl, helped kill Captain Cosgaya
Marcos Tec, former Indian magistrate of Cisteíl
Francisco Mex, regidor (councilman) of Cisteíl
Tomás Canul, regidor of Cisteíl
Hilario Canul, topil (law enforcement officer) of Cisteíl
Ignacio Caamal, topil menor (assistant law enforcement officer) of Cisteíl, helped kill Diego Pacheco
Luis Cauich, choirmaster of Cisteíl, refused to recognize Jacinto Uc as the king
Pedro Cauich, fiscal menor (assistant church warden) of Cisteíl
Nicolás Cauich, beggar-vagabond, convicted of being a sorcerer
Simón Puc, teniente (assistant to the cacique) of Tiholop

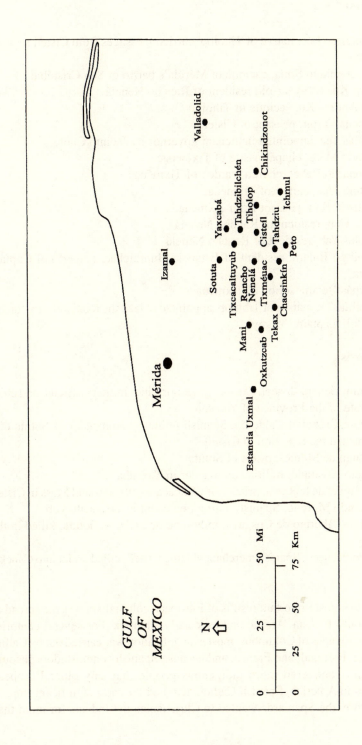

Map 5 **Cisteil and Vicinity**

+Francisco Puc, native of Tiholop, carried messages from Cisteíl to other villages

Don Domingo Sima, cacique of Mérida's barrio of San Cristóbal

Pedro Ku, 100-year-old resident of Rancho Nenelá

Don Andrés Ku, cacique of Tiholop

+Pascual Yupit, peasant of Cisteíl

Nicolás Tec, appointed lieutenant governor by Jacinto Canek

+Simón Maas, chapelmaster of Tixméuac

+Leonardo Bebet, church warden of Tixméuac

Ventura Hau, cantor of Tixméuac

Augustín Hau, peasant from Tixméuac

Pedro Can, resident of Rancho Nenelá

Nicolás Yah, resident of Rancho Nenelá

Domingo Balam, resident of Estancia Huntulchac, helped kill Captain Cosgaya

+Tomás Balam, scribe of Tixméuac

+Mathías Uc, native of Tiholop, appointed to lead the rebel military forces, helped kill Captain Cosgaya

Spaniards

Captain General Joseph Crespo, governor, chief military official, and chief magistrate of the Province of Yucatán

Captain Cristóbal Calderón, Spanish military commander of Sotuta district, crushed the rebellion in Cisteíl

Dr. Juan de Montes, priest of Sotuta

Ignacio Alvarado, militia commander in Yaxcabá

Br. Miguel de la Ruela, priest from Tixcacaltuyub who said Mass in Cisteíl

Fernando Moreno, Spanish militia lieutenant in Tixcacaltuyub

Captain Tiburcio de Cosgaya, militia commander in Sotuta, killed in the uprising

Diego Pacheco, Spanish merchant visiting Cisteíl, killed on Jacinto Canek's orders

One of the most important results of European colonialism was the spread of Christianity to Asia, Africa, and especially America. For several centuries after the voyages of Columbus, most evangelization was carried out by Catholic Spain, Portugal, and France, and because Spanish conquistadors encountered and conquered more indigenous people than any other European invaders in America, Spanish Catholicism had the most significant impact. To be sure, the Spaniards wanted to Christianize the Indians for more than just altruistic reasons. Very importantly, the conversion of the native Americans was carried out because it assuaged the invaders' conscience: it convinced the Spaniards that what they were doing was good despite the violence, extortion, and frequently gross exploitation that were inextricably linked to conquest and colonialism. In effect, Christianity became the justification, if not the cause, of colonialism. It undoubtedly helped greedy people sleep better at night. At the same time, Spaniards wanted the Indians to be converted to the Christian religion because they thought that Christianity, by teaching that paradise would be in the next but not in this world, would help pacify and control the native people. They would unconsciously have agreed with Marx that their religion was the opiate of the masses.

These assumptions proved wrong. Christianity itself, of course, included subversive teachings that could undermine any social order; after all, that is why Jesus was executed. Just as importantly, however, the native people of America already had religions, and these could not be simply forgotten as Indians converted—usually not that voluntarily—to Christianity. Religion is an intrinsic part of a culture and one religion thus cannot simply be replaced by a different one. Inevitably the old and the new religions not only conflict with but also interact with each other. Among Indians in the Spanish empire, Christianity came to occupy a large part of formal public religion, while native belief systems and practices continued to occupy realms of reality wherein Christian dogmas seemed irrelevant. Hence, among the Maya, the people participated in Christian rites and eagerly occupied the "offices" in the local church open to laymen such as church warden, choirmaster, choir member, catechism instructor, sexton, head of the religious brotherhood, and so forth. However, at the same time they continued the rituals associated with the milpa and the gods of the cornfields, of rain and others. Rejection of the latter deities was risky, for those gods, it was believed, had given maize to mankind and could always take it back.

Yet even where Christian forms prevailed, as in public worship in the village, underlying indigenous belief systems did not disappear. On the contrary, those cultural structures frequently gave the people an explanation, in non-Christian terms, of Catholicism. In other words, often what took place was not syncretism—the mixing of two religions into a unique third one combining the original two—but rather adaptation: the Maya continued to adhere to their own way of thinking, and forced Christian concepts into preexisting molds. In many cases, in other words, what changed was the form but not the substance. A core of shared non-Christian values and belief systems remained.[2]

Maya religion thus survived the conquest, and to a certain extent survives to this day. Some indigenous people continue to carry out the age-old ceremonies required by milpa agriculture and to worship the age-old gods of their ancestors. In the eighteenth century the Maya would have been even closer to their original belief systems, for European domination was only two centuries old when, in 1761, in Yucatán their cultural understanding of the cosmos and of human history gave them a reason for calling into question the legitimacy of Spanish colonial rule. As had been the case in Chiapas earlier in the century, Maya religion and culture led to revolution.

The Scene of the Action

Yucatán is most unlike the regions of Guatemala in which the other revolts discussed in this book took place. The Guatemalan Maya revolts occurred in the highlands, in mountainous regions where earthquakes are frequent, cultivatable land is scarce, and winters are chilly or downright cold. Yucatán, on the other hand, is entirely in the lowlands and therefore is extremely hot almost year-round. It is also extraordinarily flat. In the northern half of the Peninsula, where the great majority of the people lived, there are some hills in the area just to the northeast of the modern border between the states of Campeche and Yucatán. This is the Puuc region, which in colonial times was grandiosely called the Sierra. This was probably just to call attention to the existence of hills in an otherwise completely flat topography stretching from coast to coast.

The absence of mountains reflects the fact that in Yucatán volcanic and even seismic phenomena are nil. Soil for agriculture is not restricted to valleys, for there are no valleys; it is everywhere except on the coasts, which are frequently protected by mangrove swamps. But the soil on the Yucatán Peninsula is thin, for the underlying limestone bedrock is never far from the surface, and thus it is easily exhaustible. In such conditions the natural human response is the development of shifting (swidden or "slash-and-burn") cultivation, that is, the burning off of the forest (which in practice recycles the nutrients found in the trees) and the planting on the land, usually for only two years, after which the farmers move to other lands to burn off and plant.

These geographic, climatic, and topographic characteristics influence human history. Since thick forest rather than impenetrable mountains are usually all that separate one locale from another, movement throughout the Peninsula is easier in Yucatán than in highland Guatemala, and thus regionalism within Yucatán is weaker than in Guatemala. Indeed, a single Mayan language— Yucatec—is spoken all over the Peninsula for several hundred kilometers in all directions. Yucatán is by far the largest area occupied by any one Maya language group. This ability to communicate with and thus recognize others as members of the same cultural group facilitated the movement of people throughout the Peninsula, as some moved into villages, some moved out, and some founded new communities altogether. The environment, in turn, contributed to migration within Yucatán, for the easily exhausted soil caused villagers to leave overpopulated areas and move to less populated places.[3]

One such new settlement, founded by people from many villages in central Yucatán, was Cisteíl, the site of the 1761 Maya revolution. The village no longer exists, for the Spaniards systematically destroyed it. Its location has not yet been definitively identified, but it certainly was located somewhere to the south of the village of Tixcacaltuyub, north of Tahdziu, east of Nenelá (in 1761 only a *rancho*, that is, a village lower in status than a *pueblo*), and west of Tiholop. It is possible that Tahdziu (to the south) was the closest, for Doctor Juan de Montes, a priest in the large village of Sotuta (35–50 kilometers to the north-northwest) reported at the time that Tahdziu was "the large village immediate to" Cisteíl.[4] Tiholop, to the east, could not have been as close, and indeed there was no direct road between Cisteíl and Tiholop; to go from one to the other it was necessary to go through Tahdzibilchén (twenty kilometers northwest of Tiholop).[5] On the other hand, when Captain Cristóbal Calderón, the Spanish military commander who would lead the attack on Cisteíl, was preparing his assault, he reported that there were six different routes into and out of the village.[6] Hence there must have been two in addition to those going to Tixcacaltuyub (north), Tahdzibilchén (northeast), Tahdziu (south), and Rancho Nenelá (west).

Cisteíl appeared in no records at all, neither civil nor ecclesiastical, until 1755. Since Spaniards were meticulous with regards to the registering of settlements (because people in settlements were potential taxpayers), it is safe to conclude that the village was newly founded. Yet when Cisteíl finally did appear in the records, it already had a functioning village government and a church. This demonstrates that the Yucatec Maya, far from abandoning or escaping from civilization as a result of emigration, in fact recreated all their traditional institutions as they colonized new lands by moving to what was for them an internal frontier.

The inquest into the events of 1761 provides us with information about the nature of the new village. Ignacio Alvarado, a Spanish militia leader in Yaxcabá (30–40 kilometers north-northeast) identified Cisteíl as a *parcialidad* or "annex" of the village of Tixcacaltuyub just to the north.[7] A parcialidad would have been an autonomous unit within a village. This would mean that Cisteíl was originally part of Tixcacaltuyub and was made up of people who moved out of that village to set up new settlement at a nearby site. This was certainly done at least in part to be closer to lands being worked by the migrants. Institutionally there remained a connection between Cisteíl and its home village, for Father Miguel de la Ruela, an assistant to the pastor of Tixcacaltuyub, was the priest who officiated at Mass in Cisteíl;[8] hence the latter was a village belonging to Tixcacaltuyub parish to the north.

Another institutional connection to other villages is also suggested by

Cisteíl's political structure. Unlike most settlements in Yucatán, Cisteíl was not ruled directly by a resident cacique. Rather, the chief local official, Joseph Chan, was identified as a *teniente* (lieutenant), that is, someone's assistant. We know that the village of Tiholop had at least two tenientes who served as assistants to the cacique of that village.[9] The teniente of Cisteíl was certainly the assistant of a cacique of another village, most likely Tixcacaltuyub. Nevertheless, Joseph Chan, who held that post, showed considerable independence and initiative when it came to making the enormously important decision of whether or not to support a revolution.

Many of the founding fathers and mothers of Cisteíl were undoubtedly still alive when the revolution broke out. They had not yet been replaced by a generation born in the village, for of the 258 adult males captured and sentenced as a result of the events of 1761, only one person was identified as a native of Cisteíl, and even that "fact" may have been simply a clerical error caused by confusion. The largest single group came from Tixcacaltuyub, whose people made up 18.6 percent of the total. The very nearby villages of Tahdziu, Tiholop, Tahdzibilchén, and Tixméuac (to the southwest) contributed together another 26.4 percent, so Cisteíl and those settlements immediately around it comprised 45 percent of the males captured and sentenced. Not all these people were necessarily residents of Cisteíl, however, for many people from the surrounding area flooded into the village in the days just before the successful Spanish attack (to be explained below).

What is noteworthy, then, is the large proportion of people who came from further away. In fact, 55 percent of all the adult males sentenced came from villages that probably did not join the revolution en masse; their presence was more likely the result of migration from the densely populated northwestern and central parts of Yucatán to the land-rich areas east and southeast of Sotuta.

This in-migration is most clear in the case of the civil and ecclesiastical leaders of Cisteíl in 1761. Their positions and places of origin were as follows:

Name	Governmental Position	Village of Origin
Joseph Chan	Teniente	?
Joaquín Xix	Senior alcalde	Tixcacaltuyub
Pedro Chan	Second alcalde	Tixméuac
Marcos Tec	Former alcalde	Mocochá
Antonio Manuel Uitz	Escribano	?
Marcos Sulu	Escribano	?
Francisco Mex	Regidor	Tixcacaltuyub
Tomás Canul	Regidor	Temax
Hilario Canul	Topil	Temax
Ignacio Caamal	Topil menor	San Cristóbal (Mérida)

Name	Ecclesiastical Position	Village of Origin
Pedro Chan	Fiscal de doctrina	Ekmul
Pedro Cauich	Fiscal menor	?
Francisco Chan	Maestro de capilla	?
Luis Cauich	Choirmaster	Tekantó
Pedro Dzul	Sacristan	?
Felipe Chan	Cantor	Tixméuac

The information, of course, is incomplete, for six of the sixteen people never testified because they escaped, died in the fighting, or were summarily executed. Still, it is notable that not one leader could be identified as a native of Cisteíl. A village in existence for thirty years or more would probably have some locally born people in positions of power and authority. Cisteíl, therefore, was new.

This does not mean that the villagers somehow escaped their taxes by setting up new communities. The visit of the priest to Cisteíl proves that the Church knew of its existence, and it is certain that the clerical authorities would have tried to get the Indians to pay their ecclesiastical taxes. They more than likely succeeded. The Bulls of the Holy Crusade (indulgences sold to raise money for a supposed crusade against the infidels), another source of the Church's income, were also known in Cisteíl, for various people mentioned it during the trial.[10] Indeed, the person in charge of the sales—made on credit[11]—for the region was Captain Cristóbal Calderón himself, who was away from his post selling indulgences when the revolution broke out.[12]

The Maya villagers of Cisteíl would also have been subject to civil taxes in the form of tribute. This was being collected in Cisteíl, for when Canek (Jacinto Uc), the king and leader of the revolution, took over the village, he ordered all tribute receipts—that is, proof of payment—collected and burned.[13] At his trial, Canek even claimed to have paid his tribute.[14]

Nevertheless, taxes are never popular, and Indians certainly did not like to pay tribute. The Maya official Simón Puc, teniente (assistant to the cacique) of Tiholop, testified that when tribute collection time came around, Indians frequently ran away,[15] and since Puc's job included tax collection, he knew what he was talking about. The people in Cisteíl may have been particularly reluctant to pay up, for early in 1760—almost two years before the revolution—the Spanish authorities had to send Don Domingo Sima, the cacique of Mérida's barrio of San Cristóbal, to the village to ensure payment. But he had difficulty collecting, for when he threatened the villagers, they responded with brazen disrespect ("con valentías"), asserting that for every three years they owed, they would pay only one.[16]

The new settlement of Cisteíl was also subject to the repartimiento system, which had been legalized in Yucatán since 1732. The major enterprise was the advanced payment of money or credit to the Maya in return for repayment at a later date in woven cotton cloth.[17] This practice served to enrich the governor of the province. By 1761, however, Spanish government officials had also begun on a small scale to sell mules to the Indians, who repaid their debts in installments. Both kinds of repartimiento were mentioned by people from Cisteíl who testified in the proceedings resulting from the uprising of 1761.[18]

Clearly, therefore, Cisteíl was firmly tied into the colonial system of economic exchange in which the fruits of Maya labor were extracted to support the colonial regime. There is no indication, however, that Cisteíl was worse off than any other village. Nor is there any suggestion that the level of surplus extraction was suddenly increased to the point of being unacceptable to the Maya. There is no evidence at all, therefore, of a Spanish violation of the moral economy that frequently was the cause of Indian rebellions in Spanish America.

What, then, if anything, did economic factors have to do with the outbreak of revolution in Yucatán in 1761? The cause of the uprising, as will soon be seen, was more of a cultural than an economic nature. But material factors clearly did play a role in making the situation ready for revolution. For the Maya resented their economic subjugation and understood that they were at the bottom of the social order. Their culture, in turn, taught them that eventually the tables would be turned—the historical cycle would change—and then they would be on the top and the Spaniards would be on the bottom. Moreover, the Spaniards would pay them tribute![19]

The Man Who Would Be King

To explain the cultural factors that caused the revolution in Yucatán in 1761, it is best to begin with the principal leader of the revolutionary movement. This was Jacinto Uc, a native of one of the barrios of Campeche. Thirty years old at the time of the revolution, Uc was a widower. This is noteworthy, for he was one of only two unmarried males who testified at the trial. (Even sixteen-year-old Ignacio Caamal and 100-year-old Pedro Ku were married.)[20] The other man who was unmarried, Nicolás Cauich, was a self-confessed beggar and sorcerer who drifted from one place to another and claimed to have participated in witchcraft and diabolism in the wilds of the thinly populated southern lowlands of the Peninsula.[21] Jacinto Uc identified himself as a vagabond who neither lived in nor belonged to any village. One can understand why, among the very practical Maya, neither Nicolás Cauich nor Jacinto Uc was married. Neither carried out milpa agriculture, the economic role of a Maya man, and thus neither warranted a Maya wife to complement his labors.

Jacinto Uc, known in history as Jacinto Canek, was not a simple vagabond. When asked his profession, he responded that he was the "Majordomo of Lord Jesus of Nazarus." Nicolás Cauich claimed that he had accompanied Uc to the south where they participated in devil worship, but the revolutionary leader himself, when asked what kind of witchcraft ("brujería") he used, responded that he did not use any.[22] All the evidence indicates that Jacinto Uc/Canek was a shaman. He may have participated in pagan rituals, but we have only Nicolás Cauich's word for that. Several people, however, testified that Jacinto Uc showed up in central Yucatán in 1761 claiming to have come from the east, possibly brought by an English ship.[23] He himself stated that "he had come from the East, and an English ship brought him."[24]

Jacinto Uc first made his appearance in the village of Chikindzonot in October 1761. The beggar Nicolás Cauich also showed up and later testified that the village priest asked him if he knew the newly arrived Uc, who was already calling himself Canek (to be explained below).[25] What happened next is unclear, but what is certain is that the priest of Chikindzonot had Uc whipped. This is probably because he was claiming to be either the Messiah or Jesus Christ. It is also possible, however, as Nicolás Cauich claimed, that Jacinto Uc first went south and engaged in pagan rituals, and then when he returned to Chikindzonot, the village priest had him whipped for his suspicious behavior. Finally, according to Jacinto Uc himself, he was whipped and expelled from the village because the priest thought he was a wayfarer (*paseador*).[26] In any case, he resented the corporal punishment, and later, when king, he spoke about his desire to go back to Chikindzonot to take revenge on the priest.[27]

Paradoxically, the events in Chikindzonot worked to the advantage of Jacinto Uc. For now he had been scourged and bloodied. He was ready to be a Christ figure. And by mixing Christianity with traditional Maya beliefs, he could now claim to be the king sent to redeem his people.[28]

Uc next showed up in Tiholop, a village twenty kilometers to the west. By moving west, he was coming from the east. He arrived in Tiholop, it was later said, on November 5, 1761.[29] According to his own testimony, he met with members of the village government, "whom he told that he came from the east, he, King Jacinto de los Santos Uc Canek, and that he was going to be crowned in the village of Cisteíl as the King of all the Province because the day had finally come when all the Spaniards would die."[30]

The meeting with the village government was important. Had the leaders wanted to, they could have run Jacinto Uc out of town. Instead, they listened to him. Most important of all was the attitude of Don Andrés Ku, the cacique. Later, during the trials following the revolution, Fernando Moreno, the Spanish military commander in Tixcacaltuyub, would write to the governor–captain general, who was the principal magistrate handling the cases of the rebels, informing him that Ku was an important figure. Moreno had pursued and caught Ku, he wrote, "because he was the principal head who gave force to the rebellion of the Indians of Cisteíl."[31] Fortunately, the cacique of Tiholop lived to testify.

Don Andrés Ku was fifty-eight years old at the time. He related that Jacinto Uc, who called himself Canek King Montezuma, arrived in Tiholop on November 5 and asked him what he was doing. Upon learning that Ku was going about collecting the cotton cloth owed to the encomendero (that is, the goods in kind owed as tribute), Jacinto Uc told Ku that he should give the cloth to the boys of the village instead. The cacique must have been impressed with the strange visitor, for he gave the stranger as a gift some britches (*calzón*) and a shirt.[32] Canek's testimony also mentioned those gifts, and he also explained that he had given orders to the cacique of Tiholop to be "ready with all the Indians when he should call on them," to which Don Andrés Ku was said to have replied that Canek should "go and be crowned."[33]

After passing a short time in Tiholop, Jacinto Uc moved further west, to Cisteíl. Once again, he was coming from the east. He now caused a sensation. Pedro Chan, the junior Indian alcalde (*alcalde de segundo voto*) of Cisteíl—a man who would pay with his life for his role in the revolution— testified at the trial right after Jacinto Uc. Chan stated that in early November an Indian showed up in the village calling himself Canek, and that the stranger "began to do his abilities," that is, perform what we would call magic. The junior Indian alcalde remembered one of these: Jacinto Uc jumped around, "making us believe that he could fly." He also went to the village hall carrying jasmine flowers, "and he told all of us present that he lived on flowers, and he began to chew the said jasmines." Uc also said that the time had come for the Spaniards to pay him tribute, and that it was no longer necessary for the Indians to go to Mérida to see the Spanish governor to have their elections confirmed because he was now in charge of doing that. Chan and the others then proclaimed Jacinto Uc Canek to be "King Montezuma."[34]

Former Indian alcalde Marcos Tec added more details of Jacinto Uc's arrival in Cisteíl. Uc went to the town hall and presented himself before Joseph Chan, the teniente. Joseph Chan was the senior Indian government official in the village, since Cisteíl, as already noted, did not have a cacique. According to Marcos Tec, Jacinto Uc informed Teniente Chan that he was "Canek, King Montezuma," and that he was in Cisteíl because "he was going to take possession of the said village" so that all elections would be confirmed there. To this, Joseph Chan replied that "he well knew that King Montezuma would succeed [to the throne] of this Province, but he had to come dressed as a King." Jacinto Uc, however, had a good answer to this objection: he was King Montezuma but had come dressed as an Indian so that he would not be recognized by the Spaniards. He also said that it was time to kill all the Spaniards of the province, "without any escaping," and that they should also kill all their pigs "because each one was the soul of a Spaniard."[35]

Shortly thereafter, according to Pascual Yupit (a peasant who would be executed within a few days of his testimony), Teniente Joseph Chan gave the order to kill the pigs.[36] Francisco Mex, a village councilman (*regidor*), of Cisteíl, also reported that Canek ordered the pigs killed because they had souls of Spaniards.[37] Junior Indian magistrate Pedro Chan stated that Teniente Joseph Chan's orders were carried out; the pigs "were killed and left to rot."[38]

Another view of Jacinto Uc's arrival in Cisteíl was provided by a second person named Pedro Chan. This second Pedro Chan held the important ecclesiastical post of *fiscal de doctrina* (chief Indian ecclesiastical magistrate, or church warden), that is, the chief Maya religious official in the village. He was in charge of aiding the priest—a Spaniard—in his tasks. That meant enforcing attendance at Mass and instructing children in catechism. To carry out his duties he was aided by an assistant church warden, the *fiscal menor*.

Fiscal de Doctrina Pedro Chan testified at the trial that Jacinto Uc came into Cisteíl claiming to be Canek King Montezuma in early November. At first he stayed at the house of Pedro Cauich, the fiscal menor. Two weeks later he moved in with the fiscal de doctrina. Being accepted into the house of the chief Indian church warden undoubtedly meant that the stranger was being taken seriously, which the villagers undoubtedly did not fail to notice. While living with Pedro Chan, Uc helped care for Chan's wife, who had just given birth. According to the fiscal de doctrina, Uc claimed to be from the village of Canek, "which was in the south in a strange region." The visitor ate neither meat nor lard (used copiously in Maya cooking) but only bread, eggs, chili peppers, and cooked or boiled beans. (Perhaps bread was a poor translation for a general term for food made from maize.[39])

Then, said Fiscal de Doctrina Pedro Chan, on November 19 Jacinto Uc ordered the village government to come to see him. He told them that "God had communicated to him what they had to do, and that the day to begin [their task] had arrived." He told them to bring him all receipts of tribute and of the repartimiento of mules, and after reading them—for perhaps Jacinto Canek could read—he ordered all the papers burned, "telling them that from then on they did not have to pay tribute or accept mules loaned to them, and he hoped that they had already received a lot of mules" because now they would not have to pay for them. He later clarified that although tribute (a civil tax) would be abolished, the people would still have to buy the bulls of indulgence of the Holy Crusade, "because that was his concern." And he ordered the Maya leaders to kill all the pigs in the village, "because in each one of them was enclosed the soul of a Spaniard, and as many pigs as they could kill, that many Spaniards they would kill, and sure enough they left and killed all [the pigs] that were in the village, and they were not to eat them."[40]

A final description of Jacinto Uc's arrival in Cisteíl comes from a hostile source: Luis Cauich, the *teniente de coro* (choirmaster, or perhaps assistant choirmaster) of the village. Luis Cauich was the only Indian official, civil or religious, who refused to believe Uc's claims. He testified at the trial that in early November "an Indian newcomer" (*yndio advenediso*) showed up and stayed at the house of assistant church warden Pedro Cauich, who told choirmaster Luis Cauich to come and meet the visitor. But what he had been told about Jacinto Uc must have disconcerted him, for he felt that "no le cuadraban sus propociciones" (his claims did not fit him).[41]

Still, the choirmaster agreed to meet with Jacinto Uc, who told him the following: "brother, you should know that I was captured by Captain David, and he put me under the balcony of Lord St. James [Santiago], and I have come only to see how you get along with the priests and the Spaniards, who have a pig's soul." He claimed to be from a place called Canek. Choirmaster Luis Cauich asked him where that place might be, since he had never heard of it, to which Jacinto Uc responded that Canek, a village, was in the hills to the south. Upon hearing that, Luis Cauich told assistant church warden Pedro Cauich "that he should not believe the nonsense [*disparates*] of that Indian," and he then told the village leaders to be careful, for if anything bad happened they would be held responsible. But the Maya leaders refused to listen to his warnings.[42]

On Saturday, November 8—choirmaster Luis Cauich recounted—Father Don Miguel de la Ruela, the assistant pastor of the parish of Tixcacaltuyub (and the son of a Belgian immigrant), arrived in Cisteíl to celebrate Mass the next day, Sunday. But when Father Ruela entered the village, Jacinto Uc grabbed the reins of the priest's horse, and the Indian government had to restrain Uc and confine him for a while to the living quarters of the priests, next to the church building. The next day during Mass someone yelled "fire!" and the church was quickly evacuated. According to Luis Cauich, this had been a ruse concocted to kill the priest in the confusion, but the plan went awry. Father Ruela then left the village, apparently after setting Jacinto Uc free. When the latter went back to his old ways, with the support of the village government, the choirmaster sent a message to the religious authorities, probably in Sotuta or Tixcacaltuyub, requesting aid. But none was forthcoming.[43]

On Thursday, November 19—choirmaster Luis Cauich again remembered—Canek met with some of the villagers, who were "carrying out thousands of reverential acts" (in Cauich's words). Then he told them, "see my head, which has been crowned with a crown of thorns, and my scourged back, and by toes all injured because they dragged me to the House of Pilate." He said he had redeemed them by shedding his precious blood. Pedro Dzul, *sacristán mayor* (chief sacristan—the number of religious posts seems endless) then showed up and began to set the church up for Mass—a Mass to be celebrated by none other than Jacinto Canek. Choirmaster Luis Cauich told the sacristan "not to commit such an absurdity, because it was all the deception of the Devil," but again no one listened. The choirmaster then went home, which is where he was later that day when he heard a great commotion in the village: the people were killing their pigs, because Canek had said that "each pig was the soul of a priest or a Spaniard."[44]

Thus all the accounts, even the hostile one, are remarkably similar: Jacinto Uc had become Canek and proclaimed himself King Montezuma. He achieved this status because of the success of his craft. And what was his craft? The evidence suggests shamanism. Several of the survivors from Cisteíl noted that Canek carried out rituals usually associated with the healing propensities of shamans. Pascual Yupit, for example, said that Canek made a holy oil out of squash and honey, saying that it was to serve as an unction so that the Indians could go to heaven.[45]

Chief Indian church warden Pedro Chan, who eventually blamed everything on "the tricks of the Devil," also remarked on Canek's unction made of squash and honey. On the night Chan's wife was in labor, Canek made another preparation made from oil derived from the *nin* plant, which he had wrapped up and placed on a table with candles and a cross. The rite was apparently for the purpose of helping the birth of the child. The fiscal de doctrina recounted how Canek anointed the sick people of the village with the oil made in his house. After the first acts of violence, Canek cured the wounded with burned maguey (that is, aloe vera). Chan also noted that the newly crowned king had a special relationship with birds, which he allowed to fly about in the church.[46]

Not all that Canek was said to have done was benevolent. Because of all the activity going on in the village, senior Indian magistrate Joaquín Xix got sick with "the evil eye"[47]—a spell that someone, perhaps Canek, was assumed to have placed on him. Of course, because of the important decisions that he was making—to support a revolution—Indian magistrate Xix may have been suffering from severe stress. And once the threat of a full-scale battle loomed over Cisteíl, Canek, as we shall see, used his powers to bolster both the village's defenses and the villagers' courage. We shall leave beggar-sorcerer Nicolás Cauich's account of Canek's powers until a later time.

Very importantly, Canek's craft quickly merged with the existing Catholic religious activities of the village. As we have seen, after living in the houses first of the fiscal menor and then of the fiscal de doctrina, Canek moved into the living quarters of the Catholic priests. Soon he was appropriating all that he could of the Catholic Church. He used the wounds inflicted on him in Chikindzonot to present himself as the image of Jesus Christ scourged at the pillar and crowned with a crown of thorns. He now chose a new crown: he took the one off the statue of the Virgin in the church and put it on his own head.[48] According to village councilman Francisco Mex, wherever Jacinto Canek went, "all the Indian women went about him with candles, bowing before him, kissing his feet, begging him to forgive them their sins, because he made them believe that he was Jesus Christ."[49]

Soon the people of Cisteíl had set up their own version of the Catholic Church. Jacinto Canek, aided by several assistants, dressed in the vestments of the Catholic priests and celebrated Mass, heard confession, and baptized children. He gave sermons and presumably gave out communion. He led the people in praying the rosary.[50] In short, he became a full-fledged priest who administered the sacraments as the mediator between God and human beings. The Maya religious officials of Cisteíl participated in all this. Sacristan Pedro Dzul and the *mayordomo de velas* (majordomo of candles—still another religious post), someone named May, both served as deacons or "prophets."[51]

Canek also added touches of Maya culture to his priestly practices. At least two witnesses testified that he took out a statue of an Indian carrying either a bow, arrows, and quiver or a staff set on a small stone, which was incensed with copal as a holy image.[52] Yet he also used in these ceremonies the statues of the Blessed Virgin and St. Joseph, which were carried in processions.[53]

Certainly one of the aspects of Jacinto Canek that most disturbed the Spaniards was the relationship that he claimed with the Blessed Virgin Mary. Indeed, when the revolution was over the city council of Mérida officially stated that "the most execrable deed that the said King [Canek] committed [was] the sacrilegious evil of giving the name of wife to the Image of Most Holy Mary Our Lady."[54] He may have felt a special devotion to the Virgin, for according to his own testimony right after arriving in Cisteíl he asked for three pounds of wax (presumably for candles) "in order to carry out a novena for Our Lady."[55] (The Feast of the Immaculate Conception, especially popular in Yucatán, was only about three weeks away at the time.) Several witnesses testified that Canek proclaimed the Blessed Virgin to be his wife.[56] As Pascual Yupit put it, Jacinto Canek told them to "adore Our

Lady, who was the wife of St. Joseph, because she was his wife too, as King of the Earth."[57] Cisteíl's junior Indian magistrate, Pedro Chan, stated that Canek slept in his hammock in the same room with the statue of the Virgin.[58] And Jacinto Canek himself testified that "he told the Indians that Our Lady was the wife of St. Joseph and his wife too because he was King of the Earth."[59]

While he was taking over the church, Jacinto Canek was also taking over the village government. In effect, what he did was elevate the status of the local officials, for Teniente Joseph Chan, the number one man, was appointed by Canek to the post of "governor–captain general," which was the office held by the number one Spaniard in Yucatán. On the other hand, Canek appointed Nicolás Tec, who held no office in Cisteíl, as "lieutenant governor," because Tec was thought to be particularly bold and daring.[60] The Maya king was well aware of the necessity of the symbols of power. According to the cacique of Tiholop, Don Andrés Ku, Canek took the staff of office used by Spanish captain Tiburcio de Cosgaya, who had been killed (a subject soon to be explained), and gave it to Teniente Joseph Chan, the proclaimed governor–captain general, as his staff of office. According to Fiscal de Doctrina Pedro Chan, Jacinto Canek gave Teniente Chan the staff saying "here you have the staff of office of the Governor and Captain General of all the Province, which mercy I bestow on you so that you can kill all the Spaniards." Chief Church Warden Chan stated, however, that Joseph Chan was at first reluctant to take up his office. He undoubtedly was concerned about the revolution's chances of success. But finally he agreed to accept it and gave Canek his thanks.[61] Still another witness, Marcos Tec, a former Indian village magistrate, stated that Canek first stuck a coin onto the staff before awarding it to the teniente of Cisteíl. Tec also testified that once the revolution was in full force, the Spanish Royal Arms were removed from the town hall.[62] (The importance for the Maya of the staff of office will also be discussed in the last chapter).

Jacinto Canek thus assumed the powers of king, for as king he appointed the governor–captain general. He also began to spread his jurisdiction beyond the village he had just taken over. He called on Don Andrés Ku, cacique of Tiholop, to come to him and witness his kingship, as he had promised he would do when he was in that village only a week or two before. Moreover, people from the surrounding villages of Tahdzibilchén (to the northeast), Tahdziu (south), Tixméuac (southwest), and Rancho Nenelá (west) suddenly began to go to Cisteíl in large numbers, and since they were almost always led by their caciques it is likely that Canek had communicated with the leaders of those villages too. The capital of the new Maya kingdom thus began to fill up with visitors wanting to see the king who ruled in this small and formerly unimportant village in central Yucatán.

The investigation following the revolution provides us with a great deal of testimony regarding the motives of those who left their homes to go to Cisteíl. Simón Maas, *maestro de capilla* (chapel master—yes, another religous post) of Tixméuac, said that he left his village "to recognize one Canek who, he had been informed, was chosen King, in order to render obedience and venerate him, in case he was such a king," (but then he added, probably for the benefit of the judges, "but when I saw he was just an ordinary Indian, I did not do it").[63] *Alguacil de Doctrina* (probably the same as fiscal de doctrina) Leonardo Bebet, the brothers Ventura and Augustín Hau (the former being the cantor, that is, lead singer of the church), and Gerónimo Tec, all from Tixméuac, went to Cisteíl thinking they were going to see "an Indian governor."[64] Pedro Can, from Rancho Nenelá, gave the same explanation for his journey.[65] However, Nicolás Yah, the senior Indian magistrate from the same rancho, said that he went to Cisteíl because he had heard about "a King."[66] Similarly, Domingo Balam, resident of Estancia Huntulchac, stated that he went to see "the King" because he wanted to join him.[67]

Don Andrés Ku, cacique of Tiholop, stated that he received the summons from Canek on Thursday, November 19. He and the other officials of the village, accompanied by several other people, including Ku's three sons, went to Cisteíl on the following Saturday. He found the local leaders providing Canek with honey, turkeys, and cacao "as gifts to the King." Ku said that he "knelt before him and kissed his feet, telling him 'Here I am to receive your orders.'"[68]

As a result of the influx of people, Cisteíl came to be filled with people. Since there were no Spaniards around, there were no controls on Maya activity except for those imposed by the Maya themselves. Unquestionably these were heady times, for whether they knew it or not, the indigenous people had assumed not local autonomy but full-fledged religious and political independence. They had a king and ran their own church. The Maya had become a sovereign people, and although they may not yet have realized it, by carrying out a revolution they had become revolutionary.

Unfortunately none of the witnesses to these events had the time to write or dictate a detailed report of all that the Maya did in Cisteíl during their days of freedom. Consequently we are left with only fragmentary comments made through interpreters, mostly by men who were scared by the prospect of the punishment that awaited them. Indeed, some were executed within a week or two of their testimony. Nevertheless, these comments are all that are available and thus will have to be used to give us some idea of what the Maya did when ruled by their own king.

Tomás Balam, the scribe of Tixméuac, reported that Canek ruled as a king with a court—the courtiers "entertaining him day and night with harp and guitar."[69] Many other witnesses also mentioned the music that always accompanied the king.[70] Some mentioned dancing—even a "fandango"—at the court as well.[71] All who approached Canek treated him as royalty or divinity: they bowed their heads, took off their hats—for the Maya regularly wore hats—kissed his hands and feet, knelt before him, pledged their obedience, incensed him, venerated him with candles, and carried him in processions.[72] People from the other villages also offered the king gifts of what for them was valuable: bananas, turkeys, limes, and honey. To feed the multitudes, cattle were purchased from Estancias Huntulchac (a few kilometers to the west or southwest) and Xcatmis (about forty kilometers to the southwest), and the Maya indulged themselves by eating meat.[73]

While all these activities were going on, the Maya king did not forget his political goals. Over and over again, the witnesses who testified stated that Canek preached that the time had come to kill all the Spaniards.[74] As Fiscal de Doctrina Pedro Chan remembered one such occasion, Canek told those around him not to fear for "he had waged war against Spaniards in other places to defend his own people, his brothers, who he left in peaceful and quiet possession, and he was going to do the same for them, and they should not fear, for his Father—pointing with his hand toward heaven—had ordered him to carry out this conquest."[75] Moreover, "his Father had determined that they should enjoy their lands peacefully without the Spaniards."[76] Not even the priests would be spared; in fact, to make them hand over their goods, Canek said that the priests should be hung up in hammocks and then cut down suddenly.[77]

Nevertheless, several people stated that Canek sometimes suggested that not all Spaniards would have to die. The chief Indian church warden, Pedro Chan, stated that the king said he would spare those Spaniards who would give up their goods, as long as they agreed to pay tribute to the Indians. Moreover, those who wanted to leave the province would be allowed to do so.[78]

Spanish women would also be exempted from the general rule that all Spaniards would be killed. According to Francisco Puc of Tiholop, who was the very first person to testify at the trial, the Maya would kill "all the Spaniards of the Province, women as well as men, except for some of the principal women; for the King would marry them."[79] And again Fiscal de Doctrina Pedro Chan, who was particularly close to Canek, stated that the king "would let live those Spanish women born in the Province, in order to marry them to Indians."[80]

The Culture of Revolution

Here we should stop and consider what had taken place in Cisteíl up to this point, and why it had happened. It is important to add that all of this was going on apparently without the knowledge of the Spaniards. This in turn speaks volumes about the reality of the colonial regime: it did not require the presence of very many Spaniards. Cisteíl was visited by a priest every week or so, but there was no Spanish official in the village. The same was true of the great majority of villages in the Maya area, that is, Chiapas, Yucatán, and Guatemala. There also were no Spanish residents in most Maya settlements. The coercion of colonialism in fact was exerted indirectly, not by Spaniards but by the Maya themselves. The village governments—made up of caciques (or substitutes like tenientes, as in the case of Cisteíl), alcaldes, regidores, and escribanos—were the people who exercised power and authority. The Maya had a long tradition of a strong local ruling class, and this survived into the colonial period and beyond. The village government collected tribute and religious taxes, organized whatever labor drafts were demanded by the Spaniards, and administered the repartimiento on behalf of colonial officials. When the leaders talked, the people listened—and they followed their leaders.

Jacinto Canek in retrospect succeeded because he got the local Maya governments and local Maya religious leadership to support him. And once they supported him, they obeyed him. This explains why he got nothing but a sound beating in Chikindzonot, where he was not believed, probably in part because of the presence of a permanent, resident Spanish priest, the curate of the village. Jacinto Uc was more successful in Tiholop, and then almost completely successful in Cisteíl. Eventually the caciques of several other villages also threw their support to the new king. And the people followed their leaders.

But why would there be such support for a whipped Indian who claimed to be able to fly and to have come from "the East" to rule as a king in place of Spanish authority? Francisco Puc, the first person to testify, said it was in part "because they were bored with serving the Spaniards."[81] But clearly material factors were involved, for as we have seen, many people spoke of their desire to get rid of tribute. Yet here it is important to remember that at least one person stated that the desire was not simply to escape from Spanish taxes but also to have the Spaniards pay tribute to the Maya. Hence material exploitation was important, for the revolutionaries did not want to pay taxes to the Spaniards. In short, they resisted surplus extraction. On the other hand there is no evidence of any recent violation of the moral economy as occurred elsewhere in the Maya area and led to local revolts. Penetration of the area around Cisteíl by Spanish landowners had hardly begun at all, and thus intrusive commercial stock-raising was insignificant and commercial agriculture was nonexistent. Therefore, there was no pressure on the land nor increased demands for labor. Nor was exploitation through the repartimiento or religious exactions any worse than before.

The real importance of material factors like tribute is that they clearly subordinated the Maya to the Spaniards. It was that inferior, degraded—colonial—condition that was crucial. For it fitted in with long-standing indigenous cultural traditions. The Maya had always believed that human history moved in long cycles, and that eventually those on top would be put on the bottom. They saw themselves as people who had once been on top but were now on the bottom, as was proved by their material exploitation by Spaniards. But the historical process must go on, and thus one day the cycle would come along again in which they would be on top and for that very reason the Spaniards would be on the bottom.

This is why so many people testified that they *expected* a king to appear to lead them in the conquest of the Spaniards. In their past they saw their future, and from their past would come a king to lead them there.

That king was Canek. The name "Canek" is important. Canek may have been a place in some people's minds, but it clearly was the name of the kings of the Itzá Maya of the Petén region (the northern lowlands of Guatemala, at the extreme south of the Yucatán Peninsula). The Itzá Maya had remained unconquered for a long time. Spaniards had made incursions into the south but had been unwilling to spend scarce resources to subdue the Petén and its people because neither the people nor the place seemed to be worth anything. But eventually, in the 1690s, the Spaniards thought it necessary to bring the Petén under their control, and after an arduous and expensive campaign the governor of Yucatán, Martín Urzúa y Arizmendi, succeeded in capturing the Itzá capital and subjecting the Maya of the region to what turned out to be rather weak colonial control.[82]

Yet the Maya understanding of history actually contributed to this defeat in the Petén. The priestly class that surrounded the Itzá King Canek became convinced that the change of the historical cycle was at hand and would mean that the Spaniards would conquer them. The Itzá King Canek believed this and actually negotiated a surrender since he though defeat to be inevitable. Not all of his people went along with this policy, though, and as a result the Spaniards had to use military force to conquer those who would not submit peacefully. In 1697, once the conquest of the Petén was complete, King Canek—the last independent king of the Maya—trudged off into jail or house arrest in Santiago de Guatemala. He then disappeared from the historical record.

But he did not disappear from memory. Since many Yucatec Maya, including probably Jacinto Uc, had contact with the people to the south or even went there themselves, the history of King Canek became a legend. Moreover, Maya belief in the inevitable change of the historical cycle was written down in their chronicles called the *Chilam Balam* (the existence of which, as we shall see, was known to the Spaniards). It survived both colonialism and Christianity. Indeed, Maya culture even borrowed from Christianity, for the promise of the Messiah fitted in nicely with the change of historical cycle brought about by the arrival/return of a king of liberation. Thus Jacinto Canek's portrayal of himself as the image of Christ was seen not as sacrilege but as the fulfillment of prophecy.

Yet the king who was expected was also known as Montezuma. Unfortunately no explanation whatever was given at the time of the significance of that name, and as far as I am aware this is the only time in the history of the Yucatec Maya—and possibly of all the Maya—that it is mentioned. Montezuma, of course, was the Hispanicized version of the name of two Aztec emperors, including the famous last one. But we can only speculate regarding its meaning to the Yucatec Maya in 1761. In what is now the U.S. Southwest, the Indian people under Spanish rule understood Montezuma to have been a great leader who brought prosperity to his people and then left promising to return sometime in the future.[83] He was also sometimes seen as the protector of native religion against Christianity. It is very possible that Spanish priests told the Maya of Montezuma, if they had not heard of him before, and then the Maya chose to develop their own meaning for the name. We do not know what that meaning was. It is likely, however, that at a minimum Montezuma's name signified legitimate authority.

Whatever the meaning of Montezuma, the books of *Chilam Balam*, and historical cycles, it is clear that prophecy played a key rule in the events of 1761. It is possible, as Mexican historian Pedro Bracamonte has suggested,[84] that behind this was the great Mesoamerican myth of Quetzalcóatl, the king of the Toltecs who, having been betrayed, abandoned the land and promised to return one day. Since he departed and went eastward, his return would be from the east. The myth of Quetzalcóatl ("feathered serpent") entered the Maya region, possibly brought by migrants from central Mexico. Among the Yucatec Maya the figure became Kukulcán, the feathered serpent that appears in the art and architecture of the Post-Classic Period, such as on the great pyramid at Chichén Itzá (where during the equinox the sun casts a shadow in such a way that the feathered serpent seems to be descending from the pyramid).

As is well known, Hernán Cortés claimed to be Quetzalcóatl in order to make his triumph over the Aztecs seem inevitable, having been foreordained. The importance of the myth in Yucatán is less clear, and it appears to have played no role at all in the conquest of the Maya. Nor does it appear in the written record of the colonial period. Consequently, if the myth of Quetzalcóatl/Kukulcán was still alive in 1761, it undoubtedly was the result primarily of oral transmission from generation to generation. For that reason, of course, it is virtually impossible to know anything about it, such as what Kukulcán was supposed to do upon returning. It is impossible even to prove the myth's continued existence.

Whatever the case may be, there is no question that in 1761 the Maya of Yucatán expected a king to come. When Jacinto Uc came, it became possible that he was the king whose arrival or return was expected. As Tomás Balam, the scribe of Tixméuac, said, he "believed that he was the King, because it was said he would come, and he came, from the east."[85] Once someone of importance—such as the village leaders of Cisteíl and Tiholop and later Tixméuac, Tahdzibilchén, Chacsinkín, and Rancho Nenelá—believed it, and once such people in authority proclaimed Uc to be true, the people followed their leaders. For the Maya, Jacinto Uc became Canek the king. The past, therefore, should once again become the present. The Maya would now, it was hoped, rule over the Spaniards.

Therefore, although material factors were the indispensable background for the revolutionary movement—for only those who are down can dream of one day being on top—the factor that caused the revolution to happen was cultural in nature. Despite two centuries of Christian indoctrination and Spanish colonialism, the Maya still believed that history moved in cycles. They held on to core cultural beliefs, and thus saw Spanish rule as simply a phase that would eventually pass. Spaniards thus became simply one more conquering group (like the Toltecs or Putún Maya before them) who would eventually be overthrown and absorbed by the native people. That is why it was said that Spanish women would be made to marry Indian commoners, with the best ones reserved for Canek. (Kings, it seems, always get first choice.) The Maya also may have held on to their legend of Kukulcán, who was expected to return from the east. And had the revolution of 1761 succeeded, the history of Yucatán and of the Yucatec Maya would have been very different.

The Revolution Turns Violent

The trial record does not always provide clear and consistent evidence. Even chronology is not always easy to establish. But what is clear is that shortly after Jacinto Uc became Canek King Montezuma and before people from surrounding villages flocked to see the man who would be king in Cisteíl, two acts of violence took place. The violence, in turn, helped convince more people that Jacinto Uc was indeed the Maya king.

The first concerned a small-time Spanish traveling salesman named Diego Pacheco. He had business dealings with people in Cisteíl, as a result of which he was owed money. This means he must have sold on credit, although no information was given regarding the goods he dealt with. In any case, Diego Pacheco had the supreme bad luck to show up to collect debts in Cisteíl shortly after the arrival of Jacinto Canek. By the time the Spaniard got there, Canek had already convinced some of the village leaders, and half-convinced others, to accept his authority.

Most villages had a special building called the *mesón*, or *casas reales*, where itinerant Spaniards were lodged, and it was to Cisteíl's mesón that Diego Pacheco retired on Thursday, November 19, 1761. Not all the surviving accounts agree on exactly what happened next. According to Pedro Chan, the chief church warden, while in the mesón Pacheco was visited by Jacinto Canek, who asked him what he was doing in the building. Pacheco, undoubtedly clueless as to what had been going on in the village, responded "Get out of here, you drunkard." Canek then called on the local officials known as *topiles* (deputies, who assisted the cacique and village alcaldes in law enforcement) and ordered them to kill the Spaniard. There were three topiles present, all armed with shotguns. They all fired at Pacheco, two hitting their target but the third firearm misfired. The wounded Spaniard then crawled out of the mesón and spoke to his murderers, asking "Brothers, why are you trying to kill me? How have I offended you? Don't kill me, for are not you and I Christians?" By then the third shotgun had been properly loaded, and was fired at point-blank range, killing Pacheco immediately.[86]

Another version was provided by Pascual Yupit, a peasant. According to Yupit, he and Choirmaster Luis Cauich, discovering that Pacheco was in town, warned him to get out fast because the Indians were going to kill him. Pacheco either ignored them or did not move fast enough, for soon Canek showed up at the mesón and asked the Spaniard whether he was aware that the building belonged to him (Canek), and therefore, why was he there? Pacheco asked Canek if he was joking, for surely he knew that the mesón was for Spaniards. He added that he intended no harm to anyone, for he had come to collect a few small debts owed him. According to this account, Canek then grabbed a shotgun from one of the topiles, but when he tried to shoot, it misfired. He therefore gave the gun back to the topil and ordered him to kill Pacheco. This was done. Canek then left the mesón, saying "See how I kill Spaniards!"[87]

Choirmaster Luis Cauich, the doubting Thomas of Cisteíl, gave a different version, one that failed to corroborate Yupit's testimony. Cauich said that he was at home at the time, when his wife told him that she had seen some Indians leading Pacheco's horse away, and she had heard them say that the Spaniard was to be killed. Cauich hurried to the mesón but was too late, for Canek and his men had also arrived. In other words, there was no time to warn Pacheco, as Yupit claimed to have done with Cauich. Canek's men then threatened the choirmaster, who was forced to leave. As he looked back, he saw the group kill the Spaniard. Luis Cauich quickly ran away to Tixcacaltuyub to tell the local priest what was happening in Cisteíl.[88]

Both Indian alcaldes of Cisteíl, Joaquín Xix and Pedro Chan, identified Hilario Canul, Ignacio Caamal, and Ambrosio Balam as the topiles who did the killing.[89] Of these three, Balam was killed in the revolution.[90] The other two lived to testify. Hilario Canul, twenty years old, admitted that he was one of those who killed Pacheco, but he participated in the killing, he said, because he received orders from the king to do so. He also claimed that there was a total of eight people who carried out the murder.[91] Ignacio Caamal was only sixteen, and he identified himself as *topil menor* (assistant deputy). After first claiming not to be involved at all, he later admitted his guilt. Like Canul, he said he was simply carrying out orders, but unlike Canul he said that the orders were given not by Canek but by the village leaders.[92]

Finally, in this Rashomon-like story, we have the testimony of Jacinto Canek, which is as follows: "On Thursday, November 19, in the morning, a traveling merchant arrived at the casas reales [mesón]. The witness [Canek] went to him and said, 'Don't you know these casas reales are not yours? So why have you come here?' The other having responded to the effect that he must be joking, for the casas reales were for Spaniards, and he did not come to harm anyone but only to collect some debts, to which the witness responded, 'Now you will see how I kill you,' and asking for a shotgun, he tried to fire, but having misfired he gave the shotgun to another Indian deputy, telling him 'kill that Spaniard,' and the said Indian killed him, and then he [the witness] began to scream, saying 'now you see how I kill the Spaniards!'"[93]

From these versions it can be concluded that Pacheco was killed by the topiles, who acted on the orders of either Canek or the village leaders, or both. In fact, it is unlikely that the topiles would have acted without orders from their immediate superiors, the village leaders. Canek's order to kill therefore was crucial. Had the teniente, Joseph Chan, and the village alcaldes, Joaquín Xix and Pedro Chan, refused to go along with the king, there never would have been a revolution. That moment was the turning point of all the events of November 1761. The village leaders went along with Canek, and Pacheco was killed. The die was cast. There was no turning back.

Pacheco's body was dragged away and thrown into a lime pit (*sahcabera*).[94] But Choirmaster Luis Cauich had escaped. According to Fiscal de Doctrina Pedro Chan, Cauich had to run for his life, for people were shooting at him.[95] He got to Tixcacaltuyub unharmed, however, and spread the alarm. Word quickly reached Tiburcio Cosgaya y Solís, the *capitán a guerra* (war captain, that is, district military commander) of Sotuta. Cosgaya did not waste a moment. On Friday, November 20, the day after Pacheco's death, the captain sent a message to Governor–Captain General Joseph Crespo, informing

him that a rebellion had broken out in Cisteíl, and that it had the support of
the village leaders and even of the children. Cosgaya reported that he was
mobilizing his men, and was confiscating all the guns in his district. He
awaited his orders.[96]

But for reasons known only to him, Cosgaya did not wait for orders from
the Governor–Captain General. Before Crespo could possibly have responded,
the captain had already acted. He assembled a force of between ten and fifteen men, some of whom were mounted, and with temerity rivaling that of
George Armstrong Custer, he moved on Cisteíl. But someone in Cisteíl had
some sense, for sentries were posted along the roads leading into the village.
The sentries heard the sound of the horses in Cosgaya's troop apparently
coming south from Tixcacaltuyub, and gave the alert.[97]

The Spaniards arrived in Cisteíl in the late afternoon or evening, between
five and six o'clock, on Friday, November 20. It was still only one day after
the death of Pacheco, so Cosgaya had obviously moved fast. Yet if in fact his
first (and only) report to Governor–Captain General Crespo was accurate
and there was indeed an uprising in Cisteíl, then he was clearly not display-
ing caution. Rather, he probably felt contempt for the people who had dared
to defy Spanish authority.

In this study we have seen several cases of Spanish militiamen entering
Maya villages. Usually they were attacked by mobs of stone-throwing men
and women, and even when unhorsed never suffered more than a severe
blow to their dignity. Usually the Spaniards ran away and returned with larger
forces to restore order nonviolently. In short, in the other cases, the Maya
killed no Spaniards and peacefully, albeit reluctantly, submitted once again
to Spanish authority when threatened by a significant military force.

Entrance into Cisteíl was different. None of the accounts mentions women
being involved in the fighting, which is virtual proof that the villagers' actions
were not spontaneous but organized by leaders. Indeed, the men were armed
with a few shotguns and some machetes, and had already sharpened wooden
stakes to be used to kill Spaniards. The Maya, in short, were deadly serious.

The accounts of what followed differ, but clearly between fifty and one
hundred Maya men faced fifteen or so Spaniards.[98] The intruders succeeded
in getting to the central plaza, but this was because they were being allowed
to walk into an ambush. Near the plaza, the Indians attacked. Captain Cosgaya
was wounded by a bullet, and fell or was pushed from his horse. The Maya
then beat him to death and literally cut him to pieces. Several other Spaniards were unhorsed, and probably all those on foot, including the foot soldiers, were beaten and hacked to death. Only four men, all of them wounded,
managed to fight their way out and escape back to Tixcacaltuyub. The Maya
who survived to testify disagreed over the number of dead. Francisco Puc of

Tiholop—who carried messages from Jacinto Canek to the caciques of other villages and was caught doing it, was the first person to testify at the trial and was among those executed—said six Spaniards and twenty Indians died.[99] Mathías Uc, who after the battle with Cosgaya's force was named by Canek to command the rebel Maya troops, said the count was eight Spaniards and an equal number of Indians,[100] while Fiscal de Doctrina Pedro Chan said that among the Indians only one died and eight were wounded (and then cured by Jacinto Canek).[101]

Canek himself denied having anything to do with the attack on Cosgaya and his men.[102] But according to the chief Indian church warden, Pedro Chan, the king was present at the battle, "encouraging his brothers with a stake, sharpened at both ends, in his hand."[103] Mathías Uc also said that Canek was there.[104] Whatever the case, the Maya had now rebelled against Spanish authority and had killed several Spaniards. Canek's movement in Cisteíl was a challenge to colonial rule.

When the fighting was over, the Maya disposed of the bodies and possessions of the dead Spaniards. Canek received whatever jewelry and fancy buckles were found. The king also probably ordered his men to cut off Cosgaya's right hand or arm. This was done, and Canek hung it to his rear end, where it served, according to two witnesses, "like a tail."[105] It is also possible that the victors cut out the eyes of the vanquished. Francisco Puc of Tiholop later testified that Canek used Spanish eyeballs in the sacrificial ceremonies "to his God."[106] (It is worth noting that the Maya underworld—Xibalbá in the *Popol Vuh*—was inhabited by devils or demons who made necklaces out of eyeballs.) The bodies were stripped and thrown into a lime pit.

As the placing of sentries demonstrates, the rebels were organizing. According to Mathías Uc, a twenty-year-old from Tiholop, the cacique of Tiholop presented him to Canek and recommended that he serve as *cabo* (local commander) of their forces, and the king said, "very good."[107] Work on defensive fortifications began immediately. This involved a great deal of work, for stones had to be carried to the site to build a wall (*albarrada*) strong enough to help repel an attack. The wall was in front of the church and enclosed a well and the cemetery. Construction continued right up to the final battle of November 26, which was only five days after the ambush of Cosgaya's command.[108] The fortifications were completed on time, but the wall was apparently not well constructed, as we shall see.

The leadership in Cisteíl also tried to strengthen themselves by gaining the support of other villages. Someone wrote letters and sent them to numerous villages. Francisco Puc, the messenger who was the first person to testify at the trial, carried letters addressed to the caciques of Teabo, Maní, Maxcanú, and Yothilín, as well as to the foreman of Estancia Uxmal.[109] Jacinto

Canek testified that he sent letters to the caciques of Tahdziu, Tiholop, Ichmul, Tinum, Tixméuac, Tahdzibilchén, Chacsinkín, Rancho Nenelá, and Estancia Huntulchac, and "although not all the caciques came to join him, Indians from all those places did."[110] Later in his testimony he added to the list the villages of Tixcacaltuyub, Ichmul, Sabán, Uaymax, Chunhuhub, Polyuc, Telá, Ekpedz, Tepich, Chikindzonot, Tekax, Yotholín, and Bolonchén—in short, practically all the villages east, west, southwest, and southeast of Cisteíl.[111]

Three such letters, which the Spaniards called "cartas convocatorias" (letters convening a meeting or a combining of people), were later introduced as evidence at the trial. One, dated November 21, was ostensibly from Don Andrés Ku, cacique of Tiholop, to the village government of Tinum. The letter read: "My lords, with this I inform you that you have in your hands the venerable letter of Lord Governor King Matasuma [sic], who is to be found in the village of Cisteíl, so that you and all your people get on the road quickly, quickly, and once you have read this, return it to us. My lords, there are powerful reasons for this."[112]

Another of the captured letters was from Joseph Chan, the village leader of Cisteíl, and the scribe, Antonio Manuel Uitz, to the cacique of Tahdziu, inviting that village's people to join the movement. The letter said, "even if you have no guns, come with clubs, come with machetes, everyone in the village, come quickly, open your eyes when you walk, do not harm the houses, send the women to the bush [to hide] for a while."[113]

The third letter was ostensibly from the cacique and village government of Cisteíl to their counterparts in the villages of Ticul, Nohcacab, and "all those of the district of Camino Real." It informed the people of those villages of the writers' intention to fight the Spaniards, and asked for their help. It is dated, however, October 1760 not November 1761,[114] and the people who claim to be the village government are not found anywhere else in the record. Moreover, the leader of that government was one Don Juan Canul, "former cacique," yet nowhere else it is ever suggested that Cisteíl had, or had ever had, a cacique. The document is possibly a bad translation of a letter written the previous year, or a letter from a village government other than that of Cisteíl. It is also possible that the document was incorrectly dated or that the Spanish scribe who wrote the translation made an error as he wrote down the evidence. In short, the document is an enigma that is too ambiguous to be taken by a historian as proof of anything.

Don Andrés Ku, the cacique of Tiholop, vigorously denied writing the letter attributed to him, and so did the other caciques so implicated. They all had one good argument on their side: they could not have written the letters because they were illiterate. That placed all the blame on a few village scribes who were conveniently dead. And as for the letter supposedly written by

Cisteíl's teniente, Joseph Chan, the latter was either dead or missing and thus was unavailable to confirm or deny the letter's authenticity.

Despite this, these letters and the ones allegedly sent by Canek or the village government of Cisteíl are significant. There is no question that some letters, if not these, were written, and that efforts were made to spread the revolution not only to the east but also to the west, to the political districts of the Sierra and the Camino Real, where there was a larger Spanish population than in central and eastern Yucatán. Moreover, the very mention of Uxmal—far to the west—is astonishing. In 1761 the site was nothing but an estancia, that is, a cattle ranch, without a significant Maya population, and its importance to the ancient Maya was completely unknown to the Spaniards (who showed no interest in, and had no knowledge of, ancient Maya civilization). The mention of Uxmal thus suggests that somehow the Maya thought the place was important. Perhaps oral history had kept memory of the place alive, and the Maya knew more about their history than anyone gave them credit for.

The letters are also of interest because they are a good example of Maya adoption of what was useful from the Spaniards. For the writing used was of course not ancient Maya glyphs but (colonial) Maya written in the phonetic Latin alphabet taught them by the Spaniards. Thus when the Maya tried to gather support for revolution, literacy was used as a tool against colonialism. It certainly would suggest to some Spaniards the value of keeping all the Indians illiterate, as one priest did in 1785 when referring to the danger represented by the revolt of Jacinto Canek.[115] Neither church nor state, however, took such suggestions seriously.

Finally, the letters might have had some effect. Word of what was going on in Cisteíl, especially the arrival of the long-awaited king, spread to the nearby Maya villages and caused a commotion. Many people went to Cisteíl, with or without their caciques, just to see for themselves.

We have seen, then, that the revolutionaries in Cisteíl were preparing defensive fortifications and trying to gain the support of other villages. Still another defensive measure was to gather or manufacture the arms they would need to fight the expected battle with the Spaniards. The Maya did have some rifles or shotguns, some captured from Captain Cosgaya's command. Others were the Indians' personal possessions. For example, Don Andrés Ku, cacique of Tiholop, brought his gun with him when he left his village and went to Cisteíl.[116] Similarly, when a group of eight men from Tixméuac left their village on November 21—the day Cosgaya's men were ambushed—to go to Cisteíl, three of them took their firearms with them.[117] Tomás Balam, the scribe of Tixméuac, who was among this group of eight, stated that he heard that in all there were fifty-two firearms in Cisteíl,[118] while Leonardo

Bebet, another one of the eight from Tixméuac, said that there were only thirty guns as of Tuesday, November 24.[119] Those without guns armed themselves the best they could. Some had machetes. The most common weapon was the sharpened stake.

Nevertheless, the revolutionaries were not as strong as it seemed. Despite the firearms available, there was a severe shortage of powder and shot, especially the former. Indeed, those armed with guns who survived the battle said that they had no more than one or two rounds at the time of the fighting. According to the above-mentioned Tomás Balam, there was not enough powder to provide even one round for every firearm.[120] It is possible that this severe shortage of powder and shot eased a bit just before the Spaniards attacked, for Mathías Uc, who directly commanded the Maya forces, stated that by November 26, the day of the battle, there was enough powder for four rounds per gun.[121]

But even if there were thirty guns with four rounds each, there would have been a severe shortage of powder. Jacinto Canek tried to come to the rescue. He expanded the supply by adding lime juice and lime rinds to the powder.[122] Fiscal de Doctrina Pedro Chan testified that one of the Indians tried the concoction and found that it worked.[123] Marcos Tec, former Indian magistrate of Cisteíl, claimed that he witnessed the successful firing of a gun loaded with Canek's preparation.[124] Pascual Yupit, a peasant, however, said that when someone asked him if they could try the mixture out on birds, he recommended against it because they were going to need it all for the battle.[125]

Jacinto Canek tried to encourage his followers in other ways as well. According to church warden Pedro Chan, Canek claimed that he would soon be receiving aid from the English and the Miskito Indians.[126] This was not as absurd as might be thought, for the English had a settlement in Belize, and the Miskito Indians had raided into eastern Yucatán just a few years before.[127] To counteract the perceived Spanish superiority in weapons, Canek told his people that they should fear nothing, for on the day of the battle Spanish firearms would shoot not bullets but water. Moreover, he told his forces that Spanish bullets would not kill them. All they had to do was keep their courage and not scream out in fear; therefore if they kept their mouths closed, all would be well, and if they should fall in battle, he would bring them back to life.[128]

The Maya king also thought about what he would do if victorious. According to Pascual Yupit, Canek told his followers that after defeating the Spaniards, he would "cut off the balls of all of them and eat them" ("les cortaría a todos los huevos para que se los coma").[129] The king also spoke about returning to Chikindzonot to take revenge on the curate there, and going to the villages of Tahdzibilchén and Yaxcabá. There, according to second village alcalde Pedro Chan, the king would order the Indian women to leave their houses, taking their kitchenware with them, and then he would set fire to the houses, so that when the Spaniards assembled to put out the fire, they would be killed. Only the church in Yaxcabá would be left standing.[130] Canek also told Mathías Uc, his local military commander, that one day he would go to live in Maní.[131] Since Maní was the capital of the preconquest Maya state ruled by the Xiu dynasty, once again we see suggestions that the Maya knew something about their history.

Finally, we should draw attention to what the revolutionaries did not do. In the cases of revolt discussed in this study, the Maya villagers tried to make use of Spanish institutions to ameliorate the response of the colonial state to their actions. They went to the audiencia in the capital, they asked priests to intercede for them, they even hired lawyers. None of this happened in Yucatán in 1761. The people in Cisteíl made no attempt whatsoever to contact, hold a dialogue, or negotiate with the Spaniards. It is clear why. There was nothing to negotiate. Unlike the Yucatec Maya of the Caste War in the nineteenth century, who tried to negotiate with the non-Indians to resolve their grievances (and whose grievances can be studied as causes of that conflict)[132], the rebels of 1761 wanted independence and separation from the Spaniards. Those were non-negotiable demands from both the Spanish and the Maya points of view. Both sides pursued a policy of winner-take-all. No other outcome was possible. Therefore, the Maya revolutionaries waited for and expected a violent Spanish response. It was not long in coming.

6
The Yucatec Maya in 1761, Part II:
The Counterrevolution

I have come to know that it was only because of the fear of being cruelly punished that they have not risen in rebellion.[1]

—Captain Cristóbal Calderón, Spanish commander

PARTICIPANTS

+ = executed after a trial

Maya

+Jacinto Uc (Canek), Canek King Montezuma
Joseph Chan, teniente, chief political official in Cisteíl
Joaquín Xix, senior Indian magistrate of Cisteíl
+Pedro Chan, junior Indian magistrate of Cisteíl
Pedro Chan, fiscal de doctrina (church warden) of Cisteíl
+Felipe Chan, cantor of Cisteíl, helped kill Captain Cosgaya
Marcos Tec, former Indian magistrate of Cisteíl
Francisco Mex, regidor (councilman) of Cisteíl
Tomás Canul, regidor of Cisteíl
Hilario Canul, topil (law enforcement officer) of Cisteíl
Ignacio Caamal, topil menor (assistant law enforcement officer) of Cisteíl, helped kill Diego Pacheco
Luis Cauich, choirmaster of Cisteíl, refused to recognize Jacinto Uc as king
Nicolás Cauich, beggar-vagabond, convicted of being a sorcerer

156

+Francisco Puc, native of Tiholop, carried messages from Cisteíl to other villages, implicated others in the rebellion

Don Domingo Sima, cacique of Mérida's barrio of San Cristóbal

Pedro Ku, 100-year-old resident of Rancho Nenelá

Don Andrés Ku, cacique of Tiholop

+Pascual Yupit, peasant of Cisteíl

Nicolás Tec, appointed lieutenant governor by Jacinto Canek

+Simón Maas, chapelmaster of Tixméuac

+Leonardo Bebet, church warden of Tixméuac

Augustín Hau, peasant from Tixméuac

Pedro Can, resident of Rancho Nenelá

Nicolás Yah, resident of Rancho Nenelá

Domingo Balam, resident of Estancia Huntulchac, helped kill Captain Cosgaya

+Tomás Balam, scribe of Tixméuac

+Mathías Uc, native of Tiholop, appointed to lead the rebel military forces, helped kill Captain Cosgaya

Melchor Aké, native of Tiholop who spied for the Spaniards and was rewarded for doing so

Antonio May, jailer of Cisteíl, ordered to defend the women the day of the battle

Ambrosio Bec, scribe of Cisteíl, executed without trial

Don Pasqual Puch, former cacique of Tecoh

Miguel Xol, cowboy from an estancia near Tecoh

Magdalena Maas, wife of Tomás Balam, only woman to testify at the trial

Juan Antonio Cuitun, choirmaster of Mérida's barrio of Santiago

Mulato

Diego Cuero, foreman of Estancia Huntulchac

Spaniards

Captain General Joseph Crespo, governor, chief military official, and chief magistrate of the Province of Yucatán

Captain Cristóbal Calderón, Spanish military commander of Sotuta district, crushed the rebellion in Cisteíl

Dr. Juan de Montes, priest of Sotuta

Ignacio Alvarado, militia commander in Yaxcabá

Fernando Moreno, Spanish militia lieutenant in Tixcacaltuyub

Pedro Joseph Lizarraga, teniente de capitán general of the Sierra region

Captain Tiburcio de Cosgaya, captain of Sotuta district, killed in the uprising

Captain Estanislao del Puerto, teniente de capitán general of the Costa region

Juan de Vergara, city councilman of Mérida

Pedro Simón Lizarraga, assistant brigade commander (sargento mayor), son of Pedro Joseph Lizarraga

Francisco Méndez, commander of Spanish forces moving east from the Sierra region

Captain Manuel García Rejón y Pérez, commander of forces to the north of Cisteíl that never participated in the battle

Diego Pacheco, Spanish merchant visiting Cisteíl, killed on Jacinto Canek's orders

Licenciado Sebastián Maldonado, lieutenant governor and legal advisor of the governor

The Spanish Response

The wounded survivors of Captain Cosgaya's command reached Tixcacaltuyub several hours after the ambush in Cisteíl on November 20. That same night Fernando Moreno, the militia lieutenant who had been left behind to hold Tixcacaltuyub, sent a message to Pedro Joseph Lizarraga, the *teniente de capitán general* (captain general's lieutenant, that is, the governor–captain general's military assistant who outranked all the district captains) in Oxkutzcab, a large town to the west, in the heavily populated region called the Sierra. Moreno informed Lizarraga of the death of Captain Cosgaya, reported that the villagers of Cisteíl were armed with "rifles, machetes, and stakes," and requested immediate help because a large part of the command had been wiped out.[2] He also sent a message to Governor–Captain General Joseph Crespo, pointing out critically that Captain Cosgaya, "without waiting for more men, threw himself" on the rebellious village with only twenty men. He also noted that those missing in action were undoubtedly dead.[3] In a subsequent message to the Captain General, Moreno reported that the people of Rancho Nenelá and Estancia Huntulchac had apparently joined the revolt and were thought to be marching on Tixcacaltuyub. He begged for help, for his command was so small that he could not even place sentries.[4] He also sent messages to the local militia leaders in Teabo and Maní, even though those villages (to the west) were under the jurisdictions of other captains.[5]

While Fernando Moreno was trying to shore up Spanish control of Tixcacaltuyub, Father Juan Montes was fleeing that village. He decided that Tixcacaltuyub, with only a handful of soldiers under Lieutenant Moreno present, was too dangerous. He therefore fled to Sotuta (about sixteen kilometers to the northwest), leaving behind not only Moreno and his men but also the assistant pastor (probably the same priest who had barely escaped assassination in Cisteíl). Upon arrival in Sotuta, Montes sent a message to Governor–Captain General Crespo informing him of the disaster in Cisteíl. He thought that Cosgaya's force had numbered fifteen. Montes pointed out that the large village of Tahdziu (to the south of Cisteíl) had apparently also joined the rebellion, and many Indians of the region had fled to the bush in terror to see what would happen next. He also reported that the Indian rebels were said to be marching on Yaxcabá (twelve kilometers northeast of Tixcacaltuyub). The assistant pastor who stayed behind was playing it safe: he kept his horse saddled at all times.[6]

Within a day or two of the death of Captain Cosgaya and his men, all the district military commanders had received news of the revolt. Most of them showed considerable individual initiative by acting even before receiving orders from their commander-in-chief, Governor–Captain General Crespo. They all called up the local militia, posted sentries, and began to confiscate firearms from the Indians. The local official in Izamal (sixty or seventy kilometers north of Cisteíl) was able to dispatch 100 men for the relief of Tixcacaltuyub in less than twenty-four hours.[7] By Monday, November 23— only three days after the ambush of Cosgaya's command—Lieutenant Moreno was able to report that no less than five hundred Spanish militiamen had arrived in Tixcacaltuyub. He sent 100 of them to occupy Tiholop[8], thus blocking the roads to the north and east of Cisteíl. By the next day Moreno's force had grown to 931 men (541 from the Sierra region to the west, 180 from Izamal to the north, and 150 from the local area). Still another 140 were soon to arrive in Tixcacaltuyub from Yaxcabá, to the northeast.[9]

Meanwhile, to the south, more Spanish forces were gathering. They were under the command of Teniente de Capitán General Cristóbal Calderón, the military commander of the Sotuta region. Since Cisteíl was in Calderón's military region, he would be the overall commander of Spanish forces mobilized to fight the Maya under the rule of Jacinto Canek. As already noted, Captain Calderón was away from his post when the uprising broke out; he was carrying out his family business—the sale, on credit, of bulls of indulgence. He never got back to Sotuta at all. Rather, he set up a command post in Peto, nine kilometers south of Tahdziu (which was between twelve and eighteen kilometers south of Cisteíl) in order to be nearer to the troops that were being mobilized in the Sierra region (to the west) by Teniente de Capitán General Pedro Joseph Lizarraga. As Lizarraga sent the militiamen forward, Calderón took charge of them. By November 23 he had moved north and occupied Tahdziu, and found that all the people of the village were gone.[10] The revolution was now boxed in on three sides (north, south, and east).

But the west was still wide open, and the Spaniards had considerable difficulty stopping the flow of people to, and the spread of ideas from, Cisteíl. To be sure, the colonial officials moved fast when it came to weapons. As noted, all the local military commanders started confiscating firearms from the Indians even before they had orders to do so. This happened even in districts as far away as Chancenote (150 kilometers to the northeast) and Hunucmá (120 kilometers to the northwest). Indeed, the local official in the latter rounded up not only guns but also axes, machetes, knives, and lances.[11]

However, it was not always easy to enforce confiscatory policies. From Sotuta it was reported that the government official was unable to round up many guns, for the Indians who owned them usually took them with them to their corn fields[12] (which the Maya still do, in order to hunt for game along the way). It was thus easy to hide weapons once the confiscation order had become known. Furthermore, it was reported that in the villages to the east of Mérida, the provincial capital, the Indians were refusing to obey the order to hand in their guns.[13] By November 26 it had occurred to Pedro Joseph Lizarraga in the Sierra region to prohibit the sale to the Indians of powder and shot, on pain of death.[14] A few days earlier, however, Lizarraga had strongly suggested to Governor–Captain General Crespo that the confiscated guns, which were being used to arm the militia, should never be returned to their former owners, in order to avoid rebellions in the future and that the militiamen be threatened with "grave penalties" should they sell their guns to the Indians.[15]

Probably more effective as means of stopping the rebellion was the detention of the Maya caciques. This was done not only in villages close to the rebellion but also in some far away, and even in Mérida's barrios of San Cristóbal and Santiago.[16] The idea here was that the Indians were unlikely to support the rebellion unless their leaders ordered them to do so. That proved to be true for the most part, but the policy was already too late in Tiholop, Tahdziu, Chacsinkín, Tixméuac, and Rancho Nenelá—all close to the center of the uprising.

The killing of Spaniards by Maya sent a shock wave over the Peninsula. The dominant colonial people must have been frightened, and this fear soon led to exaggeration and rumor. For example, in cases already mentioned above, when Father Juan Montes, the priest in Tixcacaltuyub, reported that the rebels were marching on Yaxcabá, and when Fernando Moreno informed the governor–captain general that the rebels were marching on Tixcacaltuyub, both erred and passed the incorrect information on and misled others. Captain Cristóbal Calderón, the Teniente de Capitán General of the Sotuta region, reported to Pedro Joseph Lizarraga, his counterpart in the Sierra, that he had a heard that a thousand Indians "were to be found in the convent" (church) of Tahdziu. Lizarraga in turn informed the governor–captain general of this, but embellished it by saying that a thousand Indians were not "to be found in" (as Calderón had said) but were "dug in" (atrincherados) the church.[17] Thus the scale of events grew in people's minds, but once again there was no truth in the report. Ignacio Alvarado, the official in Yaxcabá, told the teniente de capitán general in the Costa region (which included Izamal) that he believed the Indians were marching on his village.[18] But as we have seen, this was not true. With rumors flying around, of course, it was difficult for commanders to get a grasp of what was actually happening.

The discovery of correspondence—some of which, as we have seen, may have been apocryphal—greatly added to the fear of the Spaniards. The colonial rulers became jumpy, and responded to the slightest suggestion of abnormality with almost paranoid fear. In Yaxcabá, where officials were afraid they might be attacked, some Indians laughed when told that the captain of Izamal had threatened to kill any Indian who tried to leave that village on horseback. The Spaniards arrested all those who had laughed, and had them punished (although it was not clarified what the crime or the punishment was).[19]

In Izamal, the chief town in the Costa region, Teniente de Capitán General Estanislao del Puerto, the local military commander, reacted quickly to the slightest rumor. Through hearsay he learned that a mulata woman supposedly reported that the cacique had told her while drunk that the number of Spaniards in the region would not be enough to contain the villagers if he ordered them to rebel. She also was said to have been told by the former cacique of Izamal's parcialidad of Pomolché that he was glad to be out of office, for people had shown up and tried to convince his village to join the revolution. An investigation revealed nothing. Del Puerto also found it suspicious when an Indian messenger took way too long to deliver a message to him. Several days later the captain ordered his men to search the houses of suspicious persons and to examine all their correspondence. Again, nothing turned up.[20] But it was with soldierly disdain that he reported the request from city councilman of Mérida Juan de Vergara for a personal bodyguard of twenty-five men.[21]

In Tecoh (thirty kilometers south-southeast of Mérida), the Maya were reported to be becoming disrespectful. One Indian beekeeper caused a commotion by pointing out that the Maya did not need guns to kill Spaniards; rocks would do fine. The local officials wrote on November 25 that examples like this show "the extreme haughtiness of the Indians of the whole district."[22]

Given this situation of fear, it is understandable the one of the most frightened officials in Yucatán was Pedro Joseph Lizarraga, the teniente de capitán general of the Sierra. His jurisdiction touched the western edge of the insurgent zone, and he feared that the insurrections would engulf the Sierra, where the largest Yucatec Maya villages were found. That is why he had recommended, as we have seen, that the firearms confiscated from the Indians not be returned to their owners. When he found out on November 22 that the rebels of Cisteíl were sending envoys into his district, he wrote to the captain general and requested that 200 mulato soldiers in Mérida be sent to the Sierra. He wanted to use them to garrison Peto, a large village to the southeast, for according to Lizarraga, Peto "is where the root of the rebellion was born." Later the same day he sent another message to Governor–Captain General Crespo claiming that the rebellion "could be a deeply dug mine that could cause the whole country to blow up."[23]

Lizarraga also became extremely anxious for Tekax, one of the largest villages in Yucatán, in the heart of the Sierra region. When he thought that the Indians of that village were becoming rebellious, he informed the captain general that he had to garrison Tekax, "which appears to be the frontier of the rebels."[24] Two days later, on November 24, having been informed that Tekax was about to explode in rebellion, he repeated the request for 200 mulato soldiers from the capital, for the villages of his district were anything but calm.[25]

By November 25 Lizarraga was reporting that the rebellion was spreading throughout the whole Province of Yucatán. Many Indians of Tekax, he reported, had disappeared, and he feared that they had joined the rebellion. He feared that the Maya might try to poison the Spaniards, and therefore he suggested that the militia purchase its food exclusively from the province's vecinos, that is, non-Indians.[26] On the next day he sent to Mérida a man thought to be a spy (but who would later be acquitted of the charge).[27]

Lizarraga had to vent his frustration over all that was going on or alleged to be going on in his region and in the province. What with all the militiamen coming and going, orders for mobilization, receipt of military intelligence (not all of good quality), and so on, he informed his commander, Governor–Captain General Crespo, on November 24 that "I find myself extremely confused."[28] He repeated his frustration over the "confusion" in still another message to the captain general that same day.[29] Meanwhile, upon arriving in Tahdziu, a soldier named Manuel Montalvo summed up the situation to the assistant brigade commander, Sargento Mayor Pedro Simón Lizarraga (the son of the confused Lizarraga in Oxkutzcab), by saying that "it is nothing but pure confusion."[30]

Unfortunately, none of Crespo's orders to his subordinates have survived to provide us with evidence of what the governor–captain general was doing to handle the crisis. In fact, the only act that Crespo is known to have taken is to send a company of dragoons (that is, mounted regulars rather than militiamen) to the Yaxcabá area.[31] It is not known whether these dragoons took part in the battle.

Nevertheless, Spanish forces were gathering and closing in. As early as November 22 a detachment under Captain Francisco Méndez moved into Tixméuac, the westernmost village whose people had gone over to the revolution. The Spaniards found that everyone but the cacique and one village councilman had left, taking with them all their food and beasts of burden. All the people were said to have gone to Cisteíl; the Spanish captain emphasized that in the village "neither Indian men nor Indian women are to be found," and that there was not enough food in Tixméuac even for a breakfast. Méndez and his men then headed northeast toward Rancho Nenelá, just west of Cisteíl. There the Spaniards once again found no food and the village deserted, with the exception of two people who seemed to have been left behind. And in both Tixméuac and Nenelá the Spaniards found what for them was eerie: the villagers had killed all their pigs before leaving.[32]

Meanwhile, on November 23 Cristóbal Calderón set out from Tahdziu and headed north toward Cisteíl with sixty men, leaving behind a garrison of 100 men. But upon entering a savannah and approaching within a few miles of the revolutionary village, the column ran into about twenty-five Indians. The Spaniards took nine men and four women prisoner. Questioning of the prisoners revealed that more than 1,500 Indians were in Cisteíl. Calderón decided not to act like Captain Cosgaya and George Armstrong Custer. He moved east to Tiholop and waited for reinforcements. Sometimes the better part of valor is discretion.[33]

The Spaniards also made efforts to gather intelligence about their enemy. A Maya named Melchor Aké, a native of Tiholop, served as a spy. He entered Cisteíl to reconnoiter, and returned to inform Captain Calderón of the best place to make his attack.[34]

It was possibly for this reason that Calderón rejected the opinion of Captain Manuel García Rejón y Pérez, who was in command of the troops assembling in Tixcacaltuyub, just to the north of Cisteíl. García Rejón, whose force of 600 Spaniards was now joined by 200 Maya who were willing to fight on the side of the colonial regime, wanted to attack from the northeast, from the village of Tahdzibilchén.[35] Fernando Moreno, who had been holding Tixcacaltuyub since the beginning of the revolt, also wanted to move on Cisteíl through Tahdzibilchén. Calderón, however, wanted to attack from the east, from Tiholop, because, as he put it, "this is the village that came up with the evil intent and therefore it is necessary to make the attack from it."[36]

Yet there was no road to Cisteíl from Tiholop. By heading west, therefore, Calderón would deliberately lead his troops into the bush. Since he eventually attacked what he knew in advance to be a weak point in the defenses, it is likely that the weak point was on the eastern side of the church that the revolutionaries had fortified. Calderón also had noted the ease with which

Indians came and went from Cisteíl through the savannah, called Sibak, to the south of the village, and therefore he stated his intention to occupy that savannah in order to cut off the revolutionaries' escape route.[37]

Before the attack was made, however, the Spaniards prepared themselves mentally for what they were about to do. They started to dehumanize their enemy. As early as November 23 Calderón had written to Teniente de Capitán General Pedro Joseph Lizarraga of the need to notify Governor–Captain General Crespo "of the whole reality of the intent of these dogs."[38] "Dog" was a word used by Spaniards elsewhere in the Maya region to insult the indigenous people,[39] and it was used in Yucatán too. That same day Calderón again referred to the rebels as "dogs" in a message to Fernando Moreno.[40] By characterizing the Maya revolutionaries as dogs, the Spaniards were getting ready to treat them as less than human.

Still more of the Spaniard's mind was revealed in the next two days in additional messages written by Captain Calderón. In the first, dated November 24 and written to Fernando Moreno, Calderón referred to the rebels as "Indian heretics."[41] The next day, writing to Captain General Crespo, the Spanish field commander reported that he had captured some fifty Indians who were thought to be recruiting people for the rebel side. Calderón informed Crespo that "I am punishing these [prisoners] like the heretics they are in order that they serve as an example to those who are now enlisted in our service, since I have come to know that it was only because of the fear of being cruelly punished that they have not risen in rebellion." Moreover, he went on, it had been necessary to make examples of the prisoners since he entered Tiholop two days previously. He thought this to be necessary because he had found out that the rebel King Montezuma had been preaching to his people that while Spaniards would die, none of the Indians would. He also noted that his sentinels reported smelling copal—a sign of non-Christian rituals.

Finally, returning to the topic of "cruel punishment," Calderón explained his political strategy as follows: "had these people not been treated with such rigor, I would not have made them understand that we would be tracking them down in the wilds and searching them out even in tree trunks and in caves, and in this way I have gotten many to join us, and they remain loyal. These people I treat with love."[42] Salvador del Castillo, who was in Tiholop the day of Calderón's arrival, explained what "rigor" and "cruel punishment" meant: he informed another official that the thirty prisoners in the jail "have been very well whipped."[43]

As the battle drew near, nerves were on edge. In Izamal, Teniente de Capitán General Estanislao del Puerto reported that "I have my boots on to go to Cisteíl,"[44] but not everyone was so eager to fight. Del Puerto was convinced that one of the province's assistant brigade commanders was shirking his duty, and although the latter's father, city councilman of Mérida Juan Joseph de Vergara, claimed that his son was sick with fever, del Puerto thought he was faking and should be sacked.[45] On November 25 del Puerto left Izamal with 150 men, but arrived too late to fight at Cisteíl. Meanwhile, the always nervous Lizarraga reported from Oxkutzcab that his villages were vulnerable to attack because many able-bodied men, far from flocking to the colors, had gone into hiding.[46]

On November 26, or perhaps the night before, a skirmish took place near Estancia Huntulchac between the Maya revolutionaries and militiamen under the command of Manuel García Rejón, the commander in Tixcacaltuyub. The Spaniards, numbering fifty in all, were on their way south to reinforce Tahdziu when they found themselves attacked from two or more sides. The Maya, estimated to number 1,000—surely a gross exaggeration by frightened men—used the estancia corral (which was likely reinforced with stone) for protection as they fired their guns. One Spaniard was killed, two were wounded, and six were missing as a result of the skirmish, which the Spaniards considered an ambush. Nevertheless, Fernando Moreno, who informed Teniente de Capitán General Lizarraga of the attack, was confident of success. Spanish forces in Tixcacaltuyub were said to be "filled with resolve," and would attack from the north the next day, November 27.[47]

By then, however, it was all over. For early on November 26 Calderón led his force of about five hundred men westward from Tiholop and attacked Cisteíl. The Spanish commander made no attempt to hide his presence, for the assault, which began at around three o'clock in the afternoon, was preceded by the sound of the drums and bugles used to encourage the militia troops and frighten the enemy.[48] Calderón said that he decided not to wait for García Rejón's force to join or even to coordinate its movements with his. He estimated the Maya enemy to number some 2,500, including some who were, he thought, well armed with firearms. The Spaniards probably had one or more small cannons, for Fiscal de Doctrina Pedro Chan, a witness, would testify later that the battle began with a cannon shot.[49] However, because of the shortage of powder and shot, the Spanish forces used mostly what were called armas blancas, that is, swords.[50] The battle, then, was waged in the old-fashioned style of the time of the conquest, and like the conquest was decided by cold steel.

As the Spaniards prepared to attack, some of the Maya began to doubt Canek's promise that Spanish guns would shoot water and that no one would die, as long as they kept their mouths closed. Indeed, a number of the people from Tixméuac who testified at the trial—Simón Maas (choirmaster), Leonardo Bebet (church warden), Tomás Balam (scribe), and Augustín Hau—stated that they ran away before the fighting started, and several others probably did the same.[51]

In Cisteíl, the Maya prepared for battle. The women went to the rear and worked in food preparation. Antonio May, the jailer of the village, was put in charge of guarding them (but once things started to go bad, he and they got out fast).[52] Canek himself commanded the defenders and formed his men into squads of five to guard the length of the wall. Each squad had two men armed with firearms and three with sharpened stakes. The idea was that the gunners would shoot from behind the breastworks, and when Spaniards tried to scale the wall, the Maya with stakes would stab them.[53]

Captain Calderón, however, had no intention of attacking all along the wall. He knew where there was a weak spot, identified by his spy, and it was here that he aimed his artillery. One shot from a cannon struck the wall, and four Indians were killed either by the ball or by the splinters of rock that went flying with deadly force. Soon the wall was breached, the Spaniards rushed inside, and the killing began. Some Spaniards were undoubtedly killed or wounded by gunfire, but the Maya did not have enough powder for a pitched battle. Thus it was sword against wooden stake or machete. There was little doubt over the outcome. By the time the fighting was over, some 500 Indians were dead. Spanish losses totaled 40 killed and a large number of wounded. The battle lasted two hours.[54]

Many Maya managed to escape. Antonio May and the women he had been guarding got away. So too did Jacinto Canek and village councilman Francisco Mex, who, "having seen the king break through a side of the wall and head for the bush, followed him"; they heard gunshots until nine o'clock that night.[55] But Spanish patrols were active for a week or more after the battle and captured many important leaders, who were brought to Mérida for trial.

Not all of the Maya who died in Cisteíl perished in battle. Mathías Uc, named by Canek to be the local military commander, and who by his own admissions on the day of the battle fired two rounds from his gun and then ran away, managed to put into his testimony a statement to the effect that the Spaniards had hanged Ambrosio Bec, a scribe of Tiholop, in the plaza of Cisteíl.[56] Uc probably either saw the execution himself or heard about it from other prisoners in the jail. The Spaniards made no attempt to deny it or force him to change his testimony.

The most incontrovertible evidence of executions without trial is provided by the Maya prisoners themselves: not one had been captured in Cisteíl. It is impossible to imagine a battle involving hundreds of combatants in which no one is captured and no one surrenders. The conclusion is inescapable: the Spaniards took no prisoners in Cisteíl; those who were wounded or tried to surrender must have met a fate like that of Ambrosio Bec. The heat of battle, plus the perception of the enemy as dogs and heretics, would have made such executions easier for the Spaniards—and for many other people in history before and after them.

The morning after the battle, the Spaniards searched the village for more Maya. Some were found to be hiding in houses, and they were understandably reluctant to surrender to an enemy that gave no quarter. The Spaniards burned eight houses down with all the people inside. Captain Calderón then left Cisteíl and went to Tixcacaltuyub, where he wrote a report to the governor–captain general informing him of the victory, which he attributed to "the favor of God."[57]

Two days later, on November 29, Calderón reported the capture in Tiholop of eight Maya involved in the uprising. One of them, the scribe of that village, confessed that Canek had told his people before the battle not to move their lips and they would be saved. Calderón was clearly astonished by this, for he informed the governor–captain general that of the 600 or more people killed—the number of dead had increased over what had been stated in his first report—not one person had made a sound.[58] He also reported that many women were hiding in the savannah south of Cisteíl, and since they were dying of hunger or in childbirth, he was trying to convince them to turn themselves in. But he felt that they might be reluctant to do so, for they still believed—or hoped—that King Canek's prophecy about the dead being resuscitated would prove to be true.[59] It did not.

Those who escaped the butchery in Cisteíl did their best to get away. But the Maya are not solitary people—among the prisoners only Canek and a beggar were unmarried—and thus all the fugitive men immediately sought out their wives and children and traveled as family units. Some fugitive families joined others. Don Andrés Ku, the cacique of Tiholop, and Pedro Chan, the fiscal de doctrina of Cisteíl, with their respective families, stuck together.[60] Many tried to hide out on their milpas (corn fields; for the Maya frequently lived temporarily at the more distant agricultural sites).

But finally, many of those who were not from Cisteíl tried to sneak back to their home villages. Pedro Can, originally from Tixcacaltuyub and later a resident of Rancho Nenelá, thought he was safe enough to go back to his original village and even participate in the procession of the Blessed Virgin (for the Feast of the Immaculate Conception was being celebrated). He obviously saw no contradiction between the ceremonies in Cisteíl officiated by Jacinto Canek and those in his home village officiated by Catholic priests. But the Spaniards did. He and many others in the procession were arrested and sent to Mérida for trial.[61] Eventually many people were arrested in or near their homes. Running away to the frontier was apparently not a viable option for everyone.

Nor was everyone as lucky as Pedro Can, who survived both the trial and the sentencing. Tomás Noh Cruz, one of the scribes of Tiholop, apparently tried to get home, got caught, and was lynched in his own village, presumably by Spaniards.[62]

Nevertheless, for the most part Spaniards turned from violence to pacification. They took prisoners and sent them to Mérida for trial. In the capital, Governor–Captain General Joseph Crespo, who as governor of the province was also the chief magistrate as well, tried to move as fast as possible to put the revolution behind him and restore peace in Yucatán.

And in Mérida, the city council gave thanks to God for their victory over the enemies of religion, and in January elected Captain Cristóbal Calderón to be city magistrate of the capital for 1762.[63]

The Trial

It seems to have been a cultural trait of Spaniards in America to blame Indian unrest or rebellion on a small number of evil men who misled the mass of the people. In Yucatán, therefore, once again the colonial authorities tried to track down the ringleaders of conspiracy that never existed. Fortunately for the Maya, the wild goose chase did few of them any harm.

The trial of the prisoners began on November 30, 1761, only four days after the crushing of the revolution in Cisteíl. The proceedings lasted until January 25 of the next year. During this time the authorities were still rounding up suspects and sending them to Mérida for trial. Thus, witnesses were called to testify as they were captured. It was a matter of luck as to when people were arrested, and it was going to be bad luck for those who were the first to be brought in.

The proceedings, held in the city jail, were presided over by Governor–Captain General Joseph Crespo, assisted by the lieutenant governor, Licenciado Sebastián Maldonado, *abogado de los reales consejos* (attorney of the Royal Councils). Since Crespo was a soldier not a lawyer, Maldonado's presence was required to ensure that the chief magistrate adhered to the law. But Maldonado must have intimidated the prisoners somewhat, for it is possible that they found out what Crespo already knew: the lieutenant governor was the brother-in-law of the late Captain Tiburcio de Cosgaya, whose command had been almost wiped out by the revolutionaries in Cisteíl.

Since the judges were intensely interested in proving a conspiracy, they immediately went after those who might reveal information to prove the case. The first witness was Francisco Puc, who had been caught carrying the letters ostensibly written by the leaders in Cisteíl to the caciques of the villages they wanted to join their movement. Puc seems to have decided that the best strategy for him would be to tell the Spaniards whatever they wanted hear. His decision may have been influenced by intimidation or physical punishment already received. Thus Puc gave good details of what had been going on in Cisteíl, the personalities involved, how Captain Cosgaya had been killed, and who had written the letters. He also claimed that the cacique of Mérida's barrio of San Cristóbal was involved, and identified a fellow prisoner, who he thought was the foreman of the Estancia Huntulchac, as one of the people who had killed Cosgaya.[64] This fitted in well with what the Spaniards wanted to believe.

The judges then called as a witness Don Pasqual Puch, former cacique of Tecoh. He was called because a Spaniard named Antonio Argaíz informed the court that Puch had told him back in March that some Indians from Peto— a village not far from Cisteíl—were excited about the arrival of the *xtol*, who was thought to be acting as the ambassador of persons whom Argaíz referred to as "kinglets" (*reyesuelos*).[65] In modern times in the region, "xtol" refers to a kind of jokester or "ugly king" of Carnaval (the period of celebratory excess before Lent) who is allowed to criticize the established authorities of the village.[66] The Spaniards may not have known what the xtol was, but the appearance in the region months before of alleged ambassadors from a king would have meant a long-existing plan to subvert the province. The judges clearly thought that they were on the track of a conspiracy.

Puch's testimony did not support the Spanish theory of a conspiracy. The former cacique of Tecoh stated that about a year before, he had had a conversation with the cacique of Dzonotchel (whose name he did not know), who had informed him that an estancia cowboy had told him that the xtol had arrived carrying letters for the caciques. Puch understood the xtol to be a kind of ambassador, but stated that neither he nor the cacique of Dzonotchel believed what the cowboy had said. He did mention the incident to two Spaniards, but they did not believe it either, "knowing the Indians' fibs." Puch also denied that any kind of conspiracy had been afoot in the area around his village of Tecoh; had there been one, he would have known, "because the [current] cacique and leaders consult him and have consulted him about all decisions to be made regarding the exercise of their duties."[67]

Still, the Spaniards pursued their xtol. The sixth witness called, Miguel Xol, a cowboy from an estancia near Tecoh, also had information on the matter. Xol testified that about a half a year before, Don Manuel Collí, the cacique of Dzonotchel, and two other people had passed by his estancia on their way to Mérida to sell bananas. They had told him that the xtol had been born. The witness "understood this to mean a dance . . . , with which the native Indians of the Province entertain themselves." (This demonstrates a connection to Carnaval, which is further suggested by references to the xtol appearing in March or April, the time when Carnaval takes place.) Xol explained that the cacique of Dzonotchel was just telling stories, and when someone took him seriously, he laughed and said something to the effect of "I've been pulling your leg."[68] The judges decided that the xtol was a wild goose not worth chasing. They dropped the matter entirely and let the former cacique of Tecoh go free.

The third witness called was Diego Cuero (or Quero, as the name was written in the records), a mulato who was the foreman of Estancia Huntulchac. He was the person arrested as a spy by Pedro José Lizarraga in the Sierra region, and the first witness had identified him as one of the killers of Captain Cosgaya. Cuero was accused not only of killing the captain but also of having gone to Tixméuac to get the people of the village to join the revolution. With hindsight, one suspects that the prisoner's race may have led the Spaniards to want to convict him even more than the Indians, and certainly his case looked bleak. But Cuero was undaunted and kept his head. He stated that he could not possibly have been involved in the killing of Cosgaya because he was at his estancia at the time in the company of three Spaniards, who would testify in his behalf. The judges thought it strange that when Cuero found out about the rebellion he went not to the nearby Tixcacaltuyub to report the news but rather to the more distant Tekax, but the prisoner pointed out that there were no Spanish militiamen in Tixcacaltuyub (except for the men of one Spanish family), while there were many more in Tekax. Finally, Cuero categorically denied that he had even been in Cisteíl or Tixméuac, and stated that the testimony against him was false.[69]

The judges tested Cuero's testimony by calling the Spaniards mentioned by the prisoner to testify. They were the seventh, ninth, and tenth witnesses who appeared, and they all confirmed the prisoner's alibi.[70] So too did the testimony of Magdalena Maas, wife of Tomás Balam, and that of still another Spaniard who was the nineteenth witness.[71] Several days later the judges acquitted Cuero and set him free. One more wild goose had gotten away.

But still there was the testimony against the cacique of Mérida's barrio of San Cristóbal, and so the judges called the cacique—Don Domingo Sima— to testify as the fourth witness. Interestingly, Sima, like all the Maya, required an interpreter to understand the questions and provide his answers. Being an urban resident of a Spanish city thus did not ensure the Hispanicization of the indigenous population, although it is possible that the cacique of San Cristóbal knew more Spanish than he let on. Sima and the other caciques of the capital's barrios had been locked up by order of the governor–captain general since November 23, and Sima said that he did not know why. Asked how he could say that when there was evidence that he had been in Cisteíl before the revolt, Sima pointed out that he had gone there in February 1760—well before November 1761—to help collect the tribute debts owed by the villagers. In other words, he went there in the service of the Spanish authorities. He also denied having received any letter inviting him to join a conspiracy, and stated that he had not even met any of the people mentioned by first witness Francisco Puc. He attributed Puc's testimony against him to the desire to put the blame on others to save his skin. Asked why he had failed to cooperate with the order to turn in his barrio's guns, he denied the charge, noting that he had turned in his own gun as well as a list of all people who owned firearms.[72]

Beating a dead horse, the judges called Juan Antonio Cuitun, choirmaster of Mérida's barrio of Santiago, as the fifth witness. He had been arrested for refusing to hand over three shotguns, but he defended himself by stating that he owned only one, which he had recently sold to a Spaniard. The judges then charged him with trying to foment revolution in Santiago, "sowing the false word that the time had arrived when the prophecy of the Chilambalam [sic] would be fulfilled, that it was time for the Spaniards to be killed."[73] (This of course proves that the Spaniards knew about the Chilam Balam.) But Cuitun denied that he was involved in any conspiracy, and claimed that he had never received or sent any letter on the matter and had not served as the voice of the prophecies. Asked why he had said that the Spaniards would have to kill him to take his guns away, he denied saying any such thing, as the people who were present could testify. Finally, Cuitun insisted that he was a good Christian and loyal vassal of His Majesty. Also, unlike nearly all the other Maya witnesses called, he signed his statement, demonstrating some degree of literacy.[74]

Shortly afterward, the choirmaster of Santiago, the cacique of San Cristóbal, and all the other caciques of the barrios of Mérida were freed. Also eventually let go was Pedro Ku, from Rancho Nenelá. When questioned, Ku declared that he had no profession. He was, after all, more than one hundred years old! He was also married. Ku was accused of being one of the prophets who had served Canek. He denied the charge, saying "How could it be him, when he wasn't even a resident of Cisteíl?" He also claimed to know nothing about anything that took place, and would not estimate how many people from Rancho Nenelá had joined the revolution. Another witness said that he did not see Ku in Cisteíl. The judges apparently found that witness and Ku himself to be credible, and they dropped charges.[75]

Consequently, what we see is a system of criminal justice that, while certainly bent on revenge, was bound somewhat by its own laws to let people defend themselves, and defend themselves they did. The Spaniards in turn were unwilling to punish everyone who was innocent. The whole legal process, then, far from being a "kangaroo court," was like the colonial system itself: something that was negotiated and contested.

Because of all the wild geese that were chased, it was not until December 4, the fifth day of the trial, that the judges started to focus on what could be proved. On that day they called Tomás Balam, the scribe of Tixméuac, to testify. Then, after the witnesses who confirmed the alibi of Diego Cuero (the foreman of Estancia Huntulchac accused of fomenting revolution in Tixméuac and killing Captain Cosgaya), the judges called to the stand the prisoners whose testimony, like that of Balam, shed light on what had actually happened. Most of those questioned were from Tixméuac. The sixteenth witness was Magdalena Maas, wife of Tomás Balam. She was the only woman to testify at the trial and one of the very few Maya women called to testify in the revolts discussed in this book. But her statement did not help her husband. Rather, she confirmed Cuero's testimony,[76] and, as noted, the foreman of Estancia Huntulchac was freed shortly thereafter.

By the time the judges finally acquitted Diego Cuero, they had questioned twenty-one witnesses, seven of whom would soon be executed. The twenty-second witness, called on December 8, was the king himself, Jacinto Uc, Canek King Montezuma. This must have been the dramatic high point of the trial. Uc stated that he had been captured going to Tiholop on November 30, four days after the battle and the very day the trial started in Mérida.

One can only speculate as to Uc's mental condition at the time. He probably had been beaten, for the Spaniards worked on the presumption of guilt. We will never know the factors that influenced his testimony. He was a rather talkative witness, and gave evidence that tended to confirm much of what others had said about him. He admitted giving orders to kill Diego Pacheco, the traveling merchant, but denied ordering anyone to kill Captain Cosgaya and his men. He did, however, state that the person who would know was the teniente of Cisteíl, "a one-eyed Indian who is here [in jail] as a prisoner." When asked "what witchcraft did he use to trick the Indians into obeying him as King," Jacinto Canek answered "that he did not make use of any witchcraft, because he does not use it." He also denied appointing anyone to office or hanging Captain Cosgaya's arm behind him like a tail. The questioning was so detailed that it apparently took all of December 8 and half of December 9.[77]

Following Jacinto Uc—Canek—there appeared the last of those who would die: Pedro Chan, the junior Indian magistrate of Cisteíl. He also proved talkative, and his testimony took up the rest of December 9 and all of December 10. On December 11 the judges decided to start passing sentences. This decision was made even though there were still many more people who would be called to testify, and there were even more who were prisoners but would not be called.

Why was it thought necessary to act so quickly, only eleven days after the proceedings had begun and with so much more to do? The judges tell us why in their sentence: "It is necessary to carry out prompt exemplary punishment of the native people at this moment for the eventual contentment [of the Province]."[78] In short, punishment was meted out to some, but not all, the Maya prisoners in order to hurry the pacification of Yucatán.

The judges condemned the following nine men to death.

- Jacinto Uc, Canek;
- Francisco Puc (caught carrying the subversive messages);
- Tomás Balam, scribe of Tixméuac (admitted going to Cisteíl with a firearm);
- Simón Maas, chapelmaster of Tixméuac (admitted going to Cisteíl with a firearm);
- Leonardo Bebet, church warden of Tixméuac (admitted going to Cisteíl with a firearm);
- Mathías Uc, of Tiholop (appointed local commander of the revolutionary forces in Cisteíl; participated in the killing of Captain Cosgaya and his men);
- Felipe Chan, cantor of Cisteíl (participated in the killing of Captain Cosgaya and his men);
- Pasqual Yupit (lied under oath in order to minimize his role in what happened in Cisteíl);
- Pedro Chan, junior Indian magistrate of Cisteíl.

The reasons for killing Jacinto Uc/Canek are obvious. Francisco Puc would die not only because he was caught with the subversive messages but also because he lied under oath and falsely accused Diego Cuero, the foreman of Estanicia Huntulchac, and Don Domingo Sima, the cacique of the barrio of San Cristóbal. Of the eight men from Tixméuac who together went to Cisteíl, only the three who took their guns with them were to be executed. (Leonardo Bebet had tried to say that he took his shotgun in order to hunt along the way, but the judges evidently did not believe him.) Those known to have participated in the killing of Cosgaya were condemned to death. Pasqual Yupit got caught lying under oath twice, which undermined his attempts to say that he had nothing to do with killing either Diego Pacheco or Captain Cosgaya, even though he witnessed both events. Finally, Pedro Chan would die because as one of the magistrates of Cisteíl—a person in authority—

he was expected to keep the people loyal to the king of Spain, when in fact he had sanctioned Canek's assumption of power.

All but Jacinto Canek were to be hanged. Then, their heads and hands were to be cut off and exhibited on posts in their home villages. The bodies were to be quartered and strung up on posts or trees at the entrances to the city of Mérida.

Special punishment was reserved for Jacinto Canek. He was to die "being torn apart by pincers, breaking the arms and legs roughly, placed in a cage in the public plaza of this city [of Mérida], and after dying naturally after being in the cage three hours, so that everyone can see him, his body will be burned, and his ashes scattered to the wind."

The prisoners were notified of the sentences. Jacinto Uc/Canek was taken to the chapel of the jail to be in the company of two priests, one of whom was a Jesuit. Presumably he was to confess his sins to prepare for the life hereafter.[79]

On December 14, 1761, the sentence of Jacinto Canek was carried out.

The next day more sentences were handed down on 115 prisoners. The judges did not explain why it was unnecessary to question any of them. The presumption was clearly that they were guilty, that the time and expense of interviewing them would not be worth the effort, and that it was best to clear the jail as fast as possible. Such a sentence was not unprecedented, however, for we have already seen similar punishment without trial meted out to people of Tecpán and Santa Lucía Utatlán. From the Spanish point of view this represented a kind of plea bargaining, for the sentences were lighter than those given to those interrogated and found guilty. In this case, the 115 men were sentenced to 200 lashes, the mutilation of one ear, and six years of forced labor, with no salary, for His Majesty wherever it was found to be suitable. Until that location was determined, the men were to return to their home villages, register their names, and stay there.[80]

(One of the unsolved mysteries of the uprising is the fate of Joseph Chan, the teniente of Cisteíl. One witness testified that Chan was wounded in the arm during the battle,[81] and Jacinto Canek said at the trial that the teniente was the one-eyed man in jail,[82] but no Joseph Chan was ever called to testify or was among the 115 men sentenced on December 15. Possible explanations include: Canek was mistaken or his testimony was misunderstood; Joseph Chan died or committed suicide in jail; he died in Cisteíl during or after the battle; he escaped and was never caught.)

On December 16 Francisco Puc appeared before the judges and confessed to having carried the subversive letters in question. He also admitted to bearing false witness against the cacique of the barrio of San Cristóbal and begged the latter's forgiveness. The cacique forgave him, and the two embraced.[83]

Later in the day the eight remaining condemned men were led out of jail two by two, taken to the scaffold, and hanged by the hangman, Antonio Montes, a black man. The bodies remained hanging until 2:30 in the afternoon, when the rest of the sentence was carried out.[84]

But the trial was by no means over. Patrols continued to bring in suspects, many of whom had been deeply implicated in the revolution. Therefore, on December 29 the proceedings began again in earnest. The judges acquired a great deal of additional information, especially from the testimony of Joaquín Xix (Cisteíl's alcalde de mesón, that is, the official in charge of the village hall), Don Andrés Ku (cacique of Tiholop), Francisco Mex (councilman of Cisteíl), Marcos Tec (former Indian magistrate of Cisteíl), Don Ambrosio Huchim (cacique of Tahdziu), and Pedro Chan (church warden of Cisteíl). The latter in fact gave the longest testimony of the entire trial.

On January 3 the judges interrupted the questioning of witnesses to reward Luis Cauich, the choirmaster of Cisteíl who had refused to recognize Jacinto Uc as king and had run to alert the Spaniards of what was going on. Cauich was granted the status of hidalgo, that is, noble, which would thereafter be hereditary in his family.[85] Five days later the judges recognized the contributions of five other Indians. Their actions were duly certified by Captain Cristóbal Calderón. Juan Baptista Caamal and Juan Caamal, from Tihosuco, had armed a body of Maya to fight on the Spanish side. Manuel and Julián Pacheco, alias Ciau (apparently their real Maya surname), had served as treasurer and soldier, respectively, in the column led by Captain Cosgaya and had escaped and spread the alarm. Governor–Captain General Crespo granted all these men and their families tax exemption for life. The last Maya honored was Melchor Aké, the spy who had sneaked into Cisteíl and returned with valuable information about the rebel defenses. He was rewarded with the grant of hereditary hidalgo status.[86]

On January 13 the judges called to testify the man who proved to be the final witness. This was Nicolás Cauich, the beggar who claimed to know Canek from before the events in Cisteíl.[87] His testimony certainly fascinated the judges, for although Cauich said nothing about the revolution, he said a lot about what the Spaniards called witchcraft and diabolism. He testified that he met Jacinto Uc in Chikindzonot, where the latter cast a spell on him that caused him to itch all over. This caused Cauich to renounce "God and His Blessed Mother." Uc kept his professional equipment in a satchel, from which he took out whatever he needed.

Cauich then accompanied Jacinto Uc to the village of Ekpedz and then to the wilds of the south, to a hill called Kansut. Although this was said to be thirty leagues (between 210 and 265 kilometers) from Ekpedz, according to Cauich they made the journey in only three hours. Arriving at the hill, "he found a black man with horns and more than one hundred Indians around him taking on the forms of cats, dogs, pigs, birds, pumas, and other things." Cauich then asked to be admitted to their "guild" (gremio), and the black man said, "Be welcome, I receive you with all my heart. I knew you were coming." Cauich was told "not to believe in God or His Blessed Mother, but only in him, the True One."

After two days, the people at the hill broke up and went their separate ways. Cauich returned to Ekpedz, where once again he was attacked by an itching all over his body. Once again he renounced "God and His Blessed Mother." A young man appeared before him and together they "flew" back to the hill. This time he saw "the Devil with his horns, and his tail tied into a hairpiece [tucha]," and he found the others in the same forms as before, except for Canek, who was himself. Canek told him, "I am the True God, I have come to suffer for all the Indians, and just as we have gathered here, so we will gather together in Cisteíl, and from there [go on] to Mérida to wage war on the Spaniards for Christmas Eve, because I am King Montezuma."

Told by the assembled people to return in two days, Cauich did as instructed. This time, he said, "he found Canek and the others, and he was giving out human flesh to the others for supper, and to him they gave a wrist." But when he refused to eat it, they gave him 100 lashes and left him alone on the hill. Cauich then started back to the northern part of the Peninsula. It took him five days to reach the village of Hotzuc Tepich, and he never saw Canek again until he saw him arrested in Tiholop (after the revolution). The Spaniards detained Cauich and sent him and Canek as prisoners to Mérida for trial. Now at the end of his lengthy testimony, the judges asked him how he could deny "God and His Blessed Mother" with so little fear of God, to which Cauich responded that he had already repented and begged to be admitted once more to the "guild of Holy Mother the Church."

Nowhere in the testimony, except at the very end, did the judges interrupt him by asking leading questions. They must have just listened. Since they undoubtedly believed in the Devil as well as in God, we can only speculate as to what they believed in the testimony of Nicolás Cauich. Perhaps they found it bizarre. But for the Maya, not all of Cauich's testimony would have been unbelievable. For when he described how the assembled shamans changed themselves into the shapes of animals, he was manifesting his belief in nagualism. This is widespread throughout most, and perhaps all, of Mesoamerica among non-Maya as well as Maya people. According to this belief, each human at birth is connected to a particular animal, and the person's fate is intimately related to that of the animal. Shamans, because of their special powers, had the ability to transform themselves into their nagual counterpart of the animal world. Priests writing in Yucatán in the late eighteenth century reported that their Maya parishioners believed in nagualism. Many Maya therefore would have believed Cauich's account of "more than 100 Indians around him taking on the forms of cats, dogs, pigs, birds, pumas, and other things."

On January 22, 1762, Lieutenant Governor Licenciado Sebastián Maldonado drew up the sentence for 134 prisoners.[88] Once again, very few of them had been questioned under oath; their guilt was either assumed or "known" in some other way. Perhaps some chose not to defend themselves in order to avoid the ordeal of interrogation under oath and, presumably, the threat of greater punishment. Maldonado sentenced to death Don Andrés Ku (cacique of Tiholop), Marcos Tec (former Indian magistrate of Cisteíl), Nicolás Tec (supposedly appointed by Canek to be second-in-command to Governor–Captain General Joseph Chan), Pedro Chan (church warden of Cisteíl), Joaquín Xix (alcalde de mesón of Cisteíl), and Domingo Balam (one of several who personally killed Captain Cosgaya). These men, declared to be "the principal leaders of the uprising," would be paraded through the streets of Mérida with a town crier announcing their crimes, and then they would be taken to the main plaza, where they would be hanged. The bodies were then to be quartered and placed along the public roads of the city, while their heads and hands would be displayed in their home villages.

Nine others were sentenced to 200 lashes and eight years of penal servitude in the shipyards of Havana (which at the time were building some of the largest and best warships in the world). Ten more individuals, as well as all the prisoners from Cisteíl and Tahdziu, and all those from Tiholop who went to Cisteíl, were to be given 200 lashes, the mutilation of both ears, and six years of forced labor somewhere in Yucatán, to be designated later. The rest were given sentences of six years of forced labor. Twenty-four prisoners were acquitted, while Nicolás Cauich, declared to be a sorcerer (brujo), was to be given 200 lashes and perpetual confinement and servitude in a Franciscan convent.

All that remained was for Governor–Captain General Joseph Crespo to sign the document and the sentences would have been carried out. But the governor declined to do so. Crespo pointed out that he, not Lieutenant Governor Maldonado, was the superior judge in the case, and that he was allowed to disagree with his legal advisor if he thought it appropriate to do so. In this case, he did. He noted that many Indians had died in Cisteíl, nine more had been executed, and many more had been whipped and suffered the mutilation of an ear, "something never seen in the Province." If more terror were used, he feared that the Maya would be so afraid that "they would abandon their villages and live as fugitives in the wild." His job, after all, was to get the people to accept Spanish rule as peacefully as possible. Finally, he noted that Maldonado could not legally be a judge in the case anyway, because he was the brother-in-law of Captain Cosgaya.

With Lieutenant Governor Maldonado thus put in his place, Crespo proceeded to impose his own judgment. The six individuals whom the legal advisor had wanted executed were sentenced to 200 lashes and eight years of forced labor in Havana. Six others were given 100 lashes and six years of forced labor in the Presidio of Bacalar (near the Caribbean coast, close to the modern border with Belize). All the others were given sentences of either 200 lashes and six years of forced labor somewhere in the province, 100 lashes, or fifty lashes and two years of forced labor. All but those sent to Havana were to return to their villages until the governor decided on how to use their labor. Many prisoners, mostly from Rancho Nenelá, were acquitted and freed. Nicolás Cauich was declared to be a "deceitful sorcerer" (although it was not specified whom he had tried to deceive, the judges or the Maya), but no sentence was mentioned.[89]

Thus Governor–Captain General Crespo, walking a fine line between repression and pacification, chose to end the killing. Still, since nine people had been executed in gruesome fashion and hundreds of people had been flogged and had an ear cut off, Crespo can hardly be called lenient. Yet that is exactly what some Spaniards called him. Later in the year two priests who were members of the Cathedral Chapter of Mérida wrote to the king complaining that not enough punishment had been given out, and that many guilty rebels were still at large. As a result, they claimed, the rebellion was not over, and there were signs of unrest in the villages of Hoctún (near Izamal) and Chemax (east of Valladolid).[90] Neither of these villages, however, had been in the slightest bit involved in the events in Cisteíl in November of the previous year.

Yet calmer heads prevailed, and the bloodthirsty priests did not get their way. The Maya once again grudgingly accepted their colonial burden and went on with life. No further serious Maya uprisings took place in Yucatán until the Caste War of the mid-nineteenth century.

Maya Cultural Revitalization

The "Rebellion of Jacinto Canek," as the events in 1761 are known in Yucatán, was in fact a revolution, albeit an unsuccessful one. The revolutionaries asserted their right to rule themselves and have their own Maya king as their ruler. This was in reality an assertion of popular sovereignty in the face of an absolutist and foreign monarchy. But since the movement did not spread far from Cisteíl, and since the colonial authorities acted quickly and decisively, it was crushed. The Spaniards in the other revolts in this study also used force to regain control but did not have to use violence to accomplish it. What differed in Yucatán was the extent of the threat to Spanish rule, for the revolutionaries in Cisteíl wanted to eliminate Spanish rule entirely. The nature of the threat thus determined the nature of the response. When the threat was absolute, so too was the response.

The events of 1761 in Yucatán were also manifestations of a revitalization movement. Anthony F.C. Wallace has defined this as "a deliberate, organized, conscious effort by members of a society to construct a more satisfying culture."[91] The existing culture was dissatisfying to the Maya because colonialism had removed them from high positions of political and religious power and authority. Jacinto Canek incarnated the desire of the Maya to control their political system by having one of their members serve as king and to control their religious structure by investing their king with priestly powers to communicate with the supernatural world.

Moreover, as is consistent with many other revitalization movements, the form of cultural restructuring formulated during the uprising was first conceived by a single individual—Jacinto Uc—whose personal history of deviation from "normal" social behavior suggests that he was a shaman. The man who became Canek wandered about as a healer who engaged in obscure rituals beyond the pale of colonial society. He claimed to be the majordomo of Jesus Christ, and he convinced local Maya religious and political leaders that he really was the king whose arrival from the east was long awaited. Canek's ability to convince and inspire through his command of the art of healing and his personification of long-desired political goals thus places him among other indigenous shamans, such as Sitting Bull and Geronimo, who likewise succeeded, albeit only temporarily, in rolling back the wave of European colonialism and colonization in America.

Once the movement took hold in Cisteíl, cultural revitalization took place. Adherents engaged in rituals suggestive of non-Christian ceremonies and came to believe that a Maya-controlled supernatural world would protect them from Spanish guns. Canek appointed people—in fact, the already existing local political elite, for there was none at a higher level—to fill the highest levels of the civil and religious hierarchies. In effect, the Maya were recreating a complete social structure by occupying the highest political and religious positions denied to them after the imposition of colonialism. And the charismatic leader claimed to be one of the traditional monarchs of native history.

At the same time, the uprising was a nativistic movement. It intended to overthrow the colonial regime, and many adherents believed that the movement would eliminate the Spaniards altogether. Canek himself, however, apparently said that Spanish women would be spared and would be made to intermarry with Maya men. Those who joined the movement were also called upon to kill specific animals of Spanish origin—pigs. Many did so despite the detrimental effects this must have had on the native economy.

Nevertheless, the movement also chose to keep certain elements of foreign culture that accompanied colonialism. Pigs may have been killed, but the other animals of Spanish origin—chickens, horses, and cattle—were not. Bananas, also of foreign origin, were even perceived as a semi-luxury, and were often included among the gifts offered to Canek. Most important, aspects of Christianity were retained, presumably because they were appreciated or needed. The cults of the Virgin Mary and of the saints were used to reinforce and legitimize the movement. Canek supposedly placed the Virgin's crown on his own head; the Maya used the buildings, ritualistic paraphernalia —priestly vestments, the chalice, holy oils, the rosary—and sacraments of Catholicism for their own ceremonies. Canek himself proclaimed the continued legitimacy of the bulls of indulgence of the Santa Cruzada.

The revolution of 1761 left behind documentation that, while flawed, provides insight into Maya behavior and cultural imperatives. Over and over again, the prisoners claimed to have been deceived or bewitched by Canek, or to have simply followed the orders given them by legitimate authority. The prisoners also demonstrated how far removed they were from the Spanish world when it came to understanding the empire to which they belonged and the monarch who ruled them. Examples of this include the following:

Tomás Balam said he thought that he had not shown disloyalty to the king of Spain "because it appeared to him to be compatible that he reign at the same time as Canek."[92]

Gerónimo Tec, a sixteen-year-old, said, regarding his participation in the rebellion, that "as a boy, which he is, he did not know what he did, and curiosity made him follow the others, who fooled him, for he never had the wish to go against anyone."[93]

Pedro Chan, the junior Indian magistrate, said that "he knows the crime he has committed, and the punishment he deserves for having done it, only that he was fooled by the King Jacinto."[94]

Eugenio Can, one of those who personally killed Captain Cosgaya, said that he knew what his crime was but "the Devil tricked him."[95]

Domingo Balam, another one of those who personally killed Cosgaya, knew what his crime was "but his understanding was blocked."[96]

Juan Tomás Ku, son of cacique Don Andrés Ku of Tiholop, explained his action by saying that he was told by his father to obey the king.[97]

Don Andrés Ku, cacique of Tiholop, said he did what Canek told him "because of fear of the Indian King."[98]

Hilario Canul, one of those who killed Diego Pacheco, said that he was just following orders, and that everyone else was too.[99]

Ignacio Caamal, sixteen years old, another one of those who killed Pacheco, said he did it because he was simply obeying the orders of his superiors.[100]

Gregorio Ek, a thirty-five-year-old agriculturalist who fought with a sharpened stake against the Spaniards at the big battle, said that "he knows the crime he has committed, but because he is of limited understanding he did it and for that reason he asks the pardon of God Our Lord."[101]

Tomás Canul, councilman of Cisteíl, said he participated in the rebellion because he was "fooled."[102]

Nicolás Yah, senior Indian magistrate of Rancho Nenelá, said that he participated because "he lost his reason."[103]

Pedro Chan, the oft-cited church warden of Cisteíl, said he was involved as a result of "the tricks of the Devil."[104]

Agustín Cuxim, teniente (assistant to the cacique) of Tiholop, blamed his actions on "the Devil from Cisteíl."[105]

Marcos Tec, former Indian magistrate of Cisteíl, said that he followed "Canek King Montezuma" until he saw that many Indians were dying in battle, at which point "he knew that the king had tricked them."[106]

Marcos Sulu, a twenty-year-old from Cisteíl, said that a few days after the arrival of Jacinto Uc, his whole village rebelled, but he did not know why, and when asked how he could believe that an Indian could be the king, he responded that "he as a boy followed his leaders, who obeyed the Devil King Canek."[107]

Don Ambrosio Huchim, the cacique of Tahdziu, whose village went over en masse to the revolution, when asked how he could believe that an Indian could be the king when "he was obligated to know that he had no king except that of Spain," answered that "he had heard that a King Montezuma would come, and so he believed it." Moreover, "he does not know that there is a king of Spain, and that there is no king except God, and that he did not commit any crime."[108]

Don Lorenzo Puc, one of the two caciques of Tahdzibilchén, when caught lying about his role in the events of 1761 and when asked if he knew the penalty for rebellion against religion, answered "that he did these things out of fear, and as an Indian of limited [intelligence]."[109]

Don Silvestre Cauich, the other cacique of Tahdzibilchén, explained his actions by saying that "as an ignorant Indian, he erred, which is not surprising, because others who have studied and have understanding also err."[110]

Some of these statements could be simply Maya equivalents of "the Devil made me do it." Nevertheless, the testimony taken as a whole demonstrates a kind of fatalistic view of the role of the individual in society. Few Maya seem to have exercised free will. Rather, they were all bound up in a destiny that required them to obey their parents, obey their leaders, and obey their cultural imperatives. They believed, therefore, in the cyclical movement of history and in the eventual return of a king whose arrival was expected. When an individual with strange powers appeared and claimed to be that king, many Maya leaders believed him, and the people followed their leaders. Jacinto Uc's claim seemed no more unbelievable than that of a European king whom no one knew and who was from a land no one had seen. What seemed preposterous to the Spaniards was not to the Maya.

Some Maya prisoners expressed regret for their actions during the events of 1761. But under the circumstances it was to their advantage to do so. Most do not seem to have believed that they had committed heinous crimes, and one suspects that their biggest regret is that they failed, got caught, and would be punished. And as was usually the case in the colonial world, some tried to mitigate their punishment by claiming to be "Indians," that is, stupid or of limited intelligence. And as was usual, it helped, because the Spaniards wanted to hear it: such statements helped justify in their minds their right to rule over a people who, like colonized people all over the world, did not want them there.

7

Internal Conflict and the Moral Polity:
Nebaj, 1768

That is the role they play in the comedy, and they play the role
of Indian very well.

—Investigating Judge Francisco Antonio Aldama y Guevara[1]

PARTICIPANTS

Maya

Miguel Matón, administrator of the cofradía of Our Lady of the Rosary, leader of the political faction opposed to the priest
Jacinto Matón, son of Miguel
Domingo Matón, brother of Miguel
Clemente Ramírez, leader of the pro-priest political faction, elected first magistrate in disputed election
Miguel Laynez, other leader of the pro-priest faction, elected second magistrate in disputed election
Pablo Sánchez, elected first magistrate by the anti-priest faction
Miguel Bernardo, elected second magistrate by the anti-priest faction
Francisco Guzmán, scribe of Nebaj
Diego Sánchez, church warden of Nebaj
Francisco de Paz, member of the anti-priest faction
Pedro Cobo, leader of the anti-priest faction
Jacinto Brito, leader of the anti-priest faction
Pedro de León, member of the anti-priest faction

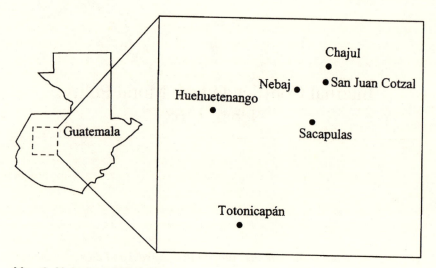

Map 6 Nebaj and Vicinity

Spaniards

Friar Eusebio Guerra, parish priest of Nebaj
Friar Antonio Toledo, priest who replaced Fr. Guerra
Juan Bacaro, alcalde mayor of the district of Huehuetenango-Totonicapán
Felipe Romana, attorney general (fiscal) of the audiencia
Pedro de Salazar, president and captain general of the audiencia
Carlos Joseph Guillén, assistant to the alcalde mayor in Huehuetenango
Dr. Francisco Vidaurre, the audiencia's advocate of the poor
Francisco Antonio Aldama y Guevara, corregidor of Quezaltenango, investigating judge in the case of the rebellion in Nebaj

Ladinos

Pedro Quezada, translator of a presidential dispatch, later a fugitive, husband of Petrona Matón

One of the most important ways in which the Maya adapted to colonialism was through religion. The Catholic Church, while trying to change fundamentally the indigenous people's understanding of the world, allowed the Indians some local autonomy by sanctioning the institutions known as *cofradías*, that is, religious brotherhoods devoted to the adoration of a particular saint. The Maya largely ran these themselves, and made them into important features of local religious devotion free from direct supervision by the Catholic clergy. Cofradías, therefore, signified considerable religious autonomy. Yet just as the Spaniards sometimes broke the agreement not to interfere with indigenous political autonomy and thereby violated the moral polity, so too did they sometimes interfere with the brotherhoods and thereby violate religious autonomy and what might be called the moral religiosity of the Maya, that is, the agreed-upon right to act on their own within a limited religious sphere.

But politics and religion often overlap, as they did in the village of Nebaj, in the chilly highlands of Guatemala, in 1768. There, the priest's decision to interfere with the management of the village cofradías necessitated intervention in local politics as well. The result was the violation of both the moral polity and the moral religiosity. The Maya response was not long in coming.

The People at the End of the Earth

Perhaps the most Indian part of modern Latin America is the mountainous region known as the Cuchumatán Highlands, located to the northwest of modern Guatemala City. The chilly environment permitted many crops to be grown but is not as propitious for agriculture as most of the rest of Guatemala, and the extremely mountainous terrain resulted in roads of the worst quality. This was especially true in the region around the village of Nebaj. Indeed, as Archbishop Cortés y Larraz noted in 1769—only one year after the revolt that we will discuss—"the road [to Nebaj from Sacapulas] is as bad as could possibly be imagined."[2] It was so narrow that in places there was not enough room for a mounted rider to pass; the archbishop had to dismount to let his mule get through. In these conditions it was difficult to get agricultural goods to market. Spaniards therefore tended to focus their economic activities elsewhere. Only a few cattle and sheep ranches were set up in the Cuchumatanes during the colonial period. Consequently, the impact of colonialism was less significant here than elsewhere, as is revealed by the small number of Spaniards and ladinos living in the area.

The three villages of Nebaj, Chajul, and San Juan Cotzal are located in the easternmost part of the Cuchumatanes. This is the region that in modern times was most devastated by the struggle between a repressive military dictatorship and a left-wing guerrilla insurgency. Many Maya were killed in the crossfire, and many more were relocated to new settlements controlled by the government.[3] The people speak Ixil Maya, which is so rare that it is spoken nowhere else. This caused problems for the colonial Church, for whereas priests could be expected to learn in the seminary one or more of the most commonly spoken Maya languages of Guatemala, no one studied Ixil because of its rarity and because the Nebaj area was considered so poor that no priest wanted to be stationed there. As a result, pastors and parishioners could barely, if at all, communicate with each other.

Spaniards clearly considered the Nebaj region to be the end of the Earth. In the late seventeenth century Fuentes y Guzmán, who usually praised Guatemala's Indians for their industriousness and good customs, had nothing good to say about the Ixil-speaking people of Nebaj and its adjacent villages of Chajul and San Juan Cotzal. They lived close to the "barbarous," pagan, and hostile Lacandón Maya who inhabited the lowland area north of the highlands, and contact with the Lacandones was allegedly one of the causes of the wildness of the Ixil. "These people are uncouth mountain men, given to idleness and vagrancy, and much prefer the hardships of the mountains to the comforts of the village," wrote Fuentes y Guzmán.[4]

Despite their state of semi-isolation, however, by the middle of the eighteenth century the Ixil people were using Hispanic surnames, which strongly suggests that they, like most Nahua people but unlike most other Maya, had no indigenous system of surnames or family names. Fuentes y Guzmán claimed that the villagers of Nebaj, Chajul, and San Juan Cotzal liked to hunt quetzals to acquire the feathers, but they did not like paying tribute and frequently were in arrears. Many of those alleged characteristics—especially resistance to tribute—continued to exist at the time of the revolt of 1768. The villages were not very large: in 1769 Nebaj was reported to have had 769 people (212 families), while Chajul had 1,160 (316 families) and San Juan Cotzal 980 (260 families).

Maya Autonomy and Meddlesome Spaniards

The brotherhood (cofradía) of Our Lady of the Rosary was an important social institution in the village of Santa María Nebaj. In 1768 it had in its treasury over one hundred pesos, a substantial sum for a poor village. The cofradía also had an altarpiece that was carried by the members in procession during religious celebrations. It had been run for years by a local village *macehual* named Miguel Matón, who was fairly well off, although hardly a "rich man" as a Spanish official would allege.

The relationship between religious brotherhoods and the Catholic Church was always ambiguous. On the one hand the institution was seen as a useful way for the Indians to learn about and participate in Christianity. Moreover, parish priests benefitted from cofradías because they received fees for saying Mass at the village religious festivals. On the other hand, the Indians believed themselves to be the owners of their brotherhoods as well as of the village properties—usually cattle or sheep ranches—that produced the revenues needed to pay for religious expenses associated with the festivals. Therefore the villagers tended to resist too much oversight by the ecclesiastical authorities, while the latter, in turn, were concerned over the proper use of cofradía revenues. These religious institutions thus could be contentious, resulting in conflict not only between the Church and the Indians but also among the Indians themselves. As one group later stated, "whenever there is conflict [the villagers] fight over the cofradías."[5] The importance of the religious brotherhoods continued into modern times: in the 1960s Nebaj had no less than twelve cofradías, while San Juan Cotzal and Chajul each had ten.[6]

Another point of contention between the Church and the Indians was obedience to basic principles of Catholicism, namely, attendance at Sunday Mass and catechism instruction for children. The people of Nebaj showed resistance to both, and for that reason the Dominican Friar Eusebio Guerra, the parish priest, appointed an exceptionally devout Indian named Diego Sánchez to the post of Indian church warden (*fiscal*). That official, who in return for his services was exempted from tribute, religious taxes, and forced labor services, was responsible for seeing that the people attended Mass and that the children attended catechism. Sánchez apparently carried out his duties with rigor and thus was disliked or even despised by many Indians of the village. (He used physical punishment when he believed it to be necessary.)

Conflict between the parish priest and the Indians resulted in complaints being made by the villagers before the *provincial* (elected leader) of the Dominicans. To avoid problems it was decided to transfer Friar Guerra and to appoint Friar Antonio Toledo as interim pastor of Nebaj. But since Guerra did not go far—apparently he was waiting around for his new assignment— he was still close at hand and able to wield influence. In any case, Friar Toledo immediately had the same difficulties as his predecessor and tried to resolve the problem by getting a village government in Nebaj that would back him in his efforts to force religious compliance as well as crack down on public drunkenness.

In addition, both Friar Toledo and Friar Guerra disapproved of Miguel Matón's administration of the cofradía of Our Lady of the Rosary. They therefore wanted a village government that would support them in their attempts to remove Matón and replace him with someone else. In short, in order to get their way the priests needed a cooperative village government in Nebaj. That, in turn, meant intervention in Indian elections, and this is what would provoke revolt.

The village elections of 1768 were crucial. Two different factions claimed victory. The one favored by the priests was led by Clemente Ramírez as senior Indian magistrate and Miguel Laynez as the junior. The other faction carried out its own elections, which resulted in the selection of Pablo Sánchez and Miguel Bernardo as the senior and junior Indian magistrates. The latter group was encouraged to do this by people from the nearby village of Chajul, who had found out what the priests were doing and were vehemently opposed to the selection of Miguel Laynez as junior magistrate. They believed that he would carry out a reign of terror that would oppress both villages.

Once again we see that, whereas among the Nahua and Mixtec peoples of Mexico it was very rare for two or more villages to cooperate and engage in joint political activity, in the Maya area people from different villages frequently acted together or tried to enlist each other's support for activities that the state considered to be subversive. In this case joint action was undoubtedly facilitated by joint ethnic membership: Nebaj and Chajul were both members of the same rare linguistic group, and they both, along with the village of San Juan Cotzal, belonged to the same parish and thus were equally affected by the actions of the priest and of the Indian church warden. It is clear that many Ixil Maya objected to the priests' intervention in their affairs and to the selection of Miguel Laynez as Indian magistrate. Moreover, as we will soon see, they also dragged their feet when it came to helping the colonial regime repress revolts by their own people.

As was the custom, the elected leaders traveled to the village of Chiantla to have their elections confirmed by the royal high magistrate, or alcalde mayor, of the province of Huehuetenango-Totonicapán. That man was Juan Bacaro, a native of Mexico City, who had paid 12,000 pesos to buy his office[7] (which in fact was one of the most expensive posts in the entire Spanish American empire). Bacaro was in Chiantla to attend the festival of the Virgin of the Candelaria, which took place on January 30. But Nebaj sent not one but two sets of elected officials. The alcalde mayor, however, later said that in fact *three* different governments had been elected, two by the different factions in Nebaj and a third supported by people from Chajul, who had no right to be involved in the other village's elections. It is likely that the magistrate either misunderstood what was happening or else made up his story to emphasize the confusion that was reigning and therefore justify his own intervention. Bacaro consulted with Friar Guerra—who just happened to be in Chiantla at the time—and chose Clemente Ramírez and Miguel Laynez to be village magistrates. He claimed that they belonged to different factions in the dispute, but neither the Indians nor the friars supported his interpretation of events. Everyone saw the Spanish official's action as the selection of the people preferred by the priests. This pleased one faction but of course antagonized the other. Immediately the new government tried to remove Miguel Matón as administrator of the cofradía of Our Lady of the Rosary.

Although the priest and the alcalde mayor did not yet know it, they had crossed an important line. They had violated both the religious and the political autonomy of the people of Nebaj, and the result would be revolt. At first, however, the new village magistrates, Clemente Ramírez and Miguel Laynez, ruled "peacefully" (as it was later said). That lasted for three weeks. Then Miguel Matón, the two Indian magistrates rejected by the alcalde mayor, and a group of dissident principales got together and came up with a plan to reverse their misfortune. A delegation was chosen to go to the capital and complain before the audiencia about the priests' and the alcalde mayor's intervention in their elections. In Santiago the Indians received a hearing (and were impressed by what was for them the strange sight of Spanish audiencia officials dressed in white wigs and black or red robes).

As a result of that hearing, on February 18, 1768, Felipe Romana, still the attorney general of the audiencia, reported to President Pedro de Salazar that magistrates were legally allowed to refuse confirmation of Indian elections for good cause, but not to appoint people or to allow the priests to interfere. In case of refusal to confirm, the proper course of action for a royal high magistrate was to order a new election. The president went along with this assessment, and ordered a dispatch to that effect be sent to Bacaro. As was the custom, this dispatch, in a sealed envelope, was given to Indians for delivery to the alcalde mayor in Totonicapán.[8] It just so happened, however, that those chosen to make the delivery were the Indians from Nebaj.

On their way back from the capital, the delegates from Nebaj began to wonder about the contents of the envelope they were carrying. Eventually curiosity killed the cat and they decided to open it, even though only one of the men present, village scribe Francisco Guzmán, knew how to read. Guzmán later would claim that he could read only his native tongue, but his handling of other documents betrayed him. Still, to help in the translation the members of the delegation, rather than going to Totonicapán to deliver it to Bacaro, chose to hurry back to their own village in search of Pedro Quezada, a ladino who could read Spanish and speak Ixil. Arriving at Nebaj the delegation found Quezada, who along with the scribe Guzmán provided what must have been a somewhat defective or misleading translation. The Indians concluded that the dispatch had given them the right to depose the undesirable village magistrates and to put their own people into power.

The revolt in Nebaj began on February 23, the very day that the delegation sent to the capital had returned home and heard the alleged translation of the dispatch. Present in the village were many people from Chajul. This may have been a coincidence, but it is also possible that they had been informed in advance that a dispatch from the president would be arriving in Nebaj. (Perhaps the scribe Francisco Guzmán really could read Spanish and had tipped off people from the neighboring village.) Meanwhile, the former delegates called on town criers, accompanied by clarion calls, drums, and fireworks, to proclaim that there would be a change in government. This was done, and a large crowd assembled. Soon rumors spread like wildfire that not only would the disliked Indian magistrates be deposed but also that the village would be exempted from tribute. Needless to say, this was not true. But the rumors helped convert a political movement into a village celebration and then into a mob of rebels.

The village officials supported by the priest were now in big trouble. The rebels went to the house of senior Indian magistrate Clemente Ramírez. He was fifty years old at the time, and was nobody's fool. He quickly resigned his post and was forced to surrender his staff of office, which the people destroyed.

A mob of rebels also showed up outside the house of junior Indian magistrate Miguel Laynez, who was sixty years old and was especially despised. He was said to have taunted the people by claiming that he would be magistrate of the village for seven years. Laynez was more determined, or perhaps more foolish, than Clemente Ramírez, for he refused to surrender his staff of office. The rebels broke into his house and then dragged him into the street. They broke his staff and began to whip him. He was given somewhere between twelve and fifty lashes. (It was later said that his back was "in pieces.") When Laynez's wife or daughter tried to protect him, she too was whipped, as were several other women, three of whom were said to be pregnant. It was later reported that at least one of the women suffered a miscarriage as result of the beating. Friar Toledo said that this was the worst crime of the whole uprising. All told, some nineteen men and eleven women were flogged. The kind of whips used, however, differed according to the gender of the person being whipped: leather for men, nettle reeds for females. Some supporters of the unpopular faction managed to escape flogging or beating by paying off their assailants. This allegedly cost somewhere between four reales and thirteen pesos, depending, one presumes, on the ability to pay and the anger of the crowd. Finally, Miguel Laynez was shackled and put into the stocks for two days. Later there was disagreement over whether he received any food or water during that time. He was eventually put into jail.

The rebels, having deposed the two unpopular Indian magistrates, also sought out Diego Sánchez, the Indian church warden. He immediately surrendered his staff of office to avoid further complications. Next, the treasury of the cofradía of Our Lady of the Rosary was taken and the money on hand was distributed among the villagers, who thereby demonstrated their belief that the religious institution belonged to them and not to the Church. The altarpiece was also disassembled, its pieces being likewise distributed among the people.

The rebels thus succeeded in carrying out what their opponents would later call a "revolution."[9] Yet they hardly acted like revolutionaries, for having overthrown the village government they tried to get the Spanish authorities to sanction what they had done. They elected a delegation of eleven men to go to Totonicapán both to deliver the president's dispatch and to get the new village government confirmed by the alcalde mayor. Included in the group were the new Indian magistrates, Pablo Sánchez and Miguel Bernardo, and Miguel Matón's son Jacinto. These people left Nebaj and got as far as the village of Sacapulas, where on March 3 they were arrested.

A few days later Friar Toledo arrived in Nebaj with the intention of calming the rebels down and freeing Miguel Laynez from the stocks. He succeeded in releasing the poor ex-magistrate but by doing so angered the villagers. The women of Nebaj retaliated by pelting him with rocks and driving him out of the village. Respect for the Catholic clergy clearly had its limits.

On February 26 the son of Miguel Laynez made it to the district chief village of Huehuetenango and reported what was happening to Carlos Joseph Guillén, the representative of the alcalde mayor in that part of the province. Guillén was called, and called himself (against his will, he claimed) the lieutenant of the alcalde mayor. During the investigation that followed it was pointed out that no such post existed and that Guillén was in the pay not of His Majesty (as a royal official would be) but of the magistrate. Bacaro claimed that he appointed such an "official" in order to help carry out tribute collection in his very large province, but the records reveal that the main duty of the "lieutenant" was to carry out the alcalde mayor's repartimiento business. To do so, however, it was thought that he needed an official-sounding title; otherwise, he said, the Indians would pay him no attention. Since a large part of the business activities of the repartimiento were illegal, Guillén's presence and title were somewhat of an embarrassment to the magistrate. Nevertheless, the investigating judge would pass over this indiscretion and report favorably on the actions of the "lieutenant" in putting down the revolt in Nebaj.

In Totonicapán on February 27 Alcalde Mayor Bacaro received notice of the revolt from his lieutenant. He immediately instructed Guillén to assemble whatever force was necessary to restore order. He also commanded that the troublemakers be arrested ánd their property sequestered, and that the people of the nearby villages of Chajul and San Juan Cotzal be warned not to give aid to the rebels. Realizing, however, that Guillén was not legally a royal official, Bacaro also gave his lieutenant a written order, signed by himself, to the people of those villages warning them not to be disobedient or join the revolt, "because if by chance you do so, you will be severely punished, as they [of Nebaj] will be."[10] Guillén, to whom the high magistrate had written "do not lose an instant of time," a few days later received another order from his boss dated March 2, commanding him to take women and children as hostages in case the men of Nebaj ran away and went into hiding.

The lieutenant acted quickly, although not precipitously. The scale of the revolt, which included people from Chajul as well as Nebaj, convinced him that the usual six or eight soldiers would not be sufficient to contain an uprising of not one but of two or more whole "villages of Indians."[11] Moreover, Friar Toledo warned him to be careful, for it was dangerous to enter Nebaj.[12] Therefore Guillén informed his boss of his intention to call up the militia. Eventually he raised a force of over fifty men, all of whom were ladinos from Huehuetenango. He also notified the Indian magistrates of the village of Sacapulas to be ready to arrest any suspicious group of people from Nebaj who might pass through on their way to Totonicapán. To facilitate the rapid movement of his force, Guillén then gave orders to the Indian magistrates of Chajul and San Juan Cotzal to provide twenty-four mules or horses each so that the militia soldiers could go mounted.

What happened next makes clear the limits of colonialism. For Indians, mules and horses were extremely expensive. A horse was worth about twice an Indian's annual tribute payment; a mule was worth five times that amount. These animals were not luxuries but rather capital goods, for they were used primarily to transport goods to market. The loss of such property could mean economic disaster for peasants. The leaders of Chajul and San Juan Cotzal weighed their options. If they provided the mounts they might never get them back, and even if they did the mules and horses might be away for weeks or even months. The chances of being paid for the rent of the animals or compensation for their loss were slim. Finally, why should they help the Spaniards repress a revolt by fellow Ixil Maya? The Indian magistrates finally just said no. In fact, it was alleged that they even tried to kill the poor Indian who delivered the order.

Guillén was undoubtedly furious. But because of the emergency he faced, he could see no way of coercing the villagers into immediate compliance. Had he tried to do so, he might have had another revolt on his hands. Guillén, who had already led his men on foot as far as the village of Aguacatán, therefore ordered most of the soldiers to return to Huehuetenango.

The disobedience of Chajul and San Juan Cotzal was brought up in the investigation of the revolt. The senior Indian magistrates did not even show up to testify; they gave excuses for not appearing in person, and sent the junior Indian magistrate of Chajul and a mere councilman (*regidor*) of San Juan Cotzal to represent their villages. These officials tried to maintain that the village government had failed to obey Guillén's instructions because the Indian magistrates were illiterate and thus could not read written orders. But the judge pointed out that their village scribe could read and was present at the time. The witnesses responded that apparently their scribe had either misunderstood the order or had mistranslated it, and that the Indian magistrates had thought the note was signed by "some Macario or other," rather than Bacaro, and thus had not recognized the name of the alcalde mayor. Other Indians from the villages testified in favor of this version of events. The judge stated for the record that the witnesses were lying—he found it inconceivable that the village officials would not recognize the name of their own alcalde mayor—but since he could not prove it he chose to let them go. The people of Chajul and San Juan Cotzal thus got away first with foot dragging and then with feigned ignorance—classic weapons in the arsenal of the weak. The colonized people won this small battle in the class war.

From Aguacatán, Guillén reported that the rebels were hiding in the mountains observing his movements. But then the lieutenant had a stroke of luck. When they saw most of Guillén's force return to Huehuetenango, the people from Nebaj entered Sacapulas in order to cross the bridge over the Río Negro and continue their trip to Totonicapán to meet with the alcalde mayor. But the Indian magistrates of Sacapulas—a Quiché Maya settlement—obeyed their orders and arrested the Ixil people of the Nebaj delegation, a total of twenty-five men and two women. At one stroke, many ringleaders of the revolt fell into the government's hands. The lieutenant therefore concluded that the rebel movement had been decapitated and that it was possible to move on Nebaj with a much smaller force than originally thought.

Guillén had figured right. Leaving Sacapulas on March 5, he entered Nebaj the next day and took control of the village. He pointed out, however, that "I accomplished this by risking my skin."[13] The villagers were obviously not happy with the arrival of the forces of repression, and demonstrated this openly. Guillén described what happened as follows:

> Upon entering Nebaj, since they were waiting for me, a large number of Indian women went to the street corners with rocks in their dresses [huipiles], but since I pretended not to notice, they chose not to use them, instead lifting up their petticoats [naguas] and they wet on me, all the while making opprobrious remarks.[14]

(One can only speculate regarding the execution of this procedure.) Since many of the men who had participated in the uprising had fled to the surrounding mountains, those remaining in the village were mostly women, children, and partisans of the faction supported by the priest. Guillén arrested twenty-two people and sent them to Sacapulas. Then, all forty-seven prisoners were remitted to Totonicapán.

The lieutenant also took steps to consolidate his control of Nebaj. He freed Miguel Laynez from jail and told him that he and Clemente Ramírez were village magistrates again. Neither man, however, wanted to serve, and Laynez even got down on his knees and begged to be excused from the burden, and pain, of office. He feared that once the occupying force had left the village the dissidents would rise up again and possibly even kill him. But eventually Alcalde Mayor Bacaro sent Guillén orders to impress upon Ramírez and Laynez the importance of doing their duty, and they eventually consented to resume their offices. It is not known whether coercion was used, or whether the two Indian magistrates received guarantees from the alcalde mayor. The lieutenant did report, however, that "it cost me a whole lot of work" to get the former village magistrates reinstated.[15]

Guillén also tried to get the priest to return to help restore tranquility in the village. He wrote to Friar Toledo, informing him that it was safe to return to Nebaj and that he was needed to reestablish order. The Friar wrote back, in somewhat unpriestly language, that "my wish was never to set foot in that damned village again," but in the end he agreed to return and do his duty.[16]

The lieutenant also followed the high magistrate's orders and began to sequester the property of the rebels. Chief rebel Miguel Matón remained at large but in his house was found the significant sum of 112 pesos 3 1/2 reales. He also owned two mules (both of which mysteriously died after being impounded), a house with a tiled roof, three religious paintings (representing St. Michael, St. Lazarus, and St. Anthony) in gold-leaf frames, and clothing, kept in a trunk under lock and key, consisting of an overcoat, woolen pantaloons, a frock coat of crude cloth, two more pantaloons of white cotton, a shirt, a sheet, and an embroidered parasol. Matón also possessed a compass and an iron tooth-puller, kept three birds (perhaps parrots, for chickens or turkeys would have been identified as such), and owned three powder flasks, a bag of bullets, and an iron mold for making bullets. It was alleged that he had sixteen shotguns, although he admitted to owning only two, neither of which was to be found. Finally, in addition to all the above, 52 measures of corn found in his house were sequestered. By any standard Miguel Matón, while perhaps not rich, as the Spanish judge later alleged, was clearly a well-off Indian. From the other rebels Guillén sequestered eleven additional horses and mules. Another important leader, Francisco de Paz, was found to own fourteen pesos worth of molasses and a still for manufacturing spirits from sugar.[17] Practically all the ringleaders owned at least one horse or mule, which means that the rebellion was led by people who were among the wealthiest members of peasant society.

The leaders also included people who were probably among the oldest in their community. The three people most often identified as the principal leaders of the revolt—Miguel Matón, Pedro Cobo (a former Indian magistrate), and Jacinto Brito—were sixty, sixty, and eighty years old, respectively. All of the other ringleaders were over fifty, and one participant, described by a sixty-year-old as "very old," was estimated to be ninety. Many were identified as principales, and some had been Indian magistrates or had held other political offices in the past. Consequently, although the three chiefs were macehuales (and were called "boys" [muchachos] by their enemies), the village political elite was well represented. This was not, therefore, a rebellion of commoners against their leaders. Rather, one faction of the elite was in conflict with the other. The dispute even cut across families and pitted brother against brother: one of the members of the faction supported by the priests was Miguel Matón's brother Domingo.

Failed Cover-up and Persistent Confrontations

As was frequently the case in colonial Spanish America, before the wheels of Spanish justice would turn, summary "justice" was meted out. First, as Guillén's men went about their task of sequestering property, they crossed the sometimes thin line between sequestration and looting. Anything of value, most notably machetes, agricultural tools, bolts of cloth, thread, and fowl were stolen and carried off. One man, who was away from the village the day of the revolt as well as the day of the looting, later said that when he returned home he found his wife crying because their food had been stolen. During the inquest the looting was brought up by both Indian factions of Nebaj, as well as by the leaders from Chajul and San Juan Cotzal. Therefore the Spanish judge was forced to admit that looting had occurred and he even went so far as to defend it, to a point. He noted that the value of the missing property was slight—only about twenty-five pesos—and that when it comes to looting, "not even the seasoned soldiers of the royal army are containable."[18] (In all fairness, the same could be said of all eighteenth-century armies.) Eventually some restitution was attempted. But many of the valuable mules that had been sequestered were never returned. This undoubtedly meant financial disaster to the owners.

Second, the prisoners were punished even before they were tried. On March 11 Royal High Magistrate Bacaro ordered his lieutenant to pardon all the unimportant participants in the uprising if they promised to obey the law in the future, but the captured ringleaders were to be given fifty lashes and a month in jail—before their trial had even started.[19] (In the official inquest, the judge would try to cover up what the magistrate had done.) Bacaro pointed out, however (or perhaps lamented), that the prisoners would not be shackled because of the lack of chains. But he promised to come up with enough to shackle the chief ringleaders.

As a result, when the alcalde mayor began questioning the captured rebels on March 14, the prisoners had been made ready to confess. Meanwhile, the villages of Chajul and San Juan Cotzal, which had failed to cooperate with Guillén, were taking action to protect themselves from their high magistrate's wrath. They appealed to the audiencia's advocate of the poor, Dr. Francisco Vidaurre, claiming that Bacaro was persecuting them. Vidaurre took action on their behalf, and as a result the alcalde mayor gave up trying to punish the two villages. The activity of the advocate of the poor would also eventually provoke the wrath of the judge at the inquest.

As always, before Alcalde Mayor Bacaro could begin officially interrogating his prisoners in Totonicapán, he first had to appoint interpreters, for the Ixil Maya of Nebaj could speak no Spanish. Also as usual, all of the Indians were illiterate, although the village scribe, who did not testify, could of course read and write Ixil. And although Bacaro did not yet know it, while his three-day trial was going on, events were taking place in the capital that would cause him to lose control of the investigation and stop his attempted cover-up dead in its tracks.

This happened because the case had come to the attention of Attorney General Felipe Romana. The fiscal by now had a lot of experience in dealing with the royal high magistrates who governed the provinces, and he apparently did not trust them. Romana therefore recommended the appointment of a special judge to carry out an official inquest and conduct the trial. The attorney general took this step because he believed that the involvement of at least three villages in the revolt suggested a scale that warranted an investigation by an impartial agent of justice. The assumption, in short, was that a royal high magistrate could not be impartial when his own actions were under review. As events proved, this was not an unwarranted assumption.

President Salazar accepted Romana's recommendation, and Bacaro's hopes of covering up his actions were soon to be dashed.

Since the alcalde mayor did not yet know of the presidential order, however, he began his investigation and trial on March 14, 1768. The proceedings lasted three days, during which time the magistrate questioned twelve men. In fact, these men were the members of the delegation that had been sent to get the high magistrate to confirm their village government and had been arrested in Sacapulas. Since they left Nebaj either the day of the revolt or the day after, they did not witness anything that happened in their village after their departure. But since they had already been in jail for several weeks and had presumably been visited by fellow villagers, they were all able to say that they had "heard" about events there. Bacaro took down the hearsay as evidence, as was the practice in the Spanish legal system.

The alcalde mayor did not intend to lose control of the proceedings. He made sure that no mention was made of the elections because of his intervention in village politics, for he had confirmed two Indian magistrates and had rejected the others. Moreover, he tried to make the uprising look like the work of a few malcontent macehuales who rejected the legitimate authority of their own principales. Therefore each prisoner/witness was carefully identified as merely an "Indian tributary," thereby implying that they were all commoners. Nevertheless, once the case was investigated by the next judge, it would be revealed that many of the witnesses interrogated by Bacaro were in fact principales. The lowering of their status turned out to be temporary.

All the people interrogated answered the usual leading questions in a manner satisfying the high magistrate. All twelve agreed on who the five men were who went to the capital to seek the help of superior authority (an action guaranteed to displease a royal high magistrate; after all, who wants powerful people prowling around in his territory and asking embarrassing questions?). Of these five men, one was Jacinto Matón, the son of Miguel, who was also a member of the delegation captured in Sacapulas and thus was among those interrogated by Bacaro. He was the only one ever questioned about the mission to the capital.

The other leading questions asked by the alcalde mayor were carefully worded to prevent anything embarrassing being said about Bacaro's role in the confirmation of elections. The prisoners admitted that they had taken part in the violent overthrow of the village government of Nebaj and that they had flogged the men and women of the opposing faction, causing one pregnant woman to miscarry (although they snuck in the information that some of the females were not flogged with leather whips but rather with nettle reeds "because they were pregnant").[20] They also confessed to proclaiming the president's order as if it gave them the right to take power and to extorting money from their enemies and then giving some of it to the Indian magistrates of Chajul. They admitted that they disliked Diego Sánchez, the village church warden, because he forced them to attend Mass and send their children to catechism, but they rightly pointed out that they could not have stoned the priest because they were in jail in Sacapulas at the time. They did see that Miguel Laynez was shackled and put into the stocks, but again they were not there to see whether he was denied food and water. Finally, they all identified the ringleaders, singling out Miguel Matón as the chief, and admitted that they got support from the villagers by promising the abolition of tribute and of magistrates.

Bacaro planned to have the participants from Chajul be his next witnesses. Eleven of the people already questioned were summoned to his presence and told to identify the Chajul people by name. The prisoners soon came up with the fourteen names. But since in this case the witnesses from Nebaj were not asked a question that could be answered by a simple yes or no like the usual leading questions, they were able to counteract somewhat the high magistrate's efforts to blame the events on macehuales. Among those identified as from Chajul were both current Indian magistrates—whom the alcalde mayor of course had just recently confirmed in office—three former Indian magistrates, and nine others identified as principales. None was a macehual.

But before Bacaro could call these people to testify, he received an order from President Salazar to cease his proceedings and send all documentation gathered thus far to the capital. The alcalde mayor wrote that "even though these proceedings are not concluded," he would comply with the order.[21]

To carry out a full-scale, and perhaps more impartial, inquest, the royal government, as was its custom, chose as investigating judge the provincial magistrate whose district was closest to that of Huehuetenango-Totonicapán. This was Francisco Antonio Aldama y Guevara (like Bacaro, a native of Mexico City), who was the corregidor of Quezaltenango. Once again we see a system of checks and balances in which the checks are not always what they were supposed to be. Aldama y Guevara may have been as good a choice as any for the post as investigating judge, but Advocate of the Poor Dr. Vidaurre did not think so. On March 23 Vidaurre told the audiencia that Aldama y Guevara was unskilled in legal procedures and that he may have sent a secret warning to Bacaro that an investigation was imminent. The magistrate of Quezaltenango denied the charges on April 6, accused Vidaurre of criminal libel, and indignantly denounced the advocate of the poor for suggesting that he was a bad judge.[22] In any case, during the proceedings Aldama y Guevara did demonstrate considerable antipathy toward indigenous people in general. He had already acquired experience in the area of Indian rebellions, for he had helped put down one in Mexico and another one in 1767 in his own district, and he managed to work this information into the proceedings.[23] As a result of that experience, he thought Indians to be crafty, cunning, and conniving people who were never to be believed or trusted.

Aldama y Guevara also undoubtedly sympathized with Bacaro, whom he may already have known (because of their common birthplace). The corregidor of Quezaltenango undoubtedly believed that when one magistrate is disobeyed, the authority of all is called into question. He even tried to cover up somewhat for the alcalde mayor of Huehuetenango-Totonicapán. In the documentary evidence is an order, dated March 11, that Bacaro sent to his lieutenant in which Guillén was instructed as follows: "For having participated in the riot of a bunch of malcontents, you are to give each prisoner fifty lashes, well laid on" (*bien dados, cincuenta azotes a cada uno*).[24] There is no reason to doubt that this order was carried out, and indeed in a statement made to the advocate of the poor less than a week later, people from

Nebaj complained that the lieutenant had given them 100 lashes.[25] Never-theless, Aldama y Guevara succeeded in getting some of the prisoners to state that they had received no punishment whatsoever other than the se-questration of their property. The judge thus succeeded in sweeping this un-der the rug and made no mention of it in his final report. However, the evidence may have been used against Bacaro in another case brought before the audiencia, and may have contributed to a presidential ruling against him.

Even before Aldama y Guevara arrived, he suffered what was for him an indignity. He had been investigating judge in Totonicapán before, and this time the leaders of the village wrote him a letter in which they said that they would like if possible to dispense with the pomp and ceremony that usually accompanied the arrival of a dignitary. The last time Aldama y Guevara had been there he had been welcomed by Totonicapán's band, and there had apparently been a party in his honor. Once was enough, the villagers were saying. Since officials were not supposed to be fêted at the people's expense, the Indians were hinting that Aldama y Guevara was a corrupt official. Once again we see the Maya trying to counteract the reality of colonialism.

The incoming judge, who received the letter a few miles outside of town, was of course furious. He reported that he did not want any band before and he did not need one now. He later called no less than thirty-three people at one time—principales representing the many calpules of the large village of Totonicapán—to explain the motives of the letter. The Indians claimed that they really were ignorant of its contents because it had been written at their request by a passer-by who knew Spanish, and that their only purpose was to show proper humility before an important official. Feigning ignorance was frequently an effective strategy. Aldama y Guevara let them go, for he could do little else.

The investigating judge arrived in Totonicapán on April 7, complaining that he was late because the Indians from Quezaltenango who carried him there by mule had failed to pick him up until nine o'clock in the morning. As a result of this foot-dragging, he had been forced to leave at an uncomfort-able hour. Aldama y Guevara then took up his duties. He presented his cre-dentials in the form of orders signed by President–Governor–Captain General Pedro de Salazar to Alcalde Mayor Juan Bacaro. The latter promised to co-operate fully, noting that he would not have to give orders to any lieutenant of his because there was none. The investigating judge therefore had to raise the awkward issue of the post held by Guillén, a subject discussed above.

After clarifying that there indeed was no lieutenant, and calling the people from Totonicapán to explain themselves, also discussed above, Aldama y Guevara went to the jail to verify the count of the prisoners. There he was told that there were no prisoners from Chajul or San Juan Cotzal; all were from Nebaj. There were eleven of them, all of whom had already been interrogated by Bacaro. Six were in shackles. Among these were Miguel Matón's son Jacinto, as well as Pablo Sánchez and Miguel Bernardo, the two Indian magistrates chosen by the anti-priest faction of the village. Aldama y Guevara asked if there were any female prisoners, and was told that there was none. Since two women were reportedly among the people arrested in Sacapulas, apparently they had been released by this time. The judge then appointed his interpreters, after verifying that they could speak what he referred to as "the language that the Indians speak." He warned them to translate "nakedly, with neither hatred nor confusion." One of the translators, Felipe Borja, was literate enough to sign his name.

Wasting no time, Aldama y Guevara then began to question the prisoners in Totonicapán. This took him two days (April 7–8). First to be interrogated were the eleven men in jail, who having been examined by Bacaro were now examined by the new judge. Aldama y Guevara followed the normal procedure and asked the men to identify themselves and give their ages, and this time five of the eleven identified themselves as principales, not macehuales. As was also normal, none of the men could say exactly how old he was. As we have seen previously, among the Maya exact age was apparently unimportant. Therefore the judge had to estimate. He guessed the first witness, Miguel Bernardo, one of the dissident Indian magistrates, to be "about sixty," and so on for the others, except for Andrés Brito, of whom it was said "he has been retired for many years because of his age."

As was to be expected, Aldama y Guevara asked leading questions. However, his questions were such that the witnesses had more of an opportunity to give their version of events. As a result, the disputed election, especially the role of Friar Guerra, now became part of the official record. The witnesses all claimed that they believed the president had given them permission to depose the priest's faction and put into power their own government, although they also confessed to having flogged Miguel Laynez. They also gave the names of the people in both factions in the dispute, and identified Pedro Quezada as the ladino who had provided the translation of the president's dispatch.

Having heard this evidence, Aldama y Guevara then decided to move the proceedings to Huehuetenango, about 30 miles to the north as the crow flies, to be closer to the scene of the revolt in order to facilitate the questioning of more witnesses. He chose not to go to Nebaj, perhaps because the road was so bad. From Huehuetenango on April 14 the judge ordered Guillén to provide him with all the documentation in his possession, and sent a similar request to Bacaro. Both men complied, although the alcalde mayor pointed out that he had already sent some material to the capital in accordance with orders from the president. The documents turned over among other things revealed Guillén's role as Bacaro's repartimiento agent in the district of Huehuetenango. Also put into the record were statements by the priest's faction in Nebaj complaining about the looting carried out by Guillén's troops and identifying the ringleaders of the revolt.

The investigating judge discovered that there were no prisoners waiting for him in Huehuetenango, and therefore he issued summons to the three people identified as key ringleaders (Miguel Matón, Pedro Cobo, and Jacinto Brito), to two other Indians (Diego Marcos and Pedro de León), and to the ladino Pedro Quezada. He then took testimony from "lieutenant" Guillén, who gave his version of events. As a result, Aldama y Guevara issued summons to two more Indians.

Most of the people called to testify showed up, for their only alternative was to be fugitives. Only the ladino and one Indian failed to appear, although the latter, after some prodding, eventually decided to testify. The investigating judge began his new interrogations on April 18. The questioning of witnesses lasted for three days. Once again the Indians were mostly old men: Matón and Cobo were sixty, Jacinto Brito was eighty, and Diego Marcos was estimated to be ninety. No wonder they turned themselves in. The unimportant Pedro de León was thirty. Indeed, one suspects that in this society age contributed significantly to a person's importance or lack thereof.

Even though Aldama y Guevara was questioning mostly old men, he was a tough interrogator. For example, when Pedro Cobo said that Indian magistrates Ramírez and Laynez had received only one vote—that of the priest—in the election, the judge vociferously interrupted to point out that the evidence hitherto gathered demonstrated that many people had voted for those alcaldes. Yet Cobo stubbornly "repeated again that only the priest had voted."[26] Similarly, whenever one of the witnesses stated that "all the village" had joined them in overthrowing the priest's faction, Aldama y Guevara interjected that some people in fact had supported Indian magistrates Ramírez and Laynez. The witnesses, however, usually stuck to their own interpretation of events.

All told, in Huehuetenango the investigating judge questioned eleven suspects from Nebaj and two from Chajul, as well as Clemente Ramírez and Miguel Laynez, the two unfortunate but reinstated Indian magistrates of Nebaj. Laynez testified that many people of his village did not want him in office perhaps because he carried out his required nightly rounds (that is, the roundup of drunks), forced everybody to attend Mass, and collected tribute properly. Among the others there was disagreement on whether any of the women whipped had been pregnant. As a result of this round of interrogation, Aldama y Guevara sent Miguel Matón, Jacinto Brito, and Pedro de León to jail and had them placed in the stocks.

On April 20 the investigating judge issued an order to Nebaj's Indian magistrates, Clemente Ramírez and Miguel Laynez, to take charge of returning the corn that had been sequestered from the villagers. They were also told to bring in two people who had failed to obey the summons and to confiscate all the shotguns in the village. Aldama y Guevara threatened those who failed to comply with sentence to a *presidio* (which usually meant forced military service in the Petén, the unappealing tropical lowlands between Yucatán and Guatemala). He also interrogated witnesses from Chajul regarding that village's refusal to provide horses and mules, but gave up trying to punish anyone for defying orders.

Then began still another struggle between the Spanish authorities and the Indians that demonstrates the limits of colonialism. Nebaj's Indian magistrates eventually ran down the last of the Indians who had refused to appear and reported that the ladino Pedro Quezada was a fugitive. But on April 23 Ramírez and Laynez also informed the judge that they were unsuccessful in confiscating the firearms. Aldama y Guevara asked for an explanation. The Indian magistrates replied that when they went from house to house the people, including Miguel Matón's wife, refused to recognize them as legitimate authority because they did not have the proper staffs of office. This certainly exasperated the judge: how it was possible, he asked, that they had gone out without their staffs? Eventually Ramírez and Laynez admitted that they had not gone personally to confiscate the guns—one suspects that they were afraid to try it—but had sent out deputies to do it. However, three people listening at the window heard the deputies' orders and ran ahead to warn everyone to hide their firearms. Aldama y Guevara then ordered those three men arrested and sent to jail, "all of which proves the wickedness of these Indians," according to the judge.[27]

In order to coerce the people of Nebaj into compliance, Aldama y Guevara went to the Huehuetenango jail on the night of April 23 and ordered the three new prisoners shackled for their role in the gun confiscation fiasco. Three days later the investigating judge claimed that without the testimony of the fugitive ladino Pedro Quezada he could not prove the guilt or innocence of the prisoners. He would free them and let them return to their homes, he wrote, but only if they turned in their guns. Since they refused, he kept them in jail, and declared them to be insolent for their continued disobedience, especially in light of his efforts to restore their property to them. He therefore went to the jail to make an official verification. There he found thirty-two people, five of whom were in stocks and three in shackles. Later that day the prisoners offered to send a message to their village with instructions to collect all the firearms and if possible capture the fugitive ladino or else hold his family hostage. Aldama y Guevara agreed (and apparently let them out of the stocks and shackles). He wrote an order to Indian magistrates Ramírez and Laynez instructing them to try again to collect the guns and to sequester the property of Pedro Quezada, the ladino who refused to turn himself in.

Three days later, on April 28, Ramírez and Laynez, Indian magistrates of Nebaj, reported back to the judge. They had searched all the houses in the village and found no guns. Moreover, when they tried to seize the house of Pedro Quezada, Friar Toledo intervened to prevent them on the grounds that Quezada's daughter was pregnant. His wife, it turns out, was named Petrona Matón—she was probably a relative of Miguel, because everyone else by that name who appeared in the records was related to him. Exasperated but determined, Aldama y Guevara, noting "the lying nature and pride of the rioters,"[28] for their goal was to keep their weapons, ordered all the prisoners to remain in jail and to be placed once again in the stocks and shackles. Miguel Matón told the interpreter that it was not his fault that the guns failed to be turned in, swearing by God and the sign of the cross. But in jail he stayed. That very day the judge, having assessed the costs of the proceedings (which came to 204 pesos 7 1/2 reales), sent in his official statement closing the case.

Aldama y Guevara's report to President Salazar of April 28, 1768, was filled with anger and vituperation. As the judge put it, "Perhaps with the reading of these proceedings one will come to know the point that the maliciousness, arrogance, and cruelty of the Indians can reach."[29] His dealings with them in his own province of Quezaltenango as a result of an uprising there convinced him that Indians were a bunch of hypocrites, "for the goal of the influential ones is to take more from the poor Indians than their malicious tongues claim the supposed greed of their corregidores and alcaldes mayores ever could."[30] They try to appear poor, innocent, ignorant, and stupid, but "that is the role they play in the comedy, and they play the role of Indian very well."[31]

It was difficult, he noted, to find the true cause of the revolt. Clearly, many people did not want Miguel Laynez as Indian magistrate because he would do what the priest wanted. And "this much is certain: that most of the Indians would like (as is evident because of their ignorance of the Law of God) there to be no magistrates to punish them nor priests to force them to learn Christian Doctrine."[32] The attack on the Indian church warden proved that. But when all was said and done, the judge wrote, "the conflict is not between Indians and the alcalde mayor or his lieutenant, but between Indians and Indians of the village of Nebaj."[33] On the other hand, he noted, if the advocate of the poor were really on the side of the poor, he would have taken the side of Clemente Ramírez and Miguel Laynez, the unfortunate Indian magistrates preferred by the priest.

Judge Aldama y Guevara also defended Alcalde Mayor Bacaro for his role in the confirmation of elections. A magistrate, he argued, should not confirm any and all persons who got the most votes. Rather, he should verify if the person is appropriate for office, and to do so the parish priest must be consulted. For in reality those best suited for office are not the rich Indians, "for they are the most audacious ones."[34] And "among vicious, lawless people, it is clear that the people will choose the most powerful delinquents" as their leaders.[35] They would choose people like Miguel Matón, who "acts like a lord, carrying arms, and contrary to what the law stipulates, he has gunpowder and bullets even though he is just a macehual and confesses to having shotguns, although he says they are for deer hunting."[36]

Aldama y Guevara also criticized his own government's reliance on Indians to deliver letters. This had been part of the problem to begin with, for rumor played a big role in the revolt. To prove his point the judge noted that he had just received some orders from the audiencia carried by a Spanish-speaking Indian from Totonicapán, who told him what the contents were. Asked how he knew, he said that the attorney general had told him. But of course the attorney general had done no such thing, and upon opening the envelope he found the documents to be of a very different nature. The communications system, then, "is worth checking into, since we know what the Indians are,"[37] namely, rumormongers.

Finally, Aldama y Guevara defended what for a Spaniard counted most: his honor. He emphatically denied that he had given warning to Bacaro of the impending investigation, and attacked the integrity of Advocate of the Poor Dr. Vidaurre, who had immediately taken the side of the Indians. The judge warned the president to "take note of the weakness of university graduates [letrados]."[38] In this he was appealing to the sentiments of President Salazar, who as a brigadier general and permanent grenadier captain of the Royal Guards Regiment (that is, an elite officer in an elite unit) was likely to feel not only sympathy for a fellow professional soldier but also disdain for people with education (a sentiment shared by many soldiers then and now). He also rejected the suggestion of corruption resulting from the affair of his welcome by the Indians of Totonicapán, and although he admitted that he had decided not to call Friars Toledo or Guerra to testify—apparently this had become noteworthy—he claimed that the priests' testimony was not needed, the confessions of the prisoners being more than enough evidence.

The judge concluded by noting that he had been unable to capture the ladino Pedro Quezada. Nor had he gained possession of the villagers' shotguns. He also claimed that he had not been prejudiced against the Indians (for he had even helped to buy tortillas and tamales to feed the prisoners); that he had not been partial to Juan Bacaro, with whom he had not had friendship; that he had not visited Nebaj because there was no need to; and that the major culprit was Miguel Matón, whose sequestered money should be confiscated to pay the costs of the revolt. Aldama y Guevara's report was received in Santiago de Guatemala, the capital, on May 6.

The day before, and almost a week after he had made his report, Aldama y Guevara, back in his own jurisdiction of Quezaltenango, received a letter from the prisoners in Huehuetenango and was presented with two old shotguns said to belong to Miguel Matón. Those in jail requested "for the Love of God Our Lord and of His Most Holy Mother Our Lady," that they be freed since the firearms had been turned in. They were afraid that if they remained prisoners they would miss the planting season and thus be unable to pay their tribute. Aldama y Guevara, however, considered his work to be done and thus passed the letter on to the attorney general in the capital.

The Spanish government had moved fast to bring the rebels to trial, but after that the wheels of justice moved slowly. The attorney general did not get around to ruling on the case until November 18, almost six months after the report by the investigating judge. Romana recommended that the less important prisoners be given fifty lashes. Ringleaders Miguel Matón, Pedro Cobo, Pablo Sánchez, Miguel Bernardo, and Francisco Guzmán (the secretary of Nebaj who was believed partly responsible for the mistranslation of the notorious dispatch) were each to be given 100 lashes and two years' exile from their village. Once again we see that from the point of view of Spanish officials it was perfectly acceptable to whip old men. Fugitive ladino Pedro Quezada was declared an outlaw, and if captured was to be forced to testify; if found guilty he was to be given 200 lashes and exile from his village, "and if he gives plausible explanations for his actions and is found less guilty, then the punishment should be moderated, and if innocent he should be absolved."[39] Finally, Miguel Matón was to make restitution for the money taken from the cofradía. The president's legal advisor went along with the attorney general's ruling and on November 28 President Salazar authorized the verdict.

Before the sentences could be carried out, however, the prisoners escaped from jail. Five were subsequently recaptured, but then the alcalde mayor chose to free them on their own recognizance. In fact, Juan Bacaro was losing control of his province, for by now he was being investigated for abuse of office and undoubtedly had more important things on his mind. Moreover, the embattled alcalde mayor got into a dispute with Aldama y Guevara regarding payment for the latter's investigation. The magistrate of Totonicapán reported that the money taken from Miguel Matón in fact belonged to the village cofradía and thus could not be used to pay the investigating judge and the others for their services. But Attorney General Romana pointed out that to deny Aldama y Guevara his salary so long after the inquest and after he had made the long journey back to his own territory would discourage other magistrates from serving the king in such cases. Therefore Bacaro was told to send the money to the former investigating judge and to find other funds to repay the cofradía. Romana also criticized the alcalde mayor for freeing the prisoners. Bacaro dragged his feet, but between April 1769 and November 1772—by which time he was no longer in office—he was coerced step by step into paying Aldama y Guevara what was his due.

Bacaro, meanwhile, had succeeded in tracking down the fugitive ladino Pedro Quezada (who was now revealed to be a tailor by profession). By February 1769, the alcalde mayor of Huehuetenango-Totonicapán had found out that Quezada was living in the village of Sajcabaja, in the jurisdiction of the magistrate of Sololá, and therefore he tried to have the ladino apprehended and extradited by the alcalde mayor there. It is not known if he succeeded or if the fugitive was ever caught. Nor is it known if those who escaped from jail were ever apprehended and given their punishment.

Patterns and Legacies

The proceedings were for the most part to the point. They do on occasion give us some insight into certain features of society at that time. One twenty-year-old witness, for example, was not in his home village of Nebaj when the conspiracy took place because he was engaged in "commerce" along the Pacific coast—a long way for an Indian from the Cuchumatán Highlands. Other sources confirm, however, that highland people did at times travel to the coastal provinces to transport raw cotton and cacao from the lowlands to the rest of the country. It is likely that Nebaj had regular contact with the Pacific coast, for one of the village's cofradías owned some cacao groves.[40] The migration to and from the highlands was not on the scale later established with the growth of the coffee industry in the nineteenth and twentieth centuries, but the pattern had already come into existence in the colonial period, if not earlier.

As in previous chapters, the inquest reveals the geographical mobility of the Spanish American population. Both Juan Bacaro and Francisco Antonio Aldama y Guevara were Mexican-born Spaniards who had managed to get appointments to lucrative positions in Guatemala. Attorney General Felipe Romana, as noted in previous chapters, was a native of Colombia. This, of course, was still a time when the crown either trusted its American subjects or else found no alternative to appointing them to office, especially since they were frequently willing to pay for the privilege, and hence the perquisites, of holding office. Nevertheless, change was just around the corner. In the 1770s the government in Spain began a policy that systematically discriminated against the American-born. By the 1780s virtually none of the magistrates in Guatemala was from the colonies. It took longer to change the audiencias because positions on those courts were frequently bought as life-time appointments, but even so by the end of the century the Guatemala audiencia was composed entirely of the Spanish-born. This turned out to be a huge political mistake, and Spain would soon pay dearly for it in the form of independence movements led not by Indians but by American-born Spaniards.

The records also reveal the importance of status and symbols in Maya society. For the Indians, it was important to distinguish between principales and macehuales. The staffs of office were essential symbols of power. They figured prominently in preconquest depictions of indigenous rulers in mu-rals and stelae, and continued to be important in colonial times. The Maya leaders would no more go around without their staffs than Spaniards would go around without their clothes.[41] At the same time, Spanish legitimization of Maya authority had become a requirement. When the dissidents in Nebaj wanted to get rid of their village government, they did not rebel; rather, they went to the capital city to get a legal writ from the Spanish government. Later, even while the rebels were overthrowing the unwanted Indian magis-trates and putting in their own village government, the leaders immediately set out to get the official stamp of approval of their election from the alcalde mayor. The goals of the rebels, therefore, were exclusively local in charac-ter. They did not attempt to overthrow the colonial regime; on the contrary, they wanted its approval.

Events in Nebaj particularly highlight once again the importance of Maya women as political actors. Although all the ringleaders were male, the fe-males played their part in the struggle. When the priest showed up to calm down the villagers, it was the women who threw stones and drove him away. They also participated in the assault on the unwanted village officials, and demonstrated their displeasure in the most extreme form upon the arrival of the force sent to put down the rebellion; their public urination on the outsid-ers was, to say the least, extraordinary. Nevertheless, although two women were among the first people arrested, not one female was called to testify. This is a reflection of Spanish cultural beliefs regarding gender: women were not thought to be suitable witnesses in a court of law. On the other hand, the Maya too had ideas regarding the importance of gender: when it came to whipping people, men and women were treated differently. It was thought that for females a more moderate punishment was appropriate. Their lashes were laid on not with leather whips but with nettle reeds, which while caus-ing pain were perceived as being less painful than leather.

The legacy of the Spanish legal system that handled this and the other cases of revolt can still be seen in Latin America. Although the colonial officials made efforts to gather documentary evidence, from the Spanish point of view the best kind of evidence was the confession. But as is true all over the world, the authorities, regardless of what the law might say, assume that the persons arrested are guilty. In the absence of checks on governmental procedures, the officials feel free to get "the truth" out of the criminals. If that requires force, then so be it. This was the working assumption of most criminal courts in Europe and America until modern times. The result in Latin America is a history of torture that has lasted till our day. This is not to say that the English-speaking world has not had its share of abuse of power. However, in Latin American police procedure more routinely includes torture. Indeed, recent history has provided gruesome evidence to that effect. One suspects in fact that in Guatemala the Indians received better treatment under the law of Spain than under that of the Guatemalan Republic.

After the submission of the investigating judge's report, the individuals who participated in the revolt in Nebaj disappear from the historical record. As was the case in the other revolts studied, the people had their chance, made their point, and then returned to anonymity. Francisco Antonio Aldama y Guevara returned to Quezaltenango and apparently completed his term in office.

But Alcalde Mayor Juan Bacaro was not so lucky. The cover page of the file on the Nebaj revolt says that the documents are part of the evidence in the case being brought against that alcalde mayor. For Bacaro had made an important political mistake. He had interfered with the business activities that the priests carried out with the Indians of their parishes. The alcalde mayor had done this not to protect the native people from exploitation, as he of course alleged, but rather to monopolize commerce in his province. Then, unlucky for him, a new archbishop, Pedro Cortés y Larraz, took possession of the diocese, and while carrying out his diocesan inspection the parish priests complained to the archbishop about the magistrate's abuses. Cortés y Larraz then brought charges against Bacaro, and as a result the latter was eventually removed from office. To make matters worse, his business partner, a merchant in the capital, abruptly broke his contract with the alcalde mayor and seized most of Bacaro's profits from the repartimiento. The ex-magistrate took his ex-partner to court, but civil suits, unlike most criminal cases such as that of Nebaj, could take years. This one did, not ending until seventeen years later. The decision was favorable to the former alcalde mayor, but by then Bacaro was dead and his widow—whose dowry had been used to purchase the magistracy of Huehuetenango-Totonicapán—got little or nothing because the ex-partner had declared bankruptcy. Such were the risks of being a royal official in Spanish America.

Conclusion

The conquest of the earth, which mostly means the taking it away from those who have a different complexion or slightly flatter noses than ourselves, is not a pretty thing when you look into it too much.

—*Joseph Conrad*, Heart of Darkness

Revolts are common occurrences in history. Revolutions are not. The Maya do not represent all rural people, nor all colonized people, and the revolts and revolutions discussed in this book do not represent even all Maya people. Nevertheless, the cases discussed do lead to conclusions regarding Maya revolts and revolutions in the eighteenth century.

Since the Spanish colonial regime rested on the extraction of a surplus from the rural population, and since the same colonial regime allowed local Spanish officials to engage in illegal business activities—it was the only way to pay them—local officials frequently tried to increase the level of surplus extraction. But the Maya, like most other indigenous people in the Spanish empire, had accepted Spanish rule in return for acceptable limits of exploitation. This was the moral economy of the colonial regime. Whenever an official tried to go beyond those acceptable limits, thereby violating the moral economy, the Maya resented it, felt that their rights were being violated, and took steps to counteract the officials' actions. This was one of the major causes of revolts within the Spanish empire.[1]

At the same time, the colonial regime rested on the political power of local Maya elites. They collected the tribute, religious taxes, and repartimiento debts, and organized the forced labor system. In return, the indigenous leaders received considerable political autonomy. As long as the Maya elites fulfilled their end of the colonial bargain, the colonial authorities did not usually interfere with how those local people went about their business. This was the moral polity of the colonial regime. But sometimes the indigenous leaders were not as cooperative as the Spanish officials wanted, especially if the level of surplus extraction was being increased. At other times Catholic priests objected to the way local politics were being run and they wanted different people—those who were more compliant and subservient or who adhered to a more rigid Christian morality—to run the villages. Spaniards therefore sometimes violated the Maya's perceived right of political autonomy, and the Maya took steps to defend their rights. This also was a frequent cause of revolts.

Yet, when Spaniards violated the moral economy or moral polity, the Maya response was likely to be limited in nature. This was because their goals were limited: restore the status quo ante, that is, go back to the acceptable level of exploitation or restore to power those whom the Spaniards had removed from power. When the Maya took violent action in these cases, the violence was also limited. Indeed, except for the revolution in Yucatán in 1761, very few people got killed in the revolts discussed in this book. No one at all was killed in three of the revolts. Moreover, since the "rebels" had limited ends and employed limited means, they used existing institutions to serve as arbitrators between themselves and the colonial officials who wanted them punished. Thus, they asked priests to intercede, they made appeals to the audiencia, they even hired lawyers to defend them.

For the "rebels" were not in fact challenging the legitimacy of authority or of Spanish rule. On the contrary, their very actions demonstrated their recognition, albeit grudging, of that legitimacy. In their eyes they had revolted against illegitimate authority, that is, the abuses of power that violated their rights. Since the "rebels" sought conciliation, and since it was in the interest of the Spanish state to pacify the "rebels," the revolts usually came to an end peacefully and at only minor cost. In this book the highest Spanish authorities showed over and over again their understanding that it was not in their interest to strangle, either through punishment or revenge, the goose that was laying the golden eggs. The law was therefore bent to make room for what was in effect both reason of state and reconciliation without severe repression. For in the long run, colonialism depended on the consent, albeit reluctant, limited, and contingent, of the governed.

At least it did during most of the colonial period. But then late in the eighteenth century the Bourbon monarchy instituted reforms that were designed to strengthen Spain's control of America and convert its American kingdoms, including the Kingdoms of Guatemala and New Spain, into true colonies. This meant giving orders regardless of popular sentiment. Thus began the process of breaking the compact between the Spanish kings and their American subjects, whose consent was no longer required, or even requested. The institution that the Maya had used to make the burden of colonialism bearable became despotic.

The Maya's situation worsened even more after Independence, for then, a monarch who was at least theoretically paternalistic and benevolent was replaced by a local creole ruling class that found neither paternalism nor benevolence to be in its interest. In a sense, this was the result of centuries of colonialism, for regardless of the law and the original intentions of the Spanish kings, local elites had developed attitudes first of cultural and religious, and then racial, superiority. Eventually the creole ruling class found it inconceivable that negotiation was necessary when deciding what to do with the Maya. This class introduced "reforms," and by the time these were completed in the late nineteenth century, the new rulers would have practically destroyed the concept of rule with the consent of the governed—or at least that was so when the governed were indigenous. The real era of terror for the Maya was not the colonial period but the centuries of postcolonial elite rule on behalf of interests that saw the Maya as obsolete obstacles to capitalist development and personal enrichment. Furthermore, the rise of agricultural exports resulted in a new state that depended mostly on export taxes for revenue; the Maya were no longer fiscally necessary. And as this took place, ruling with reluctant consent was frequently replaced by ruling with domination—that is, brute force. A delicate balance had been lost. It was no longer deemed necessary or even desirable.

Of course, the revolutions in Chiapas in 1712 and Yucatán in 1761 stand out in contrast to the Hapsburg and early Bourbon system of government through the consent of the governed. For in both cases the Maya quite simply abandoned the colonial compact and tried to rule themselves. Those rebellions were of course related to the material conditions in which the Maya lived. But history suggests that the Maya did not call into question the colonial system because of economic factors. The latter were worth fighting for but not dying for. What gave them the will to call into question the whole of Spanish colonial rule was their culture, specifically their belief that God or the gods were on their side. In Yucatán, this meant belief in the coming of a Maya king who would liberate them by turning the historical cycle as it inevitably had to turn. Religion gave the Maya of Chiapas and Yucatán an ideology, a vision of a very different future with themselves, and not the Spaniards, on top and in control. And in the history of the world—the Western world included—religion and ideology have, more often than economic factors, given people a cause to fight for that was also worth dying for.

And die they did in Yucatán and Chiapas. For the Spanish state could not permit the indigenous people to be independent. The Maya revolutionaries played for high stakes, and the Spaniards responded with massive force. In doing so they crushed not only political movements but also challenges to what was for them the "one, true religion" that had inspired their ancestors to fight the Moors, with Saint James at their side, and drive them from Spain. For Spaniards and Maya did agree on at least one principle: religion was worth dying for.

The sources used in this study are not straightforward compilations of data to be analyzed scientifically by a disinterested scientist. Historical documents never are. The inquests into Maya revolts and revolution were carried out by victorious Spaniards. The Maya appear mostly as prisoners who communicated with their captors through interpreters. A Spanish scribe wrote down what he understood—and perhaps misunderstood—to be the testimony of the witnesses.

Some would declare such sources useless as anything but a manifestation of Spanish power. But are they any worse than those that scholars have always used? After all, other than archaeological and numismatic evidence, there are no primary sources at all about Alexander the Great. Yet using accounts written several centuries later, scholars have been able to understand somewhat—and of course very imperfectly—Alexander's personality, his campaigns, his marches, his soldiers, his statecraft, and his impact on history.

My sources are not dissimilar. They are imperfect, for they are filled with mistranslations, misinterpretations, bias, and even illegibility. Yet taking them as a whole and working with them, comparing evidence from various places in the documents, I believe that I have been able to derive an account that, while imperfect, is valid—to a point.

For these sources tell us a great deal. They allow us to see how certain features of colonialism worked and the importance that colonialism had for the Maya. Moreover, they fill our social science/historical categories—to a great extent our mental creations—with real human beings who lived, loved, believed, doubted, acted with courage and cowardice in principled and unprincipled ways, threw rocks, jeered, urinated on their enemies, gave birth to children, defended their families, argued, lied, fought, and died. These people existed.

Their history, in turn, informs us. We can see the Maya as people of flesh and blood—they bled when whipped—as people with relationships of affection and of authority, with first and last names, with religious and political ideas, with a strong sense of identity and culture, and with ability to manipulate the colonial system to gain advantage or cut their losses. These people, then, tend to confirm our belief in documentation as the basis for the study of history.

The sources also give insight into colonialism as a historical process at work and having a significant impact on the indigenous people. Although the terms of exploitation and of organization differed from place to place, in all places the Spaniards subjected the Maya to colonialism. This was a kind of exploitative relationship that did not exist in Spain. (Jews and Moriscos, after all, either were acculturated or had been forced to leave in 1492 and 1607, respectively; they did not survive as identifiably different groups within Spanish society.) The colonial regime incorporated the Maya into the world economy; hence so much emphasis in this book on textiles, which were exported to colonial capitals and mining camps. This in turn meant the creation or strengthening of economic relationships between regions, relationships that would collapse because of the impact of the Industrial Revolution.

Spanish culture also tried to dominate Maya culture everywhere. It succeeded in certain ways, driving native religious rites underground, so to speak. It was also successful in the long run in terms of language, for every day the proportion of those monolingual in Maya diminishes as more and more people speak the language of the conquistadors and many become monolingual in Spanish.

These historical processes, then, show that colonialism was indeed an important factor in world history and that it greatly affected the indigenous people whose lands were invaded. The Maya may have negotiated and renegotiated the terms of domination, but they still were dominated. Their historical agency—the ability to act on their own—did not drive the Spanish colonists from their land. The Spaniards were here to stay, and even though their descendants usually are partly Maya in terms of ancestry, their culture is much more Hispanic than Maya.[2]

Nevertheless, the Maya have survived into the twenty-first century. The themes of this study help us understand how and why, as long as we believe that we can learn anything from history.

As I was writing this book in late 2000, I read in the newspaper about how a group of people in the village of Pustunich (Yucatán) violently resisted the efforts of their priest to move a statue of the Virgin from their church to that of nearby Ticul. From the point of view of the priest and the Catholic Church, the statue is just a representation. But from the villagers' point of view, it is their saint and they are afraid they will not get her back. The Maya as an independent culture, at least for now, are still with us.

Notes

Introduction

1. Edward Said, *Orientalism* (New York: Pantheon Books, 1978).

2. See specifically the following by Robert W. Patch: "La formación de las estancias y haciendas en Yucatán durante la colonia," *Boletín de la Escuela de Ciencias Antropológicas de la Universidad de Yucatán*, no. 19 (July–August 1976): 21–61; "El mercado urbano y la economía campesina en el siglo XVIII," *Boletín de la Escuela de Ciencias Antropológicas de la Universidad de Yucatán*, no. 27 (November–December 1977): 52–66; "Una cofradía y su estancia en el siglo XVIII. Notas de investigación," *Boletín de la Escuela de Ciencias Antropológicas de la Universidad de Yucatán*, nos. 46–47 (January–April 1981): 56–66; "Agrarian Change in Eighteenth-Century Yucatán," *Hispanic American Historical Review* 65, no. 1 (February 1985): 21–49; "Decolonization, the Agrarian Problem, and the Origins of the Caste War, 1812–1847," in Gilbert Joseph and Jeffrey Brannon, eds., *Land, Labor, and Capital in Modern Yucatán: Essays in Regional History and Political Economy* (Tuscaloosa: University of Alabama Press, 1991), 51–82; *Maya and Spaniard in Yucatán, 1648–1812* (Stanford: Stanford University Press, 1993); "Imperial Politics and Local Economy in Colonial Central America, 1670–1770," *Past and Present*, no. 143 (May 1994): 77–107; "Sacraments and Disease in Mérida, Yucatán, Mexico, 1648–1726," *The Historian* 58, no. 4 (Summer 1996): 731–743.

3. A survey of the riots, revolts, and rebellions of colonial Guatemala and Chiapas can be found in Severo Martínez Peláez, *Motines de indios* (Guatemala: Ediciones En Marcha, 1973, 1991). As a source this book has serious drawbacks. For the most part, the author simply lists the riots and revolts mentioned in documents in the Central American Archive and makes no systematic effort to analyze them as a group. He fails to discuss the scale of conflict involved, thus leaving the impression that all the events mentioned were of equal importance. Examples of unrest are lumped together with serious uprisings. Martínez Peláez only discusses a handful of "*motines*" (riots) in detail, and most of his work is devoted to the Tzeltal Maya rebellion—which I shall refer to as a revolution—in Chiapas in 1712.

4. Misleading and/or erroneous interpretations of the revolt in Yucatán in 1761 can be found in John Tutino, *From Insurrection to Revolution in Mexico: Social Bases of Agrarian Violence, 1750–1940* (Princeton: Princeton University Press, 1986), 266

(which does not assign enough importance to Maya religion as a causal factor); John Mason Hart, *Revolutionary Mexico: The Coming and Process of the Mexican Revolution* (Berkeley and Los Angeles: University of California Press, 1987), 24 (which grossly exaggerates the rebelliousness of the Maya in Yucatán and Chiapas); Friedrich Katz, "Rural Uprisings in Preconquest and Colonial Mexico," in Friedrich Katz, ed., *Riot, Rebellion, and Revolution: Rural Social Conflict in Mexico* (Princeton: Princeton University Press, 1988), 65–94 (which exaggerates economic causes and suggests that religion played a role only after the uprising had begun); Fred Carstensen and Diane Roazen, "Foreign Markets, Domestic Initiative, and the Emergence of a Monocrop Economy: The Yucatecan Experience, 1825–1903," *Hispanic American Historical Review* 72, no. 4 (1992): 562 (completely wrong on causation); and John Charles Chasteen, *Born in Blood and Fire: A Concise History of Latin America* (New York and London: W.W. Norton, 2001), 89 (which makes claims about the rebelliousness of the Maya of Yucatán that are not supported by any evidence or any scholar of Yucatán). On the other hand, brief but accurate and useful ethnohistorical discussions can be found in Victoria Reifler Bricker, *The Indian Christ, the Indian King: The Historical Substrate of Maya Myth and Ritual* (Austin: University of Texas Press, 1981): 70–76; and Nancy M. Farriss, *Maya Society Under Colonial Rule: The Collective Enterprise of Survival* (Princeton: Princeton University Press, 1984), 68–72.

Chapter 1. The Maya and Their History

1. Some scholars have questioned whether Yucatán had any supralocal political units before the Spanish conquest. See Matthew Restall, *The Maya World: Yucatec Culture and Society, 1550–1850* (Stanford: Stanford University Press, 1997), 28. Despite the lack of evidence in Maya language documents, however, I believe that there is more than enough information in Spanish sources to confirm the existence of some kind of alliance system or confederation, if not territorial states or provinces, at the regional level. See Ralph L. Roys, *The Political Geography of the Yucatán Maya* (Washington, DC: The Carnegie Institution of Washington, 1957); Sergio Quezada, *Pueblos y caciques yucatecos, 1550–1580* (Mexico: El Colegio de México, 1993).

2. For the unconquered Petén Maya, see Grant D. Jones, *Maya Resistance to Spanish Rule: Time and History on a Colonial Frontier* (Albuquerque: University of New Mexico Press, 1989); Grant D. Jones, *The Conquest of the Last Maya Kingdom* (Stanford: Stanford University Press, 1998).

3. For the demographic history of the Maya area, see Murdo J. MacLeod, *Spanish Central America: A Socioeconomic History 1520–1720* (Berkeley and Los Angeles: University of California Press, 1973), 1–20, 70–71, 77–79, 91–100, 104–106, 130–131, 204–206; Sherburne F. Cook and Woodrow Borah, *Essays in Population History. Mexico and the Caribbean*, II (Berkeley and Los Angeles: University of California Press, 1974), 1–179; Manuela Cristina García Bernal, *Yucatán: Población y encomienda bajo los Austrias* (Seville: Escuela de Estudios Hispano-Americanos, 1979); P. Gerhard, *The Southeast Frontier of New Spain* (Princeton: Princeton University Press, 1979), 23–30; Robert M. Carmack, John Early, and Christopher Lutz, eds., *The Historical Demography of Highland Guatemala* (Albany: Institute for Mesoamerican Studies, State University of New York at Albany, 1982); Nancy M. Farriss, *Maya Society Under Colonial Rule: The Collective Enterprise of Survival* (Princeton: Princeton University Press, 1984), 57–67; Robert W. Patch, *Maya and Spaniard in Yucatán, 1648–1812* (Stanford: Stanford University Press, 1993), 42–45,

138–139; W. George Lovell and Christopher H. Lutz, "Conquest and Population: Maya Demography in Historical Perspective," *Latin American Research Review* 29, no. 2 (1994): 133–140.

4. John Leddy Phelan, *The Hispanization of the Philippines: Spanish Aims and Filipino Responses, 1565–1700* (Madison: University of Wisconsin Press, 1967); Nicholas P. Cushner, *Spain in the Philippines: From Conquest to Revolution* (Quezon City: Ateneo de Manila University, 1971).

5. Modern-day Chiapas was created in the 1780s with the creation of the Intendancy of Chiapas. During most of the colonial period the area was divided into the *alcaldía mayor* of Chiapa (singluar) and the *governación* of Soconusco (the Pacific coast). In the 1770s Chiapa was divided into two *alcaldías mayores*, known as Tuxtla and Chiapa. These two plus Soconusco were the units combined into the Intendancy of Chiapas in the following decade.

6. MacLeod, *Spanish Central America*, 68–95, 235–252.

7. Adriaan C. Van Oss, *Catholic Colonialism: A Parish History of Guatemala, 1524–1821* (Cambridge: Cambridge University Press, 1986); Patch, *Maya and Spaniard*, 122–123 .

8. For the repartimiento in Yucatán, see Patch, *Maya and Spaniard*, 30–32, 81–93, 154–168; for Chiapas and Central America, see Robert W. Patch, "Imperial Politics and Local Economy in Colonial Central America, 1679–1770," *Past and Present*, no.143 (May 1994): 77–107.

9. Patch, *Maya and Spaniard*, pp. 30–31, 81–92, 155–168; Patch, "Imperial Politics and Local Economy," 101–104. This interpretation is essentially the opposite of that argued by Farriss, *Maya Society*.

10. Jeremy Baskes, in "Coerced or Voluntary? The *Repartimiento* and Market Participation of Peasants in Late Colonial Oaxaca," *Journal of Latin American Studies* 28, Pt. 1 (February 1996): 1–28, makes an argument that the system was not coercive because the Indians of Oaxaca were not compelled to accept the credit or goods provided by the Spanish magistrates. This ignores the fact that if the indigenous people tried to avoid paying their debts, the magistrates whipped them or incarcerated their leaders until the debts were paid. I would consider those collection methods to be coercive in nature.

11. Patch, "Imperial Politics and Local Economy," 104–106. For a different explanation of the survival of Maya culture, see Farriss, *Maya Society*, and for an interpretation emphasizing the radical transformation of the Maya economy as a result of colonialism, see Robert Wasserstrom, *Class and Society in Central Chiapas* (Berkeley and Los Angeles: University of California Press, 1983), 32–68. For an important contribution to the study of the survival and extinction of indigenous people in America, see Linda A. Newson, "Indian Population Patterns in Colonial Spanish America," *Latin American Research Review* 20, no. 3 (1985): 41–74.

12. See Farriss, *Maya Society*, pp. 227–255; Robert M. Hill II, *Colonial Cakchiquels. Highland Maya Adaptation to Spanish Rule 1600–1700* (Fort Worth: Harcourt Brace Jovanovich, 1992), 31, 33–38, 48, 53–55, 72–77. For studies of the Maya elites in the sixteenth century, see Elías Zamora Acosta, *Los Mayas de las tierras altas en el siglo XVI. Tradición y cambio en Guatemala* (Seville: Exma. Diputación de Sevilla, 1985), 382–398; Quezada, *Pueblos y caciques yucatecos*; Amos Megged, "Accommodation and Resistance of Elites in Transition: The Case of Chiapa in Early Colonial Mesoamerica," *Hispanic American Historical Review* 71, no. 3 (1991): 477–500.

13. Robert M. Hill II, "*Chinamit* and *Molab*: Late Postclassic Highland Maya

Precursors of Closed Corporate Community," *Estudios de Cultura Maya* 15 (1984): 301–321; Hill, *Colonial Cakchiquels*, 38–42.

14. This was first suggested by Alfonso Villa Rojas in his article, "Notas sobre la tenencia de la tierra entre los Mayas de la antigüedad," *Estudios de Cultura Maya* 1 (1961): 21–46. It has more recently been argued by Sergio Quezada in his *Pueblos y caciques*, chapter 1. Nancy Farriss argues that lineage groups or clans in fact had no significance among the colonial Yucatec Maya. See Farriss, *Maya Society*, 137. The evidence that she presents, however, does not support this conclusion because she confuses lineage with family.

15. Luis Reyes García, *Cuauhtinchan del siglo XII al XVI. Formación y desarrollo histórico de un señorío prehispánico*, 2d edition (Mexico: CIESAS, 1988; first published Wiesbaden, 1977), 88–118; Hildeberto Martínez, *Tepeaca en el siglo XVI. Tenencia de la tierra y organización de un señorío* (México: CIESAS, 1984), 77–123; Bernardo García Martínez, *Los pueblos de la sierra. El poder y el espacio entre los indios del norte de Puebla hasta 1700* (Mexico: El Colegio de México, 1987), in which the author leaves out the *calpulli* entirely and devotes all the analysis to the *altepetl*; James Lockhart, *The Nahuas After the Conquest. A Social and Cultural History of the Indians of Central Mexico, Sixteenth Through Eighteenth Centuries* (Stanford: Stanford University Press, 1992), 16–20.

16. Ann M. Wightman, *Indigenous Migration and Social Change: The Forasteros of Cuzco, 1570–1720* (Durham and London: Duke University Press, 1990); Karen Vieira Powers, *Andean Journeys: Migration, Ethnogenesis, and the State in Colonial Quito* (Albuquerque: University of New Mexico Press, 1995).

17. Zamora Acosta, *Los Mayas de las tierras altas*, 374–382; Robert M. Hill II, "Social Organization by Decree in Colonial Highland Guatemala," *Ethnohistory* 36, no. 2 (Spring 1989): 170–198.

18. For a detailed treatment of this theme, see Nancy M. Farriss, "Remembering the Future, Anticipating the Past: History, Time, and Cosmology Among the Maya of Yucatán," *Comparative Studies in Society and History* 29, no. 3 (1987), 566–593; also see Inga Clendinnen, *Ambivalent Conquests: Maya and Spaniard in Yucatán, 1517–1570* (Cambridge: Cambridge University Press, 1987); Hill, *Colonial Cakchiquels*, 6–8, 86–88. For an analysis of the continued Maya obsession with time, see Barbara Tedlock, *Time and the Highland Maya* (Albuquerque: University of New Mexico Press, 1982).

19. For a discussion of the significance of ideologies of the "world turned upside down," see James C. Scott, *Domination and the Arts of Resistance. Hidden Transcripts* (New Haven: Yale University Press, 1991). This book, rather than the Gramscian or pseudo-Gramscian hegemonic approach currently fashionable, is in my opinion a good starting point to approach the study of politics and social conflict in conditions of colonialism.

20. For studies of the 1712 Tzeltal rebellion, see Herbert S. Klein, "Peasant Communities in Revolt: The Tzeltal Republic of 1712," *Pacific Historical Review* 35, no. 3 (1966): 247–263; Henri Favre, *Changement et continuité chez les Mayas du Mexique; contribution à l'étude de la situation coloniale en Amérique Latine* (Paris: Editions Anthropos, 1971; Spanish translation in 1973); Robert Wasserstrom, "Ethnic Violence and Indigenous Protest: The Tzeltal (Maya) Rebellion of 1712," *Journal of Latin American Studies* 12, no. 1 (1980): 1–19, esp. p. 17; Victoria Reifler Bricker, *The Indian Christ, the Indian King: The Historical Substrate of Maya Myth and Ritual* (Austin: University of Texas Press), 55–69; Kevin Gosner, *Soldiers of the Virgin: The*

Moral Economy of a Colonial Maya Rebellion (Tucson: University of Arizona Press, 1992). A most valuable source used by all scholars is Fray Francisco Ximénez, *Historia de la Provincia de San Vicente de Chiapa y Guatemala de la Orden de Predicadores*, 3 vols. (Guatemala: Tipografía Nacional, 1929–31; written ca. 1722), especially vol. 3, 257–343.

21. John Tutino, *From Insurrection to Revolution in Mexico: Social Bases of Agrarian Violence, 1750–1940* (Princeton: Princeton University Press, 1986), 25–32.

22. Ximénez, *Historia de la Provincia de San Vicente*, vol. 3, 399.

23. Gosner, *Soldiers of the Virgin*, 124.

24. The symbolic significance of the claim from St. Peter is not noted by Klein, Wasserstrom, Bricker, and Gosner.

25. Archivo General de Indias, Escribanía de Cámara 356A, Residencia de Sargento Mayor Don Pedro Gutiérrez de Mier y Terán (1719), fol. 204r.

26. Several Spanish accounts of events that are not cited in any of the literature on the rebellion are contained in ibid.

Chapter 2. Reputation, Respect, and Role Reversal: Verapaz, 1735

1. The source for this chapter is: Archivo General de Indias (Seville) (hereafter cited as AGI), Escribanía de Cámara 358A, Testimonio de la Pesquisa en la Proa. de la Verapaz por el Lizdo. Don Antonio de Paz y Salgado Abogado de la Real Audiencia de Guatemala sobre el tumulto de los Indios de San Pedro Carcha y San Juan Chamelco contra su Alcalde Mayor Don Manuel Barrueta, Prision del, muertes executadas, y otros accidentes que siguieron a estos hechos el dia 30 de Henero del año de 1735. Unless otherwise stated, all citations of documents in this chapter are from this manuscript.

2. See E.P. Thompson, "The Moral Economy of the English Crowd in the Eighteenth Century," *Past and Present*, no. 50 (February 1971): 76–136, for an introduction to the concept; see also James C. Scott, *The Moral Economy of the Peasant: Rebellion and Subsistence in Southeast Asia* (New Haven and London: Yale University Press, 1976), for an elaboration of the concept with respect to non–European societies.

3. James C. Scott, *Weapons of the Weak: Every Day Forms of Peasant Resistance* New Haven: Yale University Press, 1990, 1986), 29.

4. Pedro Cortés y Larraz, *Descripción geográfico-moral de la Diocesis de Goathemala*, 2 vols. (Guatemala: Sociedad de Geografía e Historia de Guatemala, 1958), vol. 2, 11–19.

5. The classic study of the history of Verapaz in the sixteenth century is André Saint-Lu, *La Vera Paz: Esprit évangelique et colonisation* (Paris: Centre de recherches hispaniques, Institut d'etudes hispaniques, 1968).

6. Ibid., 12, 16.

7. Folio 47.

8. AGI, Guatemala 277, Provisiones de Alcaldías Mayores, Verapaz, 13 July 1728. For a detailed discussion of the sale of offices and the repartimiento system in Guatemala, see Robert W. Patch, "Imperial Politics and Local Economy in Colonial Central America," *Past and Present* , no. 143 (May 1994): 77–107.

9. British Library, London, Add. MS. 17,583, President Pedro de Rivera to the Marqués de Torre Nueva, 2 January 1738, fols. 222–226.

10. Stanley J. Stein, "Tending the Store: Trade and Silver at the Real de Huautla, 1778–1781," *Hispanic American Historical Review* 77, no. 3 (1997): 377–407.

11. AGI, Escribanía de Cámara 356B, Residencia de Juan Antonio Ruiz de Bustamante, Alcalde Mayor de Verapaz, 1721.

12. Fols. 94, 97–98, 100–101, 103, 106, 109, 113, 145.

13. Fols. 82, 87, 94. Alcalde Mayor Barrueta asserted that the leaders of San Juan Chamelco were all given fifty lashes: fol. 1.

14. Fols. 94–110, 113–138.

15. Fol. 98.

16. Fol. 102.

17. Fol. 140.

18. Fol. 123.

19. Fols. 98, 106, 109, 113, 116.

20. Fols. 113–114, 117.

21. Fols. 102, 114, 128, 131, 132, 134, 136, 138.

22. Fols. 43, 49, 62, 66, 70, 77.

23. Fol. 128.

24. James Muldoon, *The Americas in the Spanish World Order: The Justification of Conquest in the Seventeenth Century* (Philadelphia: The University of Pennsylvania Press, 1994).

25. Fols. 43–44, 49–51.

26. Fol. 49.

27. Fol. 50.

28. Fol. 50.

29. Fols. 50–51.

30. Fol. 52.

31. Fol. 2.

32. Fols. 51, 63.

33. Fols. 45, 52–53, 67, 71–72, 78, 83, 87–88.

34. Fols. 85, 141, 144, 146, 148, 151.

35. Fol. 46.

36. Fols. 99, 103, 108, 122, 140–144, 146, 148, 195.

37. William B. Taylor, *Drinking, Homicide, and Rebellion in Colonial Mexican Villages* (Stanford: Stanford University Press, 1979), 113–151; Steve J. Stern, *Peru's Indian Peoples and the Challenge of Spanish Conquest: Huamanga to 1640* (Madison: University of Wisconsin Press, 1982), pp. 114–137.

38. Fol. 84.

39. Fols. 55–56, 68, 73, 79, 88.

40. Fol. 56.

41. Fol. 56.

42. Fols. 68–69.

43. Fols. 88–89.

44. Fols. 46, 54–56, 64.

45. Fols. 161, 163–164, 208–210.

46. Fols. 158–159, 161, 172–173, 175.

47. Fols. 175–176.

48. Fol. 56.

49. Fol. 57.

50. Fols. 3–4 (for Barrueta's account), as well as 46, 58, 72.

51. Fols. 58–59.

52. Fol. 60.

53. Fols. 4–5.
54. Fols. 7–8.
55. Fols. 9–10.
56. Fols. 10–11.
57. Fols. 11–12.
58. Fol. 12.
59. Fols. 24–26, 37–40.
60. Fol. 17.

61. See, especially, Steve J. Stern, *The Secret History of Gender: Women, Men, and Power in Late Colonial Mexico* (Chapel Hill and London: University of North Carolina Press, 1995), 11–41, 297–319.

62. Fols. 43–90.
63. Fols. 81–85.
64. Fols. 93–97.
65. Fols. 151–152.

66. This was the American equivalent of what women in Europe sometimes did to get more lenient treatment than men. For a good example of a woman using this stratagem, see Natalie Zemon Davis, *The Return of Martin Guerre* (Cambridge: Harvard University Press, 1983).

67. Fols. 153–154.
68. Fols. 154–157.
69. Fols. 157–160.
70. Fols. 160–167.
71. Fols. 168–169, 176–177.
72. Fols. 179–183.
73. Fols. 184–185.
74. Fols. 188–193.
75. Fols. 194–197.
76. Fols. 197–199.
77. Fols. 202–204.
78. Fols. 204–206.
79. Fols. 208–235.
80. Fols. 238–245.
81. Fols. 245–247.
82. Fols. 247–249.
83. Fols. 250–253.
84. Fols. 253–261.
85. Fols. 261–262.
86. Fols. 263–264, 278.
87. Fols. 266–269.
88. Fols. 270–272.
89. Fols. 273–275.
90. Fols. 265–266, 280–281.

91. John H. Elliott, *The Count-Duke of Olivares: The Statesman in an Age of Decline* (New Haven: Yale University Press, 1986).

92. AGI, Escribanía de Cámara 358A, Residencia de Manuel Barrueta, Alcalde Mayor de Verapaz, 1738–1739.

93. Fols. 289–297.

Chapter 3. Women's Power and Spanish Colonialism in Tecpán, 1759

1. Archivo Histórico Nacional (Madrid), Consejos 20950, Quaderno de la Pesquisa Hecha Sobre los Acontecimientos en el Pueblo de Tecpangoathemala, 1759, fol. 126v. This document will be the source of all citations in this chapter unless otherwise stated. There is also a copy of the documents in the Archivo General de Indias, Guatemala 539, Expediente 11. I am using the Madrid manuscript because it contains a few documents not included in Seville. The uprising is well studied from the point of view of an anthropologist in Robert M. Hill, "Social Organization by Decree in Colonial Highland Guatemala," *Ethnohistory* 36, no. 2 (Spring 1989): 170–198. Hill used the manuscript in Seville.

2. Francisco Fuentes y Guzmán, *Recordación florida* in *Obras históricas de D. Francisco Antonio de Fuentes y Guzmán*, 3 vols. (Madrid: Biblioteca de Autores Espanoles, 1969), vol. 1, 332–335.

3. Pedro Cortés y Larraz, *Descripción geográfico-moral, de la Diocesis de Goathemala*, 2 vols. (Guatemala: Sociedad de Geografía e Historia de Guatemala, 1958), vol. 2, 172.

4. Fol. 1v.

5. Fol. 79r.

6. Fol. 79v.

7. Fol. 80r.

8. Fols. 11v, 13r, 19r.

9. Fols. 9v, 26r, 29v, 32r, 34r, 41v.

10. Eight separate calpules were identified in the documents, although it is possible that there were a few more. Several of them had two heads. The Spaniards frequently got confused over this, using the word calpul to refer to the head and to the calpul itself. See Hill, "Social Organization by Decree," 179–180.

11. Fols. 1r–2r.

12. Fols. 8r–10r.

13. Fol. 67r, 67v.

14. Fols. 68r–71r.

15. Fols. 25v, 27r, 29r, 31r, 33v.

16. These events emerge from the testimony of several militiamen, fols. 24v–34v.

17. Fols. 109–110, 112–113, 118–119, 120–121.

18. Fols. 2r, 2v, 11r, 14v, 17r, 29v, 31v, 33v–34r, 104r, 105v, 107v, 110v–111r, 114r, 116v.

19. Fols. 2v–4v.

20. Fols. 4v–5r.

21. Fols. 8r–19v.

22. Fols. 48r–53v, 55r, 55v.

23. Fols. 74r–75r.

24. Fols. 84r–85v.

25. Fols. 24v–34v.

26. Fols. 35v–40v.

27. Fols. 40v–43v.

28. Fols. 44r–46r.

29. Fols. 46r–56r.

30. Fols. 56r-71v.

31. Fols. 71r-73v, 84r–94v.

32. Fol. 73r.

33. Fols. 75r-78v.

34. Fols. 79r–81v.

35. Fols. 81v–82r.

36. Fol. 82v.

37. Fol. 129v.

38. Fols. 84r-94v.

39. Fols. 95v–96v.

40. In the final sentencing she was referred to as "Juana Tomatle, alias the one-eyed." Fol. 127v.

41. Grant Jones, in his book *The Conquest of the Last Maya Kingdom* (Stanford: Stanford University Press, 1998), pp. 307–308, notes that he found it difficult to believe that Ajaw Kan Ek', the last of the independent Maya kings of the Petén, and his cousin, AjK'in Kan Ek', did not know their ages. But since virtually no Maya ever knew his or her age, I believe it safe to conclude that for the Maya as a whole, age, measured in European terms, was unimportant. This is still frequently the case among the modern Maya.

42. Fols. 96v–97r.

43. Fol. 97r, 97v.

44. Fol. 98r, 98v.

45. Fols. 99r–100r.

46. Fol. 100r, 100v.

47. Fols. 102r–103r.

48. What follows is derived from fols. 102r–123r.

49. Fols. 108v–110r.

50. Fol. 112v.

51. Fol. 106v.

52. Fols. 123v–126r.

53. Fols. 125v–126r.

54. Fols. 126r–127r.

55. Fols. 127v–129r.

56. Fols. 129r–130r.

57. AGI, Guatemala 340, Informe del Consejo de Indias al Rey, marzo 1756.

58. AGI, Guatemala 340, Informe del Fiscal del Consejo de Indias, 1 marzo. 1748; AGI, Guatemala 550, Informe del Fiscal del Consejo, 1 octubre. 1759; ibid., Expediente sobre la creacion de las Alcaldías Mayores en el Valle de Guatemala, 1759–61.

59. AGI, Guatemala 340, Informe del Consejo de Indias al Rey, marzo 1756.

60. AGI, Guatemala 340, Acta del Cabildo de Guatemala, 26 febrero 1754; ibid., Certificacion, 26 Feb. 1754; Carta del Cabildo de Guatemala al Rey, n.d. [1754]; AHN, Consejos 20950 (1768), fols. 1–21.

61. AHN, Consejos 20952, Cuaderno 2, Pieza 101 (25 noviembre 1765), fols. 78r–99v; AGI, Guatemala 587, Expediente No. 6, Carta de la Audiencia al Rey, 3 Agosto 1798.

62. Fols. 148r–152v (including Carta de la Audiencia de Guatemala al Rey, 30 octubre 1761); AHN, 20950, 1768, fols. 1–21; AGI, Guatemala 539, Carta del cura párroco de la Ciudad de Santiago al Rey, octubre 1761.

63. Hill, "Social Organization by Decree," 185–187.

Chapter 4. Renegotiation, Injustice, and Persistence: Santa Lucía Utatlán, 1760–1763

1. AGI, Guatemala 540, Año de 1763, Quaderno No. 1. Sigue el testimonio de la real provicion y demas diligencias practicadas sobre la espera que se le concedio a Don Joseph Bentura Manso de Velasco alcalde mayor de el partido de Atitan y Tecpanatitan para la exacion de los gastos ausado en el aquartelamento de las milicias que se alistaron para la contencion de los yndios del pueblo de Santa Lucía Utatlán en el alsamto. que hicieron el dia 18 de abril del año de 1760 y en que fueron condenados por autos de vista y revista, fols. 37r, 38v. Hereafter this document will be cited as Sigue el testimonio.

2. Francisco Antonio de Fuentes y Guzmán, *Recordación florida*, in *Obras históricas de D. Francisco Antonio de Fuentes y Guzmán*, 3 vols. (Madrid: Biblioteca de Autores Espanoles, 1969), vol. 2, 304.

3. Pedro Cortés y Larraz, *Descripción geográfico-moral de la Diocesis de Goathemala*, 2 vols. (Guatemala: Sociedad de Geografía e Historia de Guatemala, 1958), vol. 2, pp. 164–165.

4. Sigue el testimonio, fol. 10r; AGI, Guatemala 540, Año de 1761. Testimonio de los autos seguidos sobre la sublevacion que executo el Pueblo de Santa Luzia Utatlan el dia 18 de abril del año proximo pasado, contra Don Joseph Bentura Manzo de Velasco Alcalde Mr. y Teniente de Capitan General del partido de Atitlan y Tecpanatitlan, y lo determinado por el Superior Govierno, y la Real Audiencia en punto de los caudales expendidos para el pago de las Compañías que estubieron aquarteladas en el tumulto acaecido en dho Pueblo con lo demas que se expresa, fol. 80v. Unless otherwise specified, all citations in this chapter are from this document.

5. AGI, Guatemala 547, Expediente 15, Testimonio de las diligencias practicadas en virtud de Real Cedula de 9 de Julio de 1765 sobre recaudacion del Común de Yndios del Pueblo de Santa Lucia Utatan, 1768. This collection of documents includes four letters written by people of the village complaining about taxes. Two of the letters were in Cakchiquel and the other two in Quiché.

6. For mules and the local economy, see fols. 44r, 48r, 51r, 53r, 54r.

7. AGI, Guatemala 441, Título del Corregidor de Chiquimula de la Sierra, Consulta, 17 marzo 1769.

8. AGI, Guatemala 442, Título del Alcalde Mayor de Atitlán-Tecpanatitlán, 23 julio 1758.

9. AGI, Guatemala 607, Testimonio de los autos instruidos a consecüencia de Real Cédula dada en San Lorenzo a 16 de octubre de 1769 (1780), fols. 9–21.

10. William L. Sherman, *Forced Native Labor in Sixteenth-Century Central America* (Lincoln: University of Nebraska Press, 1979).

11. Charles Gibson, *The Aztecs Under Spanish Rule. A History of the Indians of the Valley of Mexico, 1519–1810* (Stanford: Stanford University Press, 1964), 220–256.

12. David McCreery, *Rural Guatemala 1760–1940* (Stanford: Stanford University Press, 1994), 85–101.

13. Fol. 30r.

14. Fol. 31v.

15. Fol. 17r.

16. Fol. 1r.

17. Fol. 80r, 80v.
18. Fols. 76–77v.
19. Fols. 77v–78v.
20. Fols. 144v–146r.
21. Fols. 8v–10r.
22. Fol. 74v.
23. What follows is derived from fols. 16v–34r, 65v–76v.
24. Fol. 67r.
25. Fol. 20v.
26. Fol. 1r.
27. Fols. 1v–3r.
28. Fols. 78v–81v.
29. Fol. 3r.
30. Fol. 3r, 3v.
31. Fol. 3v–4r.
32. Fols. 147v–148v.
33. Fol. 4v.
34. Fols. 35r–37r.
35. Fol. 1r.
36. Fols. 37r–38v.
37. Fols. 15r–16v.
38. What follows is from fols. 16v–34r.
39. Fol. 39v–54v.
40. Fol. 50r.
41. Fols. 43r–44v.
42. Fol. 41r.
43. Fol. 49v.
44. Fol. 54v.
45. Fols. 54v–56r.
46. Fols. 6–8v.
47. Fol. 57r.
48. Fols. 57v–58r.
49. Fols. 59r–72v.
50. Fol. 65r.
51. Fols. 72r–76v.
52. Fol. 74r.
53. Fol. 74r.
54. Fol. 64r.
55. Fol. 74v.
56. Fol. 75r, 75v.
57. Fol. 75v.
58. Fol. 76r.
59. Fol. 76r.
60. Fols. 81v–82v.
61. Fols. 82v–83r.
62. Fols. 83v–85v.
63. Fols. 86r–87v.
64. Fol. 87v.
65. Fols. 88r–89r.

66. Fols. 90v–97v.

67. Fols. 89v–90r.

68. Fols. 108r–109v, 111v.

69. AGI, Guatemala 540, Expediente del Fiscal de la Audiencia de Guatemala sobre el alboroto acaecido con los Yndios del Pueblo de Santa Lucía Utatán, 1763.

70. AGI, Guatemala 593, Expediente 2, Carta del Presidente al Rey, 31 mayo 1760. The dispute was over a struggle for power then taking place in San Salvador, and as a result the president accused three judges, including López de Urrelo, of "crimes and disobedience" while they accused him of smuggling.

71. Fols. 106v–107v.

72. Fols. 109v–111v.

73. Fol. 108r.

74. Fols. 111v–113r.

75. Fols. 113r–119r.

76. Fol. 163r, 163v.

77. Fol. 121v.

78. Fols. 148v–149r.

79. Fols. 137r–141r.

80. Fols. 141v–143r.

81. Fols. 143r–144r.

82. Fols. 122v–131r, 149v–152r.

83. Fols. 152r–155r.

84. Fols. 157r–158r.

85. Fols. 158v–159r.

86. Fols. 164r–166r.

87. Fols. 167r–171r.

88. Sigue el testimonio . . . , fols. 1r–8r.

89. Sigue el testimonio . . . , fols. 9v–10r.

90. Sigue el testimonio . . . , fols. 10r–11r.

91. Sigue el testimonio . . . , fol. 11v.

92. Sigue el testimonio . . . , fols. 14v–15r.

93. Sigue el testimonio . . . , fols. 15r–16r.

94. Sigue el testimonio . . . , fol. 16r, 16v.

95. Sigue el testimonio . . . , fols. 16r–18r.

96. Sigue el testimonio . . . , fols. 18v–19v.

97. Sigue el testimonio . . . , fols. 19v–21r.

98. Sigue el testimonio . . . , fol. 21r, 21v.

99. Sigue el testimonio . . . , fols. 23r–24v.

100. Sigue el testimonio . . . , fols. 25v–26r.

101. Sigue el testimonio . . . , fol. 26v.

102. Sigue el testimonio . . . , fol. 27r.

103. Sigue el testimonio . . . , fol. 29r, 29v.

104. Sigue el testimonio . . . , fols. 29v–31v.

105. AGI, Guatemala 641, Carta del Capital de Infanteria Don Joseph Ventura Manso de Velasco, Alcalde Mayor de Atepan-Atitan [sic.], al Rey, 25 septiembre 1762.

106. Sigue el testimonio. . . , fols. 31v–33v.

107. Sigue el testimonio. . . , fols. 33v–34v.

108. Sigue el testimonio. . . , fols. 35r–40r.

109. Sigue el testimonio. . . , fol. 40r, 40v.

110. AGI, Guatemala 540, Expediente del Fiscal de la Audiencia de Guatemala sobre el alboroto acaecido con los Yndios del Pueblo de Sta. Lucia Utatan, 1763; AGI, Guatemala 641, Carta del Capitan de Infanteria D. Joseph Ventura Manso de Velasco, Alcalde Mayor de Atitan y Atepan-Atitan [sic.], al Rey, 20 febrero 1763; AGI, Guatemala 547, Expediente No. 15 (1768); AGI, Guatemala 423, Real Cédula de 27 enero 1771.

111. AGI, Guatemala 567, Expediente No. 3 (1782).

Chapter 5. The Yucatec Maya in 1761, Part I: The Origins of Revolution

1. This chapter's primary source is the collection of documents and trial records found in AGI, México 3050. There are two copies: (1) Año de 1761, Testimonio de Autos fhos. sobre la Sublevasion que hizieron varios Pueblos de esta Provincia en el de Cisteíl en el que se aclamaron por Rey a Joseph Jacinto Uc de los Santos Canek Yndio Natural del Barrio de Campechuelo en el Puerto de San Francisco Campeche; and (2) Autos criminales seguidos de ofisio de la Real Justisia sobre la sublevacion que los Yndios del Pueblo de Cisteil y los demas que convocaron hicieron contra Ambas Magistades el de 19 de Noviembre de 1761. I used both copies because of differing degrees of legibility and the requirements of microfilm. Hereafter I shall cite the first copy as "Testimonio de Autos" and the second as "Autos criminales."

2. Valuable works on Maya religion in the colonial period include Nancy M. Farriss, *Maya Society Under colonial Rule: The Collective Enterprise of Survival* (Princeton: Princeton University Press, 1984); Mario Humberto Ruz, *Copanaguastla en un espejo. Un pueblo tzeltal en el virreinato* (San Cristóbal de las Casas: Centro de Estudios Indígenas, Universidad Autónoma de Chiapas, 1985); Clendinnen, *Ambivalent Conquests.* Hill, *Colonial Cakchiquels,* Amos Megged, *Exporting the Catholic Reformation: Local Religion in Early Colonial Mexico* (Leiden: E.J. Brill, 1996).

3. Farriss, *Maya Society,* pp. 199–223; Robert W. Patch, *Maya and Spaniard in Yucatán, 1648–1812,* (Stanford: Stanford University Press), 62–66, 225–229.

4. Testimonio de Autos, 2v.

5. Testimonio de Autos, 49r.

6. Testimonio de Autos, 72r.

7. Testimonio de Autos, 5v, 8r.

8. Testimonio de Autos, 197r.

9. Autos criminales, 292v, 295r.

10. Autos criminales, 274r, 298r.

11. For the bulls of the Holy Crusade, see Patch, *Maya and Spaniard,* 82–84, 156–158.

12. Testimonio de Autos, 33v.

13. Testimonio de Autos, 175v, 182v; Autos criminales, 264v, 298r.

14. Testimonio de autos, 186v.

15. Autos criminales, 293v–294r.

16. Testimonio de autos, 141v–142r.

17. For the repartimiento, see Patch, *Maya and Spaniard,* 30–32, 81–93, 155–156, 198, 204, 246, 277.

18. Testimonio de autos, 155v, 158r; Autos criminales, 264v, 274r, 298r.

19. Testimonio de autos, 188v; Autos criminales, 272r.

20. Autos criminales, 241r; Testimonio de autos, 172v.

21. Autos criminales, 330v–335r.

22. Testimonio de autos, 183v.

23. Testimonio de autos, 151v (Tomás Balam), 176r (Pascual Yupit), 196v (Luis Cauich).

24. Testimonio de autos, 181r, 181v.

25. Autos criminales, 331v.

26. Testimonio de autos, 181r.

27. Autos criminales, 271v, 272v.

28. Autos criminales, 246r.

29. Autos criminales, 224r, 233r.

30. Testimonio de autos, 181r.

31. Autos criminales, 222v.

32. Autos criminales, 233r–233v.

33. Testimonio de autos, 181r. For more information about Canek in Tiholop, see the testimony of the three sons of Don Andrés Ku, 224r–226r.

34. Testimonio de autos, 188r, 188v.

35. Autos criminales, 297v–298v.

36. Testimonio de autos, 174v.

37. Autos criminales, 246v.

38. Testimonio de autos, 188v.

39. Autos criminales, 263v–264r, 268v.

40. Autos criminales, 264r–265r, 267r, 274r.

41. Testimonio de autos, 196v.

42. Testimonio de autos, 197r.

43. Testimonio de autos, 197r–198r.

44. Testimonio de autos, 198v–199r. Luis Cauich did not name the sacristán, but Pascual Yupit (178r) identified him as Pedro Dzul.

45. Testimonio de autos, 175v–176r.

46. Autos criminales, 226v–227r, 263v–264r, 270r, 278v.

47. Autos criminales, 229r.

48. Testimonio de autos, 129r, 165v, 175v, 188v; Autos criminales, 246v, 271r.

49. Autos criminales, 246r.

50. Testimonio de autos, 131r, 131v, 149v, 167v, 267v, 302r.

51. Testimonio de autos, 178r.

52. Testimonio de autos, 131r–131v, 167v; Autos criminales, 302r.

53. Testimonio de autos, 158v, 160v, 166r, 176r, 182r; Autos criminales, 265v, 267v.

54. Archivo del Ayuntamiento de Mérida, Libro 4, Acuerdos 1761–1766, 17 diciembre 1761, fol. 44.

55. Testimonio de autos, 181v.

56. Testimonio de autos, 149v, 166r; Autos criminales, 246v, 265v.

57. Testimonio de autos, 176r.

58. Testimonio de autos, 192v.

59. Testimonio de autos, 182v.

60. Autos criminales, 299r–299v, 239r, 247v, 265r.

61. Autos criminales, 265r.

62. Autos criminales, 297v–299v, 303r.
63. Testimonio de autos, 153v.
64. Testimonio de autos, 155r–163r.
65. Autos criminales, 255r–257r.
66. Autos criminales, 260r–261v.
67. Autos criminales, 221r.
68. Autos criminales, 233v–234r.
69. Testimonio de autos, 149v.
70. Testimonio de autos, 156v, 160v, 192v; Autos criminales, 302r–302v.
71. Testimonio de autos, 159v–161r, 166r; Autos criminales, 302v.
72. Testimonio de autos, 156v, 158v, 160v, 162v, 164v, 166r, 198v; Autos criminales, 246r–246v, 267v, 272r, 272v, 274r, 274v, 275r, 275v, 288v, 302r, 310r, 329v.
73. Autos criminales, 275v.
74. Testimonio de autos, 131r, 167v, 174v, 189r; Autos criminales, 246v, 265r, 298r, 309v.
75. Autos criminales, 266v.
76. Autos criminales, 267v.
77. Autos criminales, 272r.
78. Autos criminales, 272r.
79. Testimonio de autos, 131r.
80. Autos criminales, 272r.
81. Testimonio de autos, 130v.
82. The history of the conquest of the Petén is well told in Grant D. Jones, *The Conquest of the Last Maya Kingdom* (Stanford: Stanford University Press, 1998).
83. Robert Patch, "Community, Culture, and 'Rebellion' in the Yucatec Maya Rising of 1761," in Susan Schroeder, ed., *Native Resistance and the Pax Colonial in New Spain* (The University of Nebraska Press, 1998), 67–83.
84. It is likely that Pedro Bracamonte, who has also worked on the documents relating to the 1761 uprising, came up with this idea before I did and therefore I am giving him credit for it.
85. Testimonio de autos, 151v.
86. Autos criminales, 265v–266r.
87. Testimonio de autos, 175r, 175v.
88. Testimonio de autos, 199r, 199v.
89. Testimonio de autos, 189v; Autos criminales, 228r.
90. Autos criminales, 299r.
91. Autos criminales, 238v.
92. Autos criminales, 241v–242v.
93. Testimonio de autos, 181v–182r.
94. Autos criminales, 266r.
95. Autos criminales, 266r.
96. Testimonio de autos, 1r–2r.
97. Autos criminales, 269v, 299v–300r.
98. What follows is based on Testimonio de autos, 130r–130v, 166r–166v; Autos criminales, 269v–270r.
99. Testimonio de autos, 130r, 130v.
100. Testimonio de autos, 166v.
101. Autos criminales, 270r.
102. Testimonio de autos, 183v–184r.

103. Autos criminales, 270r.

104. Testimonio de autos, 166v.

105. Testimonio de autos, 130v, 166v.

106. Testimonio de autos, 131r.

107. Testimonio de autos, 167r.

108. Testimonio de autos, 148r–149v, 154r, 156v, 158r, 160v, 191r–191v; Autos criminales, 235r, 303r.

109. Testimonio de autos, 129r.

110. Testimonio de autos, 183r.

111. Testimonio de autos, 185v–186r.

112. Testimonio de autos, 204v.

113. Testimonio de autos, 205r.

114. Testimonio de autos, 204r–204v.

115. Archivo de la Mitra Emeritense, Visitas Pastorales, Mocochá, 20 enero 1785.

116. Autos criminales, 236r.

117. Testimonio de autos, 149r.

118. Testimonio de autos, 149r.

119. Testimonio de autos, 156r–156v.

120. Testimonio de autos, 149r.

121. Testimonio de autos, 167v–168r.

122. Testimonio de autos, 176v, 191v; Autos criminales, 279v, 300r.

123. Autos criminales, 279v.

124. Autos criminales, 301r.

125. Testimonio criminales, 176v–177r.

126. Autos criminales, 279r.

127. British Library (London), Additional Ms. 17569, Visita a su Obispado por el Yllmo. Fray Don Ygnacio Padilla (1755–56), 6v.

128. Testimonio de autos, 131v; Autos criminales, 279r.

129. Testimonio de autos, 177r.

130. Testimonio de autos, 189r.

131. Testimonio de autos, 167v.

132. Robert W. Patch, "Decolonization, the Agrarian Problem, and the Origins of the Caste War, 1812–1847," in Gilbert Joseph and Jeffrey Brannon, eds., *Land, Labor, and Capital in Modern Yucatán: Essays in Regional History and Political Economy* (Tuscaloosa: University of Alabama Press, 1991), 51–82.

Chapter 6. The Yucatec Maya in 1761, Part II: The Counter-Revolution

1. Testimonio de autos, 70v. The sources for this chapter are the same as those of the previous chapter, cited in note 1.

2. Testimonio de autos, 14v–15r.

3. Testimonio de autos, 4v.

4. Testimonio de autos, 5r.

5. Testimonio de autos, 15r–15v.

6. Testimonio de autos, 2r–4v.

7. Testimonio de autos, 9v.

8. Testimonio de autos, 35v.

9. Testimonio de autos, 49r–50r.
10. Testimonio de autos, 38r, 50r.
11. Testimonio de autos, 46v, 49r, 73r.
12. Testimonio de autos, 7v–8r.
13. Testimonio de autos, 87r–88v.
14. Testimonio de autos, 95r.
15. Testimonio de autos, 16r.
16. Testimonio de autos, 13v, 19v, 28r, 28v, 97v, 140v, 143r.
17. Testimonio de autos, 25r, 23r.
18. Testimonio de autos, 10r.
19. Testimonio de autos, 34r, 34v.
20. Testimonio de autos, 46v–48v, 81v–83r.
21. Testimonio de autos, 82v.
22. Testimonio de autos, 83r–84r.
23. Testimonio de autos, 22v–23r, 24v.
24. Testimonio de autos, 24r.
25. Testimonio de autos, 59v, 63v–65r.
26. Testimonio de autos, 92r.
27. Testimonio de autos, 98v–99r.
28. Testimonio de autos, 57r.
29. Testimonio de autos, 65r.
30. Testimonio de autos, 66v.
31. Testimonio de autos, 56r.
32. Testimonio de autos, 23v, 66v–69r.
33. Testimonio de autos, 38r, 38v, 50r.
34. Testimonio de autos, 305r–305v.
35. Testimonio de autos, 101r–101v.
36. Testimonio de autos, 89v.
37. Testimonio de autos, 89v.
38. Testimonio de autos, 25r.
39. See, for example, the comments made in 1769 by Pedro Cortés y Larraz, Archbishop of Guatemala, in AGI, Guatemala 553, Expte. 16, Carta del Arzobispo al Rey, 24 febrero 1769.
40. Testimonio de autos, 50r.
41. Testimonio de autos, 89v.
42. Testimonio de autos, 70r–72r.
43. Testimonio de autos, 80v.
44. Testimonio de autos, 81v.
45. Testimonio de autos, 98r–98v, 78r–79v.
46. Testimonio de autos, 91r.
47. Testimonio de autos, 101r–102r, 109v–111r.
48. Autos criminales, 276r.
49. Autos criminales, 276v.
50. Testimonio de autos, 113v.
51. Testimonio de autos, 15rv, 157r, 158v–159r, 161r.
52. Autos criminales, 229v–231v.
53. Testimonio de autos, 191r–191v.
54. Testimonio de autos, 113r–114r; Autos criminales, 276v–277r.
55. Autos criminales, 248v.

56. Testimonio de autos, 165r–165v.
57. Testimonio de autos, 113r.
58. Testimonio de autos, 117v.
59. Testimonio de autos, 118r.
60. Autos criminales, 236v–237r, 277r–278v.
61. Autos criminales, 255v, 260v.
62. Autos criminales, 293v.
63. Archivo del Ayuntamiento de Mérida, Libro 4, Acuerdos 1761–1766, 17 diciembre 1761, 43v–45r.
64. Testimonio de autos, 128r–135r.
65. Testimonio de autos, 125r.
66. Information provided by Sergio Quezada and Pedro Bracamonte y Sosa.
67. Testimonio de autos, 135r–136r.
68. Testimonio de autos, 145r–146r.
69. Testimonio de autos, 136v–140v.
70. Testimonio de autos, 146r, 146v, 151v–152v.
71. Testimonio de autos, 163r–163v, 171r–172r.
72. Testimonio de autos, 140v–143r.
73. Testimonio de autos, 144r.
74. Testimonio de autos, 143r–144v.
75. Testimonio de autos, 172r–173r, 178r.
76. Testimonio de autos, 163r–163v.
77. Testimonio de autos, 180r–187r.
78. Testimonio de autos, 194r.
79. Testimonio de autos, 196r.
80. Testimonio de autos, 200v–201v.
81. Autos criminales, 303v.
82. Testimonio de autos, 184r.
83. Testimonio de autos, 205v–206v.
84. Testimonio de autos, 207v–208r.
85. Autos criminales, 251v–252v.
86. Autos criminales, 304v–307r.
87. What follows is from Autos criminales, 330v–335v.
88. Autos criminales, 335v–339r.
89. Autos criminales, 339r–343r [although in fact nothing after 338 is foliated].
90. AGI, México 3050, Carta de Don Joseph Bernardo de Alarcón, Maestre de Escuela de la Catedral, y Br. Don Juan Antonio de Mendicuti, Canónigo de Gracia de la Catedral, al Rey, 30 agosto 1762.
91. Anthony F.C. Wallace, "Revitalization Movements: Some Theoretical Considerations for Their Comparative Study," *American Anthropologist* 58, no. 2 (1956): 265.
92. Testimonio de autos, 151v.
93. Testimonio de autos, 162v–163r.
94. Testimonio de autos, 193r.
95. Autos criminales, 220r.
96. Autos criminales, 222r.
97. Autos criminales, 225v.
98. Autos criminales, 237r.
99. Autos criminales, 240v.

100. Autos criminales, 242v.
101. Autos criminales, 244r.
102. Autos criminales, 251r.
103. Autos criminales, 261v.
104. Autos criminales, 263r.
105. Autos criminales, 295r.
106. Autos criminales, 297r, 303v.
107. Autos criminales, 308v–310v.
108. Autos criminales, 313v–314r.
109. Autos criminales, 321v.
110. Autos criminales, 323v–324r.

Chapter 7. Internal Conflict and the Moral Polity: Nebaj, 1768

1. The principal source for this chapter is AGI, Guatemala 599, Expedientes diarios, Año de 1773. Testimonio de los autos sobre las inquietudes de los naturales de los Pueblos de Nebaj, y Chahul de la Alcaldía mayor de Gueguetenango, con motibo de las elecciones de alcaldes, de que fueron principales autores Miguel Maton Pablo Sanchez y Pedro Cobo. This will be cited as Testimonio de los autos. The quotation is on folio 100.

2. Pedro Cortés y Larraz, *Descripción geográfico-moral dela Diocesis de Goathemala*, 2 vols. (Guatemala: Sociedad de Geografía e Historia de Guatemala, 1958), vol. 2, 45.

3. See David Stoll, *Between Two Armies in the Ixil Towns of Guatemala* (New York: Columbia University Press, 1993).

4. Francisco Antonio de Fuentes y Guzmán, *Recordación florida*, in *Obras históricas de D. Francisco Antonio de Fuentes y Guzmán*, 3 vols. (Madrid: Biblioteca de Autores Espanoles, 1969), vol. 3, 17.

5. Fol. 61.

6. Benjamin N. Colby and Pierre L. Van den Berghe, *Ixil Country: A Plural Society in Highland Guatemala* (Berkeley: University of California Press, 1969), 63.

7. AGI, Guatemala 603, Expediente diario No. 1, Año de 1773, Testimonio de la insta.a de Don Juan Bacaro Alcalde Mayor de Gueguetenango sobre remover las existencias de la comp.a de gananciales que ha tenido con Don Juan de Montes de Oca.

8. This important dispatch is found on fols. 5–6.

9. Fol. 55.
10. Fol. 52.
11. Fol. 6.
12. Fol. 54.
13. Fol. 9.
14. Fol. 9.
15. Fol. 10.
16. Fol. 12.
17. Fol. 59.
18. Fol. 105.
19. Fols. 29, 54.

20. Fol. 14.
21. Fol. 24.
22. Fol. 31.
23. AGI, Guatemala 441, Títulos, Quezaltenango, 20 July 1762; AGI, Guatemala 550, Representaciónes de Francisco Antonio Aldama y Guevara al Presidente, 20 enero 1769 (copied 24 enero 1769) and 23 enero 1769; AGI, Guatemala 600, Expediente No. 8 (1776), Representación de D. Joseph Arias y Quiroga, Corregidor de Quezaltenango, al Presidente, 2 noviembre 1770.
24. Fols. 53–54: "A los demas reos, que tiene Vmd. en esa carcel, por haver contribuido a el alboroto de los mal contentos, les hara Vmd. dar, bien dados, cincuenta azotes a cada uno, y un mes de carcel."
25. Fol. 29.
26. Fol. 64.
27. Fol. 89.
28. Fol. 94.
29. Fol. 99.
30. Fol. 99.
31. Fol. 100.
32. Fol. 101.
33. Fol. 102.
34. Fol. 102.
35. Fol. 102.
36. Fols. 102–103.
37. Fol. 106.
38. Fol. 107.
39. Fol. 112.
40. Fol. 61.
41. There is a picture of modern-day staffs and of the village officials carrying them, in Colby and Van der Berghe, *Ixil Country*, between pages 106 and 107.

Conclusion

1. William B. Taylor, *Drinking, Homicide, and Rebellion in Colonial Mexican Villages* (Stanford: Stanford University Press, 1979).
2. This is my own general observation, having lived in Mérida and Seville. I therefore disagree with Robert Redfield, who argued that the culture of Mérida is "mestizo" in nature. See Robert Redfield, *The Folk Culture of Yucatán* (Chicago: University of Chicago Press, 1941). That is clearly true of the urban working class, but less so of the middle class and far from true of the upper-middle and upper classes. I seriously doubt that Redfield studied the latter groups enough to justify his conclusions, and no one since him has paid much attention to the culture of the middle and upper classes of Mérida.

Index

About the Author

Robert W. Patch is an associate professor at the University of California, Riverside. He studied as an undergraduate at the University of Illinois, Urbana-Champaign, and received his Ph.D. from Princeton University. Patch is the author of *Maya and Spaniard in Yucatán, 1648–1812*, and is currently engaged in research on the economic history of Central America and the Philippines.